THE ADVENTURES

OF

JAMES CAPEN ADAMS

JAMES CAPEN ADAMS.

THE ADVENTURES

OF

JAMES CAPEN ADAMS

Mountaineer and Grizzly Bear Hunter of California

Theodore H. Hittell

TAYLOR TRADE PUBLISHING
Lanham • New York • Boulder • Toronto • Plymouth, UK

Published by Taylor Trade Publishing
An imprint of
The Rowman & Littlefield Publishing Group, Inc.
4501 Forbes Boulevard, Suite 200, Lanham, Maryland 20706
www.rowman.com

10 Thornbury Road, Plymouth PL6 7PP, United Kingdom

Distributed by National Book Network

First published 1861
Reprint edition 2012

British Library Cataloguing in Publication Information
Available

**The 1972 edition of this book was previously cataloged
by the Library of Congress as follows:**

Hittell, Theodore Hengry, 1830–1917
    The adventures of James Capen Adams.
    (BCL/select bibliographies index reprint series)
    Repreint of the 1911 ed.
    1. Adams, John, 1812–1860. I. Title.
F864.A2 1972
639'.11'744460924 [B]   78-39492

ISBN 978-1-58979-763-5 (pbk. : alk. paper)
ISBN 978-1-58979-764-2 (electronic)

♾™ The paper used in this publication meets the minimum
requirements of American National Standard for Information
Sciences—Permanence of Paper for Printed Library
Materials, ANSI/NISO Z39.48-1992.

Printed in the United States of America

CONTENTS.

v

PART II.

LIST OF ILLUSTRATIONS.

PART I.

PART II.

vii

INTRODUCTION.

A STATEMENT of the circumstances under which I wrote "The Adventures of James Capen Adams, Mountaineer and Grizzly Bear Hunter of California," may be not uninteresting. In the early part of October, 1856, while in charge of the local department of the *Daily Evening Bulletin* newspaper of San Francisco, California, my attention was attracted to a small placard at the door of a basement on the south side of Clay, near Leidesdorff, Street. It announced the exhibition there of "The Mountaineer Museum"—a collection of wild animals of the Pacific Coast, the principal of which were "Samson, the largest Grizzly Bear ever caught, weighing over 1500 pounds, Lady Washington (with her cub), weighing 1000 pounds, and Benjamin Franklin, King of the Forest."

Descending the stairway, I found a remarkable spectacle. The basement was a large one but with a low ceiling, and dark and dingy in appearance. In the middle, chained to the floor, were two large grizzly bears, which proved to be Benjamin Franklin and Lady Washington. They were pacing restlessly in circles some ten feet in diameter, their chains being about five feet long, and occasionally rearing up, rattling their irons, and reversing their direction. Not far off on one side, likewise fastened with chains, were seven other bears, several of them young grizzlies,

three or four black bears, and one a cinnamon. Near
the front of the apartment was an open stall, in which
were haltered two large elks. Further back was a
row of cages, containing cougars and other California
animals. There were also a few eagles and other
birds. At the rear, in a very large iron cage, was the
monster grizzly Samson. He was an immense creature
weighing some three-quarters of a ton; and from his
look and actions, as well as from the care taken to
rail him off from spectators, it was evident that he was
not to be approached too closely.

In the midst of this strange menagerie was Adams,
the proprietor—quite as strange as any of his animals.
He was a man a little over medium size, muscular and
wiry, with sharp features and penetrating eyes. He
was apparently about fifty years of age; but his hair
was very gray and his beard very white. He was
dressed in coat and pantaloons of buckskin, fringed at
the edges and along the seams of arms and legs. On
his head he wore a cap of deerskin, ornamented with
a fox-tail, and on his feet buckskin moccasins. An
excellent likeness of him, as well as of his favorite bear,
is presented in the illustration, drawn from life by
Charles Nahl, entitled "Adams and Ben Franklin." *

After looking cursorily at the different animals, I
became particularly interested in the bears Ben Franklin and Lady Washington. Adams seemed to have
perfect control over them. He placed his hands upon
their jaws and even in their mouths, to show their
teeth. He made them rear on their hind legs and

* See illustration facing page 178.

walk erect, growl when he ordered them to talk, and perform various tricks. He put them to boxing and wrestling, sometimes with himself, sometimes with each other; and they went through the performance with good nature and great apparent enjoyment of the sport.

One thing especially noteworthy, in addition to the docility of the huge beasts, was the fact that the hair was worn off of portions of their backs. Upon my asking the reason, Adams answered that it was caused by pack-saddles. This led to further questions, in reply to which he gave a brief account of how he had lived in the mountains for several years; how he had caught and trained his bears, and, among other things, how on occasions he had used them as pack-animals. I asked to see the pack-saddles, but was answered that they had not been brought from the mountains. At the same time Adams said he would show how the bears would carry burdens; and, after loosing Ben Franklin and jumping upon his back, he rode several times around the apartment. He next threw a bag of grain on the animal's back, and the bear carried it as if used to the task.

My interest became thoroughly aroused. Within the next few days, I inserted in the newspaper several notices of the exhibition and also a short account of Adams and the strange life he had been leading. These notices attracted attention; and, in the course of a month or two, Adams's receipts from his show enabled him to hire and fit up the spacious first floor of the California Exchange on the northeast corner of Kearny and Clay Streets, where in December, 1856, he established "The Pacific Museum." There until August, 1859, and thereafter in the Pavilion building on the site of the present Lick House until the end of 1859, he continued to give exhibitions, which were witnessed by many thousands of visitors.

During all those years Adams lived among his animals. He continued to wear buckskin; and when seen on the street, it was almost always in his mountaineer garb. He slept, on a buffalo robe or bear-skin, in one corner of his exhibition room or in a small adjoining chamber. He sometimes cooked his own meals, but usually dined at a restaurant. From time to time he added other attractions to his exhibition; but he was not a business man and did not save money; so that about the beginning of 1860—when he removed his collection to New York—he was substantially as poor in purse as when he first came to San Francisco.

Between July, 1857, and December, 1859, he narrated to me his adventures in full. He understood my purpose to be, if the story should prove sufficiently interesting, to make a book. He seemed flattered and was evidently pleased with the idea. My custom was to go to his place in the afternoon, after the newspaper went to press, and write down what he had to say. He would usually talk for an hour or two; but there were many interruptions. I told him plainly that I wanted nothing except the truth, and he assured me that he would give it. On various occasions I cross-questioned him sharply; but his replies were always satisfactory and, I believe, truthful. His memory seemed remarkably good. In writing my notes, I to some extent corrected his language, but put down in substance all he told me. And from the notes thus taken, with many omissions of unimportant details, I subsequently, in the winter of 1859–60, wrote out the following narrative.

An edition of the work was published at Boston and also at San Francisco in 1860, just before the breaking out of the Civil War, and some copies were disposed of; but, on account of business troubles, occasioned by the war, the publication was discontinued and the book went "out of print." The present new edition is issued in exactly the same form, so far as type, illustrations, and binding are concerned, as the first edition; and the only additions are this introduction and the postscript at the end.

SAN FRANCISCO, December, 1910.

THEODORE H. HITTELL.

THE ADVENTURES

OF

JAMES CAPEN ADAMS.

PART· FIRST.

CHAPTER I.

SKETCH OF MY EARLIER LIFE.

Birth. Trade. Early Hunting. Zeal in Hunting. Adventure
with a Bengal Tiger. Seriously Injured. Benefit of a Trade.
Work at Boston. Speculation. Ruination. Emigration. Cali-
fornia. Occupations in California. Struggles with Fortune.
Retirement to the Mountains. Personal Appearance and Con-
stitution. Qualifications for ˙ Mountain Life. Outfit. First
Impressions of the Mountains. Mountain Scenery. California
Indians. Indian Intercourse Buckskin Dressing. Approach·of
Winter. Mountain Economy. Mountain Life.

MY name is James Capen Adams. I was born on
October 20th, 1807, in the town of Medway, Massachusetts. My parents, who were honest and respectable people, bred me up from an early age to the
trade of shoemaking; but, being of a roving and adventurous disposition, I no sooner attained my majority than I threw aside the pegging awl, and hired
myself to a company of showmen as a collector of
wild beasts. In pursuance of my engagements with
this company, I hunted through the forests of Maine,
New Hampshire, and Vermont, and captured many
panthers, wolves, wild-cats, foxes, and other animals,

1

which were subsequently exhibited and admired
throughout the country;—but all these were small
game in comparison with what it was my destiny
afterwards to hunt.

It was a characteristic of my youth, as it has been
of my subsequent life, to take hold of a subject con-
genial to my tastes with a whole soul; and, as this
business of hunting suited my turn of mind, it would
be difficult to tell how far my zeal might have carried
me, what labors I might have attempted, and what
achievements I might have performed, had not an
accident disabled me while still a young man. This
unfortunate affair occurred in the following manner:
my employers had, in their collection of animals, a
royal Bengal tiger, which had become refractory.
They requested me to reclaim him; and, not doubt-
ing my ability, I entered his cage a number of times.
On the last occasion, however, the magnificent but
treacherous beast struck me to the floor and buried
his teeth and claws in my flesh. When taken from
the cage, I was insensible, and my injuries so serious
that for a long period recovery was problematical.
By this accident—if that can properly be called accident, which was brought about by my own rashness—my constitution was shattered; and for many
years my hunting was at an end.

The benefit of teaching a young man some honest
and useful handicraft, whatever may be his ulterior
destination in life, was well exemplified in my case
now; for, had it not been for shoemaking, I should
have become a burden not only to myself but to my

family. Fortunately, my injuries, which affected the spine, were of such a character as not to prevent the free use of my hands; and, removing to Boston, I went to work at my trade again, and more than supported myself. From that time I continued perseveringly employed for fifteen years, at the end of which period my gainings amounted to some six or eight thousand dollars; when, Yankee that I was, I must needs speculate. Accordingly, converting all my means into a cargo of boots and shoes, I shipped them to St. Louis in the hope of doubling or trebling my capital; but, instead of becoming suddenly rich, I had the misfortune to see them all consumed in a fire which occurred in that city; and in one short night I found myself a ruined man. This sad event, as it happened, took place at the time when the great gold fever broke out, and intense excitement about California prevailed over the whole country. In one year over a hundred thousand persons put themselves upon the way for the shores of the Pacific; and I could not do otherwise, I thought, than join that mighty migration. I seized the opportunity as one offered me by fortune; and, after numberless hardships and privations, arrived in California, by the way of Mexico, overland, in the fall of 1849.

From the period of my arrival in the country till I went into the mountains, my occupations were various, —sometimes mining, sometimes trading, sometimes raising stock and farming. Sometimes I was rich, at other times poor. At one time, in 1850, while farming in the neighborhood of Stockton, I possessed thousands of dollars' worth of cattle, most of which were stolen from me in a single night. At another time, I possessed mining claims, which ought to have made me very wealthy; and, at another, lands, which are now worth many fortunes; but one after the other passed out of my hands, partly on account of my own reckless speculations, partly through the villainy of others. In the space of three years, I failed three times; from the height of prosperity I was plunged into the depths of difficulty; until at last, in the fall of 1852, disgusted with the world and dissatisfied with myself, I abandoned all my schemes for the accumulation of wealth, turned my back upon the society of my fellows, and took the road toward the wildest and most unfrequented parts of the Sierra Nevada, resolved thenceforth to make the wilderness my home and wild beasts my companions.

My hair was already beginning to turn gray; and as I wore it long, with long, gray beard, and long mustaches,—such being the custom of those days,— my appearance was that of an old man, though, in truth, I was but in the prime of life, and could bear almost any degree of exposure, privation, or fatigue. My general temperance and active avocations had strengthened and hardened my frame, so that to walk during a whole day, or to endure hunger or thirst, was comparatively easy. To shoot well had been a part of my early education; and as to all that appertained to the procurement of provisions in a country of game, I considered myself well qualified for mountain life. So far as concerned my outfit, I could save but little out of the wreck of my estate. I managed, however, to retain an old wagon, two oxen, an old Kentucky rifle which used thirty balls to the pound of lead, a Tennessee rifle which used sixty, a Colt's revolving pistol, and several bowie-knives. Besides these, my effects were poor indeed,—a few tools, several pairs of blankets, a little clothing, and this was all.

Notwithstanding such scanty preparation, I drove up into the mountains with a buoyant and hopeful spirit; and it gives me pleasure, even now, to recall my lively feelings upon mounting the scarred and rugged shoulders of the Sierra. The roads were very rough; my team was none of the strongest; I had to rely on my rifle for provisions and the roadside for pasture; but the new and romantic scenes into which I was advancing, enchanted my imagination, and seemed to inspire me with a new life. The fragrance of the pines and the freshness and beauty of nature in those elevated regions were perfectly delightful to me. The mountain air was in my nostrils, the evergreens above, and the eternal rocks around; and I seemed to be a part of the vast landscape, a kind of demigod in the glorious and magnificent creation.

The country about the headwaters of those rivers, which run from the Sierra into the San Joaquin, is sublime on account of the magnitude of the mountain masses which compose it. The cliffs are of enormous size and extent; and everything conspires to render the scene grand and imposing to the last degree. In many places, the rocks rise in towering proportions, perfectly bare, from the midst of the forests which, though composed of giants in themselves, seem dwarfed in comparison. The trees are, many of them, of the most magnificent description, principally of evergreen kinds; but there are also oak, ash, and other deciduous species. The soil is generally scanty; but along the streams, there is much that is good; and there are many valleys affording abundant herbage and beautiful meadows. In almost all the defiles, gorges, and cañons, there is chaparral and brush in crowded profusion, among which are to be found manzanita, juniper, laurel, whortleberry, and many other mountain bushes; also many vines and weeds, which form tangled, and almost impenetrable, thickets. Such, briefly, was the character of the region in which I now chose out a little valley, on a northern branch of the Merced River, twenty or thirty miles northeast of the famous Yo-Semite, and a hundred and sixty miles east of San Francisco.

In the neighborhood of my camping place, there happened to be one of those restless tribes of California Indians, who are accustomed to migrate from the plains to the mountains, and from the mountains to the plains, as the seasons change and the game upon which they live goes up or down. These children of nature lived upon the fish which they caught in the streams, and the small animals which they killed on the land; also, upon nuts, acorns, berries, and roots, sometimes upon insects and sometimes upon grasses. At the time of my advent among them in the fall, though plenty still smiled upon their larders, I aided to give them abundance; for there was much game, and I was liberal with what cost me so little trouble to procure. In return for this liberality, the Indians assisted me in building a wigwam and gathering and drying grass for the use of my oxen in the winter. They also assisted in tanning the skins of the deer I killed, and in making me several complete suits of buckskin, which I then adopted as my costume, and in which, ever since, I have generally dressed. Next my body I wore a heavy woollen garment, and on my head an untanned deer-skin cap, lined with rabbit's fur, and ornamented with a fox's tail; but all the rest of my clothing was buckskin, —that is to say, coat, pantaloons, and moccasins.

Having thus provided myself in every particular, as well as I was able, I awaited the advancing winter. As it began to grow cold, the Indians moved down the river, according to their custom; the mountains became deserted; the snows fell, and soon a wild waste surrounded me on every side. From now on I was perfectly alone, and did not see another human being for months. Yet, strange to say, those months were among the happiest of my life. My habitation was warm and comfortable; my health excellent; my time pleasantly and continuously occupied. I had enough to eat and drink, for game of some kind never failed; and there was no lack of the purest and freshest water. When the little stock of groceries, which I had brought along, ran out, various kinds of grass seeds, pounded into meal, served for flour, and roasted acorns made a substitute for coffee. The sugar-pine trees furnished that sweet gum, called pine sugar, which exudes from bruises in their trunks; and many were the receipts and expedients in mountain economy, which now became my special study. In making myself comfortable, I found pleasant and beneficial occupation, and I may say that I was as happy as a king.

Such was my first experience; and it was the earnest of what, on nearer and longer familiarity, I found mountain life really to be. I was peculiarly fitted for it. Even the mountain winters, severe as they are, were better suited to my tastes than the Italian beauties of the climate on the coast; and, as will be seen in the course of my narrative, for three successive years, though wandering during the summers in distant regions, I always returned to pass the winters in the high portions of the Sierra Nevada.

CHAPTER II.

THE GRIZZLY BEAR.

Greatness of the Grizzly Bear. Character of the Lion. Character of the Tiger. Character of the Grizzly of California. Neighborhood of the Grizzly. Armed Neutrality. Object in entering the Mountains. Visit of William Adams. Comparison of Fortunes. William's Propositions. Our Contract. Preparations for Travel. William Sykesey. The Indian Boys Tuolumne and Stanislaus. The Party and Equipments. May Morning in the Mountains. The Shoulders of the Sierra. Through Oregon into Washington. A Nondescript of Southern Oregon. Range of the Grizzly Bear. The Rocky Mountain Grizzly. The Californian Grizzly. The Grizzly of Washington, Oregon, and New Mexico.

THE mountains which I have been describing are the favorite haunts of the grizzly bear, the monarch of American beasts, and, in many respects, the most formidable animal in the world to be encountered. In comparison with the lion of Africa and the tiger of Asia, though these may exhibit more activity and bloodthirstiness, the grizzly is not second in courage and excels them in power. Like the regions which he inhabits, there is a vastness in his strength, which makes him a fit companion for the monster trees and giant rocks of the Sierra, and places him, if not the first, at least in the first rank, of all quadrupeds.

The lion, celebrated from time immemorial as a noble and generous brute, is, I grant, a splendid animal. When seen in his native wilds, with head erect and black mane floating over mighty shoulders, he presents a magnificent spectacle. When standing at bay also, with eye darting fire, and lashing his tawny sides with fury, he makes a terrific picture. Hundreds and hundreds of years ago, when animals first became known to literature, the old fabulists, impressed with his proud bearing, awarded to him his splendid reputation; they clothed him with the attributes of majesty; and few, since then, have ventured to deny his royalty, none to dispute his title of king of beasts. But, if we pursue him into his lairs and follow him on his midnight prowls, we soon detect the sneaking, cat-like qualities, which are born in him, and which must and will exhibit themselves in one mode or another. In the face of the world, the lion stands noble, magnificent, magnanimous; but in private life, he is rapacious, cruel, ever watchful for advantages, and frequently a feeder on carrion.

The tiger of India occupies a place in natural history next to the lion, and is classed with him among the most powerful and mighty of brutes. His path, it is true, is always red with blood, but it is the blood of inferiors; he fears his equals and flies from those above him. Like a midnight assassin, he creeps through his native jungles and makes a desolation around him; but his is the might of blood and butchery.

The grizzly bear of California, in the consciousness of strength and the magnanimity of courage, alone of all animals, stands unappalled in the face of any enemy, and turns not from the sight of man. He may not seek the conflict, but he never flies from it.

He may not feed upon royal meat, nor feel the flow of royal blood in his veins; but he is unapproachable, overwhelming. The lion and the tiger are like the deserts with their fiery simoons and tornadoes; the grizzly bear of California, like the mountains with their frosts and avalanches.

This was the animal which ranged, monarch of all he surveyed, on every side of me. I frequently saw him; he was to be found, I knew, in the bushy gorges in all directions; and sometimes, in my hunts, I would send a distant shot after him; but, as a general rule, during this first winter, I paid him the respect to keep out of his way; and he seemed somewhat ceremonious in return. Not by any means that he feared me; but he did not invite the combat, and I did not venture it. A few months afterwards, I considered it a point of honor to give battle in every case; but at this period bear hunting was not specially an object of either my ambition or inclination.

Upon entering the mountains, indeed, it was without any idea of devoting attention to bear hunting as a business. I went to live in peace, not to levy war upon the natives of the forest, any more than might be necessary for my support or recreation. But an event took place in the spring of 1853, which gave a direction and purpose to my mountain life, and led me to undertake those hunting expeditions and undergo those dangers and perils of which the history of my career chiefly consists. This event was the arrival of my brother William in my mountain camp.

He had come to California almost as early as I; but all my endeavors to find him had been unavailing. Although there was frequent communication between different parts of the country, my inquiries were always fruitless; never could I find even a trace of him. He was a man of few words, having a tinge of melancholy in his disposition, and little disposed to mingle much in conversation; so that, on the other hand, though he may have met many of my acquaintances, he learned nothing of me. While I was struggling in the southern mines to retain what had once been mine, and was now but a rough hunter, possessing little besides my rifles and my oxen, he, who had settled in the northern mines, had gone evenly forward, accumulated thousands, and was now returning, a wealthy man, to the east. By mere accident, he had heard of my failures and my subsequent retirement to the mountains, and had followed the clue until he found me.

My brother gave me a brief account of his life in California, which had been that of an industrious, energetic, and successful miner, and concluded with an earnest invitation for me to accompany him to our home in Massachusetts, where he kindly offered to start me in business again. I could not think for a moment, however, of returning, a broken man, upon his generosity, and replied that I preferred the wild and free life of a hunter to the confinement of a city. He observed from this answer the real state of the case, and made a second proposition, as generous as the first, and one which I could not refuse. This was, that he and I should enter into partnership; he to advance the means, and I to collect wild animals of California and neighboring countries; in short, we soon drew up and signed articles, specifying the conditions of a regular contract, providing for the payment of drafts, and prescribing the disposition to be made of animals; in relation to which, it is almost needless to state, that a *carte-blanche* was given me. These arrangements being completed, my brother and I again parted. He proceeded on his way to the East, and I soon afterwards started upon my first great hunting expedition.

I had long wished to see Oregon and Washington territories, whose fame was known to the world, even before that of California; and having now a business object, I resolved that they should be the first regions I would visit. I accordingly left my mountain fastness and drove down to a place called Howard's Ranch, laid in a stock of ammunition, and such other necessaries as were required; exchanged my oxen for mules and packsaddles, and gathered such information regarding the northern countries and the roads to them as could be obtained. I also opportunely fell in with a young man, named William Sykesey, who had been in those regions before, and who willingly undertook to go with me on the expedition. This young man came originally from Texas, and seemed to have a tinge of Indian blood in his veins, which was betrayed by his high cheek bones, his long, coarse, black hair, and very dark complexion. He had a good rifle and was a fair marksman; and, being well acquainted with woodcraft, my meeting with him was fortunate.

From Howard's, Sykesey and I proceeded, with our mules and packs, to Strawberry Ranch, near the North Fork of the Tuolumne River, where we procured the services of two Indian boys, about twenty years of age. These lads, who proved to be true and faithful fellows, had lived a portion of their lives among white people, could speak the English language, and understood the use of the rifle. The elder of them, from the name of his tribe, I called Tuolumne; the younger, for the same reason, Stanislaus. Our party was now complete, consisting of myself and three vigorous young men, having two good stout mules. We were all four cased in buckskin, and three of us carried rifles upon our backs; we had also pistols and knives; and, packed upon our mules, were camp fixtures, tools, a small quantity of flour, sugar, salt, other provisions, and other articles necessary for our vocation.

It was a beautiful May morning when we finally set out, — a morning doubly beautiful at that season, in those elevated mountain regions. Nature had arrayed herself in robes peculiarly fresh and green, and Flora decked the landscape with myriad flowers peculiarly bright and lovely. The purest and most invigorating atmosphere spread around, and birds of spring carolled songs from every tree. It was, indeed, a delightful opening of the campaign, and we set out upon our travels with hopeful and glad hearts. We travelled northward from Strawberry Ranch,

keeping upon the shoulders of the mountains, with
the snowy crest to our right and the valley of the
Sacramento far to our left. It was a rough road,
chosen only for the reason that we had to provide
ourselves with provisions on the way; and, frequently,
as the view opened here and there down into the
emerald and golden world below, we could not for a
moment but regret that we ever had to pass beyond
its borders. Happy the man that can establish his
permanent home there, and never be called upon to
live under other skies!

Without stopping to examine the country, or hunt
more than necessary, we hastened on for two weeks
to the Klamath region; whence we struck down
through that wilderness which lies between the Cascade and Blue mountains. We saw much to interest
us, on this travel, in the mountains, plains, forests,
streams, and Indians of Southern Oregon, but pushed
ahead as rapidly as possible, leaving the lofty heads
of Mount Jefferson and Mount Hood to our left, and
at length, well worn with fatigue, turned the great
bend of the Columbia, crossed Lewis's River, and struck
out into the country lying to the northeastward. We
came at last to a desirable valley among the hills,
where grass and water were abundant, about ten
miles distant from an Indian village or rancheria;
and, turning out our mules, we made our camp; and
this constituted our headquarters during the entire
summer.

In the course of our journey, we killed a number
of animals, and caught two small black bear cubs,

which we carried in a hamper on one of our mules. We also, while near Klamath Lake, saw a strange beast, which resembled a hedgehog with the head and feet of a bear. We made all the endeavors in our power to catch it, but in vain; and now, in looking back and harrowing my memory of this curious animal, I am unable to describe it more particularly. It was entirely unknown to me, and I had, very unwillingly, to leave it as one of the nondescript wonders of the Pacific coast.

The region of eastern Washington, where we were now encamped, contains many fine animals; but chief among them is the powerful one often denominated the curly-haired brown bear, which is in reality, however, but a variety of the grizzly species and cousin-german of the monster of California. There are several varieties of the grizzly bear; or, to speak more properly, perhaps, the species has a wide range, extending from the British Possessions on the north to New Mexico on the south, and from the eastern spurs of the Rocky Mountains to the Pacific Ocean. He was once frequently found on the lower part of the Missouri, and on the Mississippi River; but by degrees has been driven back, until now, his range east of the Rocky chain is much circumscribed. His size, general appearance, and character, vary with the part of this great region in which he is found; for although courageous and ferocious in the Rocky Mountains, he is there neither so large nor so terrible as in the Sierra Nevada, where he attains his greatest size and strength.

The grizzly of the Rocky Mountains seldom, if ever, reaches the weight of a thousand pounds; the color of his hair is almost white; he is more disposed to attack man than the same species in other regions, and has often been known to follow upon the human track for several hours at a time. It was this bear which first became known to the enlightened world; and from him the species was appropriately named grizzly. Among hunters, he is known as the Rocky Mountain white bear, to distinguish him from other varieties.

The California grizzly sometimes weighs as much as two thousand pounds. He is of a brown color, sprinkled with grayish hairs. When aroused, he is, as has been said before, the most terrible of all animals in the world to encounter; but ordinarily will not attack man, except under peculiar circumstances. It is of this animal that the most extraordinary feats of strength are recorded. It is said, with truth, that he can carry off a full-grown horse or buffalo, and that, with one blow of his paw, he can stop a mad bull in full career. When roused, and particularly when wounded, there is no end to his courage; he fights till the last spark of life expires, fearing no odds, and never deigning to turn his heel upon the combat. It is to him that the appellations of science, *ursus ferox* and *ursus horribilis,* are peculiarly applicable.

The grizzly of Washington and Oregon territories resembles the bear of California, with the exception that he rarely attains so large a size, and has a browner coat. His hair is more disposed to curl and is thicker, owing to the greater coldness of the climate. He is not so savage, and can be hunted with greater safety than either the California or Rocky Mountain bear. In New Mexico, the grizzly loses much of his strength and power, and upon the whole is rather a timid and spiritless animal.

THE DEAD GRIZZLY AND HER CUBS.

CHAPTER III.

LADY WASHINGTON.

NOT far distant from my camp, there was an extensive tract of chaparral, covering the side of a broad
mountain and skirting a beautiful valley of tender
herbage. My attention was attracted to it by indications of large bears; and, after a short examination, I discovered on the mountain-side the den of
an old grizzly with two yearling cubs. The animals
were in the habit of descending into the valley every
night, and had worn a trail, along which they almost
invariably passed in their excursions. I immediately
determined, if possible, to slay this dam, and make
myself master of her offspring, which were two of the
finest looking young beasts I had ever seen.

To resolve to do a thing, and to do that thing, are
different matters; and so I found them on this occasion. There seemed, however, to be but one plan of
action,— to waylay the dam; and, in accordance with

it, I concealed myself one morning near the trail, when the animals were coming up from the valley. I had both my rifles well charged lying at my side; and, as the oldest approached, I drew Kentucky, and planted a half-ounce ball in her breast. She fell, but almost instantly recovered herself and rushed towards me; when, seizing my second rifle, I fired a second shot through her open mouth into her brain. It is often the case that the grizzly will live for several hours after being pierced even through the head or heart, and perform prodigies of strength; but in this instance, fortunately for me, perhaps, life lasted but a few minutes.

As soon as the dam expired, I seized a lasso, which lay at my side, and rushed towards the cubs. I had imagined it would be a matter of ease, with the dam once out of the way, to secure them; but soon learned my mistake. As I rushed at them, they retreated; as I pursued, they broke away, and, doubling, shot past with a rapidity of motion which defied all my skill. I chased a long time without success; and, finally, when they and I were nearly worn out, they suddenly turned and made so violent an attack upon me that I was compelled, for my personal safety, to betake myself to a tree, and was glad to find one to climb. Although but little more than a year old, I saw that they had teeth and claws which were truly formidable.

It was a ludicrous situation which I occupied in that tree; and it makes me laugh now to think how a hunter of great bears was thus besieged by little

ones. However, there I sat, and there was no help
for it. The cubs tried to climb after me, and it was
necessary to pound their paws to keep them down;
and I shall never forget how they snapped their jaws,
and how wickedly they looked, when they were satisfied I was beyond their reach. Had they been full-
grown grizzlies and thus driven me, like the sage
Nestor of antiquity, to seek refuge in the branches,
it might have been a long time before it would have
been their good pleasure to withdraw; but the cubs
did not understand the art of starving an enemy;
and, in the course of half an hour, went off to their
dead mother. They had shown enough, however, to
make me give up the idea of taking them by the plan
proposed; and, as I left the place, I began contriving
other kinds of expedients for their capture.

The plan hit upon at last was to procure horses
from the Indians; for it seemed to me that, if we
could chase the cubs into the plain, and pursue on
horseback, we could certainly take them with our
lassos. Accordingly, the same day, I mounted a
mule, and, taking a quantity of dried venison as a
present, rode down to the village, which I found to
be under the sway of a hard-headed but good-natured
old Indian potentate, named Kennasket. This chief,
for divers good reasons, doubtless, placed little reliance in the white man; but he seemed pleased with
my present and conversation, and finally consented to
loan me three good horses, with which, however, he
sent a brave, whom we called Pompey, to see to their
safe return.

Having thus procured horses, three of us, well mounted, took the field the next morning before daylight, and repaired to the neighborhood of the dead bear, where the cubs still remained. It was my intention to drive them down the trail to the open valley, so that our lassos could be used with effect; and I therefore directed my comrades to conceal themselves and be ready to rush forward. Having dismounted, I then made a circuit, and getting upon the trail above the position of the animals, moved slowly down towards them. In many places the bushes were so thick that I had to creep under them upon my hands and knees; and, as my rifle was never out of my hands, it may be conceived that the path was not without its annoyances.

Upon drawing near the spot, a most interesting sight presented itself to my eyes. The cubs lay, with their paws upon the body of their dead mother, as if endeavoring to draw the accustomed warmth from it. Their appearance was so pleasing, so childlike, that, for a few moments, I could only stop and gaze. At first they did not observe me; but, on a slight movement, they suddenly sprang to their feet, and, as they did so, I dashed forward, whirling my cap. They bounded down the trail; I followed, thinking we surely had them now; but, unfortunately, my comrades, too anxious to act, prematurely left their places; and the cubs, frightened by the display, bounded aside from the trail, and, getting into the chaparral, escaped.

The next morning, we endeavored to try the same

plan over; but, on going to the place, I found that
the body of the dam had been devoured during the
previous afternoon by vultures or buzzards; and of
the cubs nothing was to be seen. I was now put
to my wits to know what to do; for some time it
appeared that nothing could be accomplished; but,
finally, the idea occurred to me that, as there was
but one spring in the valley, the animals would have
to visit it for water, and that there was the place
to take them. I therefore determined to watch the
spring; and, as soon as it began to grow dark that
evening, selected a place of concealment, where, the
result of the experiment being uncertain, and the
remainder of the party choosing to return to camp,
I was left alone.

The spring was a curious one, boiling up in the
midst of the valley and making a pond, with a considerable space of moisture. For some distance
around it there was a rank vegetation of coarse and
heavy grass, called sword-grass, and a few trees and
bushes. The mountains at the borders of the valley
were high and rugged, with chaparral upon their
sides, and oak, cedar, pine, and various kinds of mountain shrubbery about their summits. It was a lone
place; no signs of human habitation were to be seen,
no sounds of human life to be heard; and, particularly at night, the place was desolate and dreary
indeed. I tried to beguile the time by a severe
exercise of thought upon other subjects; but, in a
short time, I fell into a doze, then into a sleep, and
was not awakened until midnight, when the cubs

unexpectedly passed by me. The moon shone, and
they were plainly to be seen; but they had evidently
been at the spring, and were now on their return to
the mountain. They had outwitted me! I instantly
sprang from my concealment and rushed after them;
but in vain,— before I could overtake them, they
reached the chaparral; and thus, for the third time,
my endeavors failed.

It was my intention at first, after this failure, to
return to camp; but the thought struck me, that perhaps other animals would visit the spring, and I might
still not go empty-handed. I had before noticed the
tracks of panthers, wolves, deer, and antelopes, besides those of bears, in the neighborhood; and, as
almost all wild animals are abroad in the night-time,
there were fair chances of meeting some of them.
The idea was not a mistaken one; for in the course
of a few hours a pack of wolves approached. It is
the habit of these animals, when they drink as well
as when they eat, to do so noiselessly; but, as soon as
they have satisfied themselves, they usually set up a
concert of howls, which is anything but pleasant. It
is indeed a horrible noise, the most hateful a man
alone in the wilderness at night can hear. To a person anywise low-spirited or melancholy, it suggests
the most awful fancies, and is altogether doleful in the
extreme. I am, perhaps, as little affected with squeam-
ishness as any man; but the lugubrious howl of a
pack of wolves is more than I like; and I was glad
to put the cowardly rascals to flight by sending a
ball after them.

It was nearly morning before anything else approached. The moon had gone down; dawn began to appear; and I thought for certain that nothing more would come, when a light step attracted my attention; and, by putting my ear to the ground, I recognized it as the tread of a bear. To take a prize at last, after my long watch, was a pleasant anticipation; and I was all willingness for a conflict with the beast, however large or however ferocious he might prove to be. It was not necessary to wait long; in a few minutes a large black bear approached the spring; drank heartily, stepped into the water, and, after wallowing, came out and began rolling on the grass. At this moment, before he could start off for the mountains again, I resolved to fire; and, drawing my rifle to my face, uttered a yell to attract his attention. As anticipated, he rose upon his hind legs, and presented as fair a mark as could have been desired. Though still in the gray of the morning, the light of dawn shone upon my rifle barrel; the sights aimed directly at his breast, and I fired. It was all the work of a moment; and the bear sprawled upon the ground, which he tore in his mortal agony. I was so excited that, without waiting to reload, I rushed up, planted my foot upon his neck, and plunged my knife into his throat — and for several days afterwards his meat served for provisions.

Being now certain that the grizzly cubs visited the spring, I ordered out all my forces the next evening, and concealed them about the place, with strict instructions not to move but upon a signal. We commenced at sundown and watched till midnight. Once in a while a band of antelopes, a couple of deer, or a pack of wolves would approach; but they were allowed to come and go undisturbed. The stars, which rose in the evening, passed over our heads, and had sunk far down into the west; and faint streaks of light already played upon the eastern horizon, when, all at once, a yelping on the mountain, in the direction of the den, gave the welcome notification of the approach of the cubs. We now all stood watching every shadow and catching every sound. Presently the little bears ran past us, plunged their noses in the water, wallowed a few minutes, and then, crawling out, began tumbling and wrestling on the grass. At this moment, I gave the whistle; and sinking the spurs into our horses' sides, and swinging our lassos about our heads, we dashed forwards. The cubs, frightened by our sudden and unexpected attack, separated and ran in different directions. I pursued one, and my comrades the other.

My cub, which proved to be a female, bounded into the plain, and required a long chase. She ran quite a mile before it was possible for me to throw the lasso, which was no sooner over her head than she poked it off, and started on again. I followed several miles, and threw the lasso over her again and again, as many as seven times, before it kept its place; but it did finally retain its hold, and she was mine. I immediately sprang from my horse, and, whipping out a muzzle and cords from my pockets, soon had her bound head and foot. She was so beautiful that I had to stop and admire her for some time, before going to see what my comrades had done. They, too, had succeeded. Indeed, they flattered themselves that they had excelled the old hunter,— a hallucination in which I indulged them awhile for amusement. When the cubs separated, they had pursued theirs, which proved to be a male, a long distance, until he ran into a chaparral so thick and interlaced that he became completely entangled. They then dismounted, and seized him with their hands in such a manner that, though all were more or less scratched and bitten, they succeeded in securing and binding him,— and well was he bound; never in my life before or since have I seen an animal so completely tied up and wound about. They had then procured a long pole, and slinging the bear upon it, had borne him upon their shoulders to the spring. All this they told with great glee, enjoying their supposed triumph over me. I asked to be shown the place where they had captured him; and when they pointed it out, I remarked that they had an easier place to catch their bear than I mine; but they had got bitten and scratched, which I had not. This speech puzzled them. "Look at your hands," said I; "mine are not scratched in that way; there is no blood here;" and then I told them my story. "And," said I, "she is the prettiest little animal in all the country." Sykesey and Tuolumne thought I was joking, and wanted a proof; but, looking them straight in the eyes, I asked if they had ever known the old hunter to lie. No, they replied, they had never known that he ever did.

Such was the manner in which my bear, Lady Washington, one of the companions of my future hunting life, was captured. From that time to this, she has always been with me; and often has she shared my dangers and privations, borne my burdens, and partaken of my meals. The reader may be surprised to hear of a grizzly companion and friend; but Lady Washington has been both to me. He may hardly credit the accounts of my nestling up between her and the fire to keep both sides warm under the winter colds of the mountains; but they are all true; let him only read on.

CHAPTER IV.

THE WAY TO CAMP.

As the cubs were now caught, the next matter was
to get them to camp; and upon this question various
opinions were held. Sykesey proposed taking them
bound upon horseback; Tuolumne preferred making
a drag of grass, fastening them upon it, and pulling
them along; but there were objections to both these
plans. We finally determined to make an experiment
with the male cub, by putting a strap of buckskin
about his neck, attaching lariats on both sides, and
leading him. This arrangement, however, did not
work as well as anticipated; and the animal worried
himself so much, by prancing and leaping to one or
the other side, that, by the time we got to camp, he
was completely worn out. However, we doused him
into water, and, as soon as he was cooled and refreshed, chained him up to a tree.

On account of the above difficulties, I proposed making for Lady Washington a kind of box of dry hide, and packing her in on horseback; but my Indian friend, Pompey, said, No, that he would procure a cart, which would answer much better. This cart, he said, was of a kind sometimes used by the Indians for hauling their goods from place to place, and consisted of a tongue, axle-tree, two solid wooden wheels, and a body of green hide. I had never seen a vehicle of the kind, but from the description it seemed to be the very thing required, and I sent him off at once to procure it; and he promised to meet me where the bear lay three hours before dark.

Agreeably to our understanding, I rode out about the middle of the afternoon to the spot, and found the cub lying where she had been left, but fretting considerably with her situation. I passed the time admiring her, and looking for Pompey; but it grew nearly sundown, and he did not make his appearance. I fired my rifle several times as a signal; and at last, as the sun went down, a faint shout replied, appearing to come from a great distance; but this was caused by an intervening hill; and in a few minutes Pompey, with a cart drawn by two horses, came up, followed by three Indians on foot.

I had to stand amazed at the novelty of the vehicle they had brought. It answered the description given of it, but was entirely different from my idea, being one of the most rude and aboriginal carriages possible. The harness consisted of strips of dry elk-hide, rubbed in the hands until pliable, and fastened together with strings of the same. The traces were made of like strips, twisted. There were no collars, but only broad bands of hide in place of them. The tongue of the cart was short, and held up between the horses by strings attached to the shoulder-bands; but there was no breeching, and this astonished me most of all. I asked the Indians how they could keep the cart from running upon the horses' legs when going down hill. Pompey replied, that an Indian's cart was made to go only forwards, and it was a bad horse that could not keep out of the way of it. This answer amused me, and I should have asked many more questions; but the night approached, and we therefore, without more ado, hastily lashed the cub on the cart, and Pompey, jumping upon one of the horses, started off at so round a rate that I found it difficult to keep up. The Indians on foot put themselves to a fast trot, and, being good runners, lagged not behind in the race.

On the road to camp, upon getting within a mile of it, we suddenly came upon a pack of wolves, at a spot where they appeared, by remarkable good fortune, to have found a choice bit of carrion. The Indians cried out *Lobos*, as both they and the Spaniards call wolves, and asked me to kill them. At that time, wolves had no value in my eyes; but, to please the Indians, I dismounted, and, crawling towards the pack, which had gorged themselves, and were now howling and fighting over what was left, as is the habit of these gluttonous creatures, fired at them. My shot was random, there not being light enough to see; but I succeeded, by firing into their midst, in boring one through the middle, and soon heard him draw his breath through blood. At this the Indians were exceedingly delighted, and, with almost one voice, asked for the skin. I had always supposed that wolf skins were valueless; but now learned that they are highly prized by these northern Indians, who make leggings of them. So much, indeed, did they prize it, that they would not suffer the precious carcass to be tied on the cart with the bear, for fear of its being torn, and insisted upon carrying it themselves. So anxious were they for lobos leggings, that I at once engaged them for a grand antelope hunt, by a promise of wolf skins.

After this, we proceeded, without further incident, to camp, where a quantity of roasted bear-steaks, tea made of a fragrant herb of the mountains, and a rousing, comfortable, big fire awaited us. We were now eight souls in all, and sat down flat upon the ground to a feast such as only hungry hunters could properly enjoy. Our provisions, which were heaped before us when we sat down, rapidly dwindled away; but we continued to hack and hew until after midnight, and finally had it break in upon our stores of dried venison. This we placed upon the coals, so as to make it more brittle and edible; and most earnestly did we attack it. I remarked that my rifle had never failed in the hour of need, and directed the company not to spare; and I can assure the reader that the company did not spare; these Indians, whatever may be their failings in other respects, are terrible fellows with their jaws. The meal was barely ended, when Pompey, with a ludicrous twist of his lips, asked for the leather bottle. I protested that the leather bottle contained nothing but medicine. Pompey replied that it was good medicine for red man as well as white; and I found myself obliged to bring out the brandy, though I had but a few pints. We accordingly closed the occasion with a hearty swallow, which enlivened us all; and then, having chained up the second cub as we had done the first, we crept into our blankets, in an excellent good-humor with the world and with ourselves, and went to sleep.

The next day, having no further present use for the horses which were hired of the Indians, I determined to return them, and at the same time pay a visit of respect to the village, it being not only politic to make friends of our neighbors, but a matter of common justice to acknowledge our obligations to them. Accordingly, packing up a mule, I requested Pompey to take the horses, and we proceeded to the village.

The main species of traffic among these children of the wilderness is barter; there is, it is true, a knowledge of coin, which is becoming more extended as they are thrown into more frequent intercourse with civilization, but exchanges in kind still constitute the principal trade. My agreement had been to pay a sack of dried meat for each horse each day of their use; and as the indebtedness daily accumulated, this was an additional reason for promptness in settling the account.

The village was a collection of wigwams under the government of the old chief Kennasket, a man whom I afterwards found to be of considerable dignity of character, and, for a savage, of remarkable mildness and urbanity of manner. He ruled over his people with a sort of patriarchal sway, exercising the power, not of a conqueror and despot, but of a protector and father. The whole constitution of the society, indeed, resembled what we are taught of the patriarchs, with the exception that, instead of those immense flocks which we read of, the only domesticated animals found here were horses and dogs, and the mode of life was rude in the extreme.

The chief, when I was brought into his presence, expressed himself glad to see the white man, and thanked me for the venison. He had always been disposed, he said, to look upon the pale faces with distrust, having frequently been wronged by them; but, seeing that I was punctual and honorable, he hoped we might be friends. With these words, he looked up towards heaven, as if calling upon the Great Spirit to witness the purity of his intentions, and handed me his pipe, which I smoked. We then settled the terms of our accounts; and, in this transaction, he was much more liberal than was to have been expected. After passing my faith that the score should soon be squared off, I shook hands with all the Indians, mounted my mule, and, followed by Pompey, returned to camp.

The excellent relations thus so auspiciously commenced with the Indians, afforded assurances that we would have no difficulties with them. They are a rude race of beings, but intrinsically very much like ourselves, having the same passions, differing from us more in education, or want of education, than in nature. Even the Digger races of California, though idle, shiftless, and filthy, as a general rule, are capable of being active and handy, — witness my boys, Tuolumne and Stanislaus. They have been, however, greatly abused by those whites who consider them little better than beasts; and their generally peaceful and submissive characters, instead of procuring immunity from injury, have seemed only to invite oppression. It makes my blood boil with indignation to hear of the cruelties sometimes practised towards these poor creatures; for if the truth of the oft-repeated battle-cry of "Indian Depredations" were known, few indeed would be the cases found where the red men were really at fault.

The northern tribes, being fiercer and more disposed to resent injuries than the poor Diggers, are more respected, and treated more like fellow beings; but even in their case, it is not humanity or respect that protects them but rather the fear of their retaliation. Over the whole western country, it seems to be a rule that the white man can injure the Indian with impunity, and no one steps forward to make his the common cause of mankind; but let the Indian retaliate, and the cry of "Indian Depredations" is raised, and the hounds of war and extermination are loosened to slay and ravage. I have lived much among the red men; I have seen much, and had many opportunities of knowing them intimately; but in all cases, in the north and in the south, never have I found them otherwise than as well disposed for peace and fair dealing as the white men. My tastes of propriety and cleanliness, as a white man, have frequently been shocked by their habits; but honorable and courtly dealing on my part has always been met with a return in kind on theirs. In all my experience, I have never had to quarrel or fight with them; and I am convinced that, if my disposition towards them had actuated all white men from the first, they would have been found as well disposed to all as they invariably were to me.

It is the decree of an overruling Providence that the red man shall die out, and there is no fault to be found with it, any more than with the fiat which ordered the extermination of the ancient creatures whose forms live only in the rocks; but that butchery and wrong by their own more enlightened fellow-men should be the means of destruction, seems to me not necessarily the command of a good God. It may be that everything that is, is right; but we might make it different, and it would still be right.

CHAPTER V.

ANTELOPE HUNTING.

OUR supply of fresh provisions being now entirely gone, I led out my whole party for an antelope hunt. In the course of an hour or two, we reached a grassy plain, where this animal abounded; and, as the sun rose over the misty landscape, we descried a herd of about fifty. The antelope is one of the sharpest-sighted and keenest-scented of all animals, and being also the fleetest, the hunter would have great difficulty in taking it, were it not for another peculiarity in its nature, which renders it a comparatively easy prize. I refer to its curiosity; it is so inquisitive as almost invariably to approach, rather than run from, a strange object, unless badly frightened. The attraction of highly colored cloths, particularly, is so great that it is often drawn into the very jaws of destruction by running up to look at them. Frequently I have decoyed a foolish herd within fifteen or twenty steps of my rifle, by merely holding up my handkerchief, coat, or hat, or even my hand or foot. To lie on one's back, with the feet in the air and the rifle between the legs, is a favorite and very successful mode of hunting them.

When a herd of antelopes is feeding, one of the bucks, and sometimes more than one, stands upon the lookout. He generally selects an eminence a little apart from his companions, and continually snuffs and whiffs the air, throwing his head in every direction, and noticing everything calculated to attract attention. It is easy to recognize him; and if the hunter can succeed in deceiving or escaping his watchfulness, he finds no trouble in approaching the herd. Having this knowledge of the habits of the animal, I gave my comrades instructions how to surround the game without alarming them, well knowing that if we could frighten them into a panic, there would be no difficulty in taking as many as we required. They followed my directions implicitly, and Pompey, when he reached his post, raised a red handkerchief, the fluttering of which soon attracted the notice of the antelope lookout. Upon observing it, the animal gave a sharp snort, and, bounding into the air, wheeled around and called the attention of the herd to the strange sight. Immediately, the other Indians raised their handkerchiefs at other points; and upon all closing in, the animals, seeing too late that they were surrounded, became bewildered, and, huddling up together, wheeled and tramped around in utter amazement, apparently not knowing what to do or where to go.

In the meanwhile, taking care to keep our bodies

concealed in the long grass, we had continued to approach; and, being now within sixty yards of the panic-stricken animals, I rose upon my feet, took deliberate aim, and fired into their midst. Sykesey and Tuolumne followed the example, and the Indians discharged their arrows. I reloaded as quickly as possible, and fired a second shot; then, dropping the rifle, pulled my revolver in my right and my bowie-knife in my left hand, and rushed into the thick of the herd, which continued wheeling and tramping around in a circle, seeing themselves surrounded on all sides, and too much alarmed to fly. At the same time my comrades rushed forward; and we were soon all mixed up together, myself, the Indians, and the antelopes. Having discharged the shots of my pistol, I began plying my knife; and as the Indians used theirs, we wounded several that escaped our fire-arms. In the midst of the excitement, a buck broke away from the herd and was immediately followed by all that were able to get away, some dragging lamed limbs after them. As, however, six dead and five wounded lay before us, there was no use pursuing the flying band, and they were allowed to escape, although we might easily have procured a dozen more.

The field, as it was, was a field of carnage. Within the space of half an acre lay the bodies, some struggling still with life; and the grass all around was sprinkled with blood. We soon despatched the wounded; and, dragging the eleven into a heap, surveyed our work with satisfaction. The Indians, particularly, looked on with astonishment, and said one to the other, that the white man was *muchee goodee killee muck-a-muck*, — that is, a great hunter. I said that it was no great thing for a white man to plan a slaughter in that manner; but the Indians continued to regard it as an extraordinary feat; and, from that time on, they regarded me as a very great man, a *Hyas Tyee*, a great chief.

It is usual, on the hunt, after killing large game, to open it and turn out the entrails, as well to lighten the load to be carried as to preserve the freshness and sweetness of the meat. Such would have been the course here; but considering that the hearts, livers, lungs, and other inward parts would make good provisions for our young bears, I ordered the bodies of the antelopes to be packed as they were. The mules were brought up; three antelopes placed on each, — two lengthwise, and one crosswise on top; and, being firmly lashed to the saddles, they made good loads of about three hundred pounds. Packing is an art which requires some apprenticeship; and, in countries where goods are transported on the backs of animals, a skilful hand is a man of repute.

Our mules being able to take but six of the bodies, and there being five over, I determined, as a matter of experiment, to try what the Indians were made of, and proposed that each one, who would carry an antelope to camp without stopping, should have it for his pains. At the time of making the banter, I did not expect its acceptance; but Pompey's three friends directly picked up a body each and started off. They did not calculate the distance, which was not less than three miles, but started off manfully. There being two bodies left, I directed Tuolumne to remain with them until my return with the mules; and the rest of us then proceeded after the stalwart Indians, and, in the course of a mile, overtook them. Their legs were already weakening under their burdens; and, in the course of a few hundred yards further, one suddenly threw his load down and declared that he would carry no more *muck-a-muck;* and the two others followed his example. They had, however, done so well that I freely gave them the game, and, on my return, loaned them a mule to carry it the remainder of the way.

Upon getting back to Tuolumne, I found him lying in the grass, near his antelopes, but fast asleep. The sun had by this time risen high, and was darting fierce rays upon him; but the boy was so completely overcome that he did not awake at my approach. I even packed the antelopes, and drove off a short distance; and still he slumbered, perfectly unconscious of all that transpired around him. This was culpable neglect on his part, and I determined to teach him a lesson. Accordingly, after concealing the loaded mule entirely out of sight, I encased myself in a bear-skin which ordinarily served the purpose of a blanket under the mule's saddle, and, hiding myself in the long grass near the sleeping fellow, uttered a savage growl, as nearly like that of a bear as possible. Tuolumne, being startled, sprang in an instant to his feet, and stooped to seize his rifle, which lay at his side;

but I growled louder than before, and made a jump forwards. At this demonstration, he wheeled, and ran as fast as his legs would carry him, ingloriously leaving his rifle behind. The faster he ran, the faster I followed and the louder I growled. He looked over his shoulder once, but seeing himself pursued by a most savage and bloodthirsty animal, as he supposed, strained himself to the extent of his speed; it was only with difficulty that his heels could be seen, for the dust he raised. When he disappeared, I leisurely picked up his rifle, and, taking the mule, proceeded to camp.

Upon arriving there, I found that Tuolumne had told a terrible story about being chased by a bear; and the entire camp was in a great state of excitement at his account of the monster, which he declared had pursued within a short distance of where they sat. Being willing to play the joke a little further, I did not contradict the report, but affected to believe it, and amused myself with listening to his description of the bear, which he said was not so very large, but exceedingly fierce.

When we turned into our blankets that night, I cautioned him to keep a good look-out. "That bear," said I, "has got a smell of your meat, and he will be sure to call on you before morning." This frightened the poor fellow so much that he became violently excited. I continued to aggravate all the circumstances which he had narrated, until he became positively alarmed, when I reproached him for his cowardice, and told all the particulars of my finding him asleep, packing and concealing the mule, how I had thrown the bear-skin over my head, how I growled, how far I had chased him, and, indeed, all the facts just as they occurred. But Tuolumne could not, or would not, believe otherwise than that he had really been pursued by a bear, and answered all our jokes at his expense by the reply that what he saw with his eyes he must believe. To such an extent will imagination sometimes take possession of the senses, and, on small foundation, conjure up terrors which have no actual existence!

CHAPTER VI.

TRAP BUILDING.

Determination to build Traps. Tools. Construction of the Body of
a Trap. Doors. Dead-fall Arrangement. Modus Operandi of
a Trap. Early Work. The Beauties of Morning. Distribution
of Labor. Blasting Logs. Adventure with a Black Bear. Abundant Venison. Philosophy_of our Hunting.

HAVING thus, by a few hunts and the many indications on every side, fully convinced myself of the
existence, in abundance, of fine game in the country,
I determined immediately to build traps; for it was
on them, and not on the rifle or the lasso, that any
great reliance for the capture of living animals could
be placed. We had already put off this work too
long, and it would not do to delay any longer. We
therefore at once proceeded to select positions for
three traps, choosing such places as the game most
frequented, and where the materials for the building
could be most conveniently procured. As for tools,
they were a portion of the outfit which we brought
from California, consisting of axes, saws, hatchets,
augers, chisels, picks, shovels, and drawing-knives.
With these we commenced our labors, and, having
anticipations of great success, worked with alacrity
and perseverance.

There are required, for the construction of a good
trap, about seventy pieces of timber, and a large num-

ber of wooden pins. It is usually made in size about ten feet long, five wide, and five high. When the ground is selected and levelled off, two parallel trenches are dug, into which the sleepers are laid; and upon these is pinned the floor, which consists of logs placed side by side, resembling a section of corduroy road. The sides are made by placing a number of large timbers, similar to the sleepers, one above the other, and pinning them firmly together, so that solid walls of timber are formed; and upon these are pinned the top timbers, which resemble those of the bottom. Above these, along the sides, are laid what are called string-pieces, which are not only pinned down, but at the ends they are connected with the sleepers by perpendicular ties, made of limbs with crotches or hooks at their extremities. Thus bound, the body of the trap is very strong, and might be turned over repeatedly, like a box open at the ends, without displacing a timber. But, for the purpose of making it still stronger, a spot is generally selected between two trees, into which the side timbers, besides being fastened together, are also pinned, doubling the strength. Where there are no trees, posts are generally planted for the same purpose; or where there is one tree, a post is used on the other side. Strength is the great object.

The doors are made of split boards a few inches thick, pinned together crosswise in a square form of the required size. They are intended to slide up and down in grooves, made by pinning slats at the ends of the trap. When they are down, the trap is perfectly inclosed, a complete box. But the most nice and particular work is the apparatus for setting and springing the doors. Two upright, forked pieces of wood, a few feet high, are mortised into the middle of the string-pieces, one on each side; and in their forks rests a beam. Over this beam play two levers, eight or nine feet long, to the outer ends of which, by short chains or ropes, the doors are attached. The butt-ends of these levers are sharpened, to fit the notches of a small but important piece of timber, which holds them in their places. The levers lying across the beam, with the weight of the doors at their outer ends, there is a strain tending to draw their butt-ends apart; the notched stick supports this strain, and holds them in position. While the levers, and by them the doors, are held up by the notched stick, the stick itself is held by the levers,— the whole being a sort of self-sustaining, double dead-fall arrangement. The bait is attached, by a rope running up through a hole in the top of the trap, to this notched stick; so that if an animal enters the trap, and jerks at the bait, it pulls the notched stick away, and displaces the levers from the notches; and the doors, being no longer supported, of course fall, and the animal is inclosed. Such is the common double-door trap of the mountains; but sometimes only one door is made, and the arrangement is somewhat simpler.

The three traps occupied our time for a couple of weeks; and we labored steadily, going out early every morning to our work. It has always been my opinion that an hour before sunrise is worth two afterwards; the mind is then clear and the body fresh; and it was my practice, therefore, to rouse the camp and get upon the way even in advance of Aurora. A person who has not experienced the influence of an early, calm, summer morning, with the heavens lighting up in a crimson glow above, and the birds wakening into song around him, may perhaps imagine, but cannot feel the beauty and joyousness of the scene.

During the first days of the building, we took the mules with us, for the purpose of hauling the logs together in such places as had been selected for the traps. These spots were several miles apart, but all in ravines where timber-trees were plenty. In some cases, little hauling was necessary; but in others, logs had to be brought from some distance; and this labor was generally attended to by the boys, while Sykesey and I, being more expert with the tools, hewed and hacked. Everything went well till we came to make the doors of the first trap; when, having occasion to split a straight-grained but tough log, we experienced difficulty, and for some time did not know how to manage it. The axe was not enough, nor would wedges work as well as could be wished; and, after several ineffectual trials, we found that some other plan must be adopted. I remembered a method of splitting logs sometimes practised in the forests of New England, and determined to try it. This was to bore an auger-hole in the log, and load it with gunpowder, in the same manner that blasts in rocks are charged. It succeeded admirably, rending the timber into two

equal pieces; after which it was easy to split it up
into boards with our axes and wedges. In this manner we worked up other logs, until there were boards
sufficient.

During all the period of our labor our rifles were
always within reach, and on the way to and from the
traps they were invariably upon our shoulders. One
morning, as we were thus on our way, we observed
a black bear on a hill-side ahead, which appeared to
be either eating grass or digging roots. I resolved
to slay it, and, giving the mules over to the care of
the boys, directed Sykesey to take one direction and
I would take another, to get above the beast and
shoot it. It was preconcerted that he should fire
first; and, upon reaching the spot pointed out, he did
so; but the ball struck the bowels instead of the
vitals of the beast, and seemed rather to madden
than disable. It tore up the grass and dirt at a fearful rate, and looked about for its enemy. Meanwhile,
I endeavored to procure a shot at the heart, but was
not able to do so, on account of its violent motions;
and, therefore, trusting to chances, rose with my rifle
at my face, and uttered a yell. At this, the bear
turned, and I fired; but with little better effect than
Sykesey; the animal only reeled and staggered for
a moment, and then ran towards a thicket about a
hundred yards distant. I immediately dropped the
rifle, and, drawing my revolver and knife, rushed after
it; and so closely, that, suddenly facing about, it made
at me open-jawed, within a few feet. Being prepared
for this, however, I discharged my pistol in its face;

the ball passed through the nose into the brain, and the brute fell over backwards, dead. We left the boys to quarter and pack the meat to camp, and proceeded, as usual, to our work. As the traps were completed, one after the other, we baited them with pieces of fresh venison. Deer were plenty, and fell before our rifles in unconsidered numbers, affording a bountiful supply of provisions for our wants, and for barter with the Indians. I never killed game in mere wantonness, nor allowed those under my control to do so; but the hungry stomachs of two men at constant hard labor, and of two growing Indian boys, besides the traps, captive bears, and drying-poles, required an amount of flesh, which might surprise the uninformed. The exercise of a hunter creates a keen appetite, and, if successful, he is as dainty in his palate as other good livers, accepting none but choice cuts. For this reason, unless he have animals to feed with the refuse, he sometimes makes great and inexcusable waste, giving too much cause for the reproach of indiscriminate slaughter, which is often laid at his door.

CHAPTER VII.

IN THE CHAPARRAL.

OPPOSITE where we built our last trap was a hill composed of crumbling rocks, high and precipitous. It was covered with chaparral, and by the spreading and interlacing of creeping branches and vines, the precipice appeared entirely overgrown with a thick and vigorous vegetation. One evening, as we were about giving over work for the day, my attention was attracted by a noise on this hill; and, upon casting my eyes upward, I beheld a large grizzly bear coming down, back foremost, allowing her weight to carry her, while she retarded what would otherwise have been too rapid a descent by holding on to the rocks and bushes with her claws. So ludicrous was this mode of progression, — if coming down tail foremost can be called progression, — and so droll her movements in catching at every twig and branch in her course, that, but for the danger of my situation, I could have laughed outright, As, however, laughing or any other

ADAMS AND THE ELK

noise under the circumstances, might have exposed us to imminent peril, I kept perfectly silent, and beckoned Sykesey to reach me my rifle, which was leaning against a tree near where he stood. As he did so, I whispered that we were in a dangerous situation, and that it would require all our coolness and nerve to escape destruction. At the same time, I cautioned him to reserve his fire and be ready in case my shot should prove ineffectual; and, at all events, to stand by me in case of extremity. I spoke thus, because the fellow seemed frightened; but this solemn talk frightened him still more; he, however, promised to obey my instructions, and stand by me like a man.

By this time the bear had slid down within shooting distance; but, her position not presenting so fair a mark as was desired, and there now not being light enough to procure good aim, I was loth to fire; nevertheless, feeling that it would be the only opportunity, and trusting to good fortune, I blazed away. The smoke hardly lifted, and the echoes were hardly still, when crack! went Sykesey's rifle too; and, upon looking around, I saw that he not only had fired, but had also taken to his heels, and was running as fast as his legs would carry him, leaving me to take the chances alone. There was, however, no time to reprove this cowardly conduct, for the bear now came down with a tumbling plunge, and I drew my bowie-knife in the expectation of an immediate and close conflict. Indeed, I braced myself for a deadly encounter, when, very unexpectedly, the bear rushed past, perhaps not seeing me, and bounded away for the dense thicket in the ravine below. Her motions, and a few drops of blood which stained her course, showed that she was badly wounded. Catching up my rifle, and reloading as quickly as possible, I pursued, in hopes of obtaining another shot and finishing the business; but before I was able to overtake her she gained the thicket, which was too dense, and it was now too dark, to attempt to enter.

While this was taking place, Sykesey stopped in his flight, and, retracing his steps, came up with a story that his gun had gone off prematurely, and that he supposed he must save himself the best way he could. "It is to be expected," I replied, "that a man will act according to his nature. Bravery fronts danger, and repels it; but it is the character of a coward to run, though he drag after him, not only disgrace, but danger too." Indeed, I felt crusty enough to have said still more severe things, on account of his cowardly conduct; but I well knew that many other men would have acted precisely in the same manner, under similar circumstances.

It was now dark, and we were three miles from camp. A good part of the distance, too, was through chaparral, frequented by bears and other formidable animals, where an encounter might, at any time, and particularly in the evening, be expected. Sykesey knew this, and asked what I would do provided a bear should dispute our passage. My reply was, that it would be as easy to fight a bear in the night as in the daytime; for, said I, a man has to die but once, and when his time comes, it comes. He re-joined, that I might fight in the dark, if so disposed, but not to expect his help. "It is not likely," said I, "that a man will stand fast at night, who will run in the day; but do not be alarmed, you have the choice of staying where you are." At the mention of the dreadful alternative of being left, the fellow was more alarmed than ever, and very gladly fol-lowed me, without another word. Fortunately for him, as well as for myself, perhaps, we were not ob-structed in our way, and reached camp without fur-ther adventure.

Early the next morning, as usual, we started out for the purpose of working on the trap. As we passed the thicket into which the bear had disap-peared on the last evening, Sykesey remarked that she must have been badly wounded, and might be taken without difficulty. I replied that if he would promise to exhibit a little more courage than the pre-vious evening, I was willing to enter the chaparral, and look for her. He protested that he would stand by me to the last drop of his blood; and, upon this assurance, I bade him follow. We thereupon dis-mounted, and, pursuing the bloody track of the bear, entered the thicket. The further we penetrated, the thicker became the brush; and, presently, so inter-laced and intertwined were the upper branches, that we were compelled to get upon our hands and knees, and crawl. Thus we proceeded, I in front, and Syke-sey at my heels, for at least five hundred yards, but still could see nothing of the animal.

At last, we arrived in a spot where the chaparral was particularly thick, and it was difficult to proceed further, even by crawling. I remarked to my companion that we must keep our weapons ready for instant use, for, should an attack be made upon us, there being no room to turn, and little to use our arms, we would be in great danger. Had I not been confident, indeed, judging from the blood which discolored the leaves along the trail, that the bear would be too weak to do much injury, I would hardly have ventured into that dark and tangled place; and Sykesey, upon looking ahead, at once proposed to give up the search, and return. In his opinion, it was mere foolhardiness thus to rush into the jaws of peril. I replied, that I had been taught long ago the lesson, never to commence a thing and then back out, without good reasons; and if the bear was there, I would find her. With these words, adjusting my revolver and bowie-knife, but still holding my rifle, I advanced, peering about in every direction for the beast, which, as this was the thickest portion of the chaparral, and a likely place for a den, I thought could not be far off. The idea was not incorrect; I soon perceived a heap of earth, and, cautiously approaching and looking over, I saw the bear lying in the den, with her head upon her paws, as if sleeping. I beckoned Sykesey to look, and he also saw her. I thought from his actions that he would draw back, without a blow; but, catching him by the arm for a moment, I drew my rifle, and, taking a sure and deliberate aim, placed a ball at the butt of the bear's ear. The lead broke through her skull, but there was no movement; she was already dead. I turned to Sykesey, and remarked that he need not be alarmed, she had gone to sleep forever. "What!" said he, "is she dead?" "Yes," I replied, "and cold too." We jumped down into the den, and turned the body over to find the wounds. My ball of the previous evening had passed through her lungs, and probably caused death immediately after she reached the den. We then drew our knives, skinned and cut her up, bore the quarters and hide out through the chaparral, and, packing them upon the mules, sent the boys with them to camp.

Another adventure occurred about this same time, which might have cost me my life; this was a combat with an elk. The morning of the day we expected to complete the trap, as fresh meat would be needed for bait, I sent my comrades ahead with the mules, but myself made a circuit for the purpose of killing a deer. In the course of a few miles, I discovered a band of five or six elks. There was one of them, a splendid buck, with fine antlers, and magnificent bearing, which particularly attracted my attention. Could he have been transported, as he stood there, into the midst of the world, poets and painters would have paid tribute to his beauty; no stag of Landseer has a nobler mien, or more of the spirit of freedom in his limbs.

It was impossible to approach nearer than seventy-five yards without alarming the band; and, consequently, I fired from that distance. The buck fell, and supposing him to be dead, I drew my knife, and, as is the usual practice upon shooting an animal of this kind, rushed up to cut his throat. The elk, however, was only wounded; and when I reached him, he suddenly sprang upon his feet, and jumped with his fore legs upon my shoulders. This knocked the knife from my hands; but hastily drawing my revolver, I discharged the barrels, one after the other, in quick succession, while hopping around to avoid his terrific lunges. Fortunately, one of my shots took effect at the butt of his ear, and stunned him; when, seizing the opportunity to grasp my knife, I ran up, plunged it to the heart, and the red tide of life spouted from his side. I then ripped him up to the bearded throat, and turned the entrails out upon the ground.

My neck and back were severely bruised, but not enough to prevent me from shouldering my rifle, proceeding to the trap, and working there steadily until sundown. In the evening, we passed by the spot, packed the meat to camp, and had a noble roast. While enjoying a dainty cut, I could not help remarking that it was as good as any porter-house steak; upon which observation, Tuolumne, who was of an inquiring mind, asked what was the meaning of "porter-house steak." I explained to him, as well as I could, that it was the choice cut of a beef. This casual conversation gave us a phrase of which we did not hear the last for many days; for Tuolumne was so impressed with the sound, that he used the words, "porter-house steak," long afterwards, to express the climax of excellence.

The next day after this, we completed the trap, and, as soon as it was finished, Tuolumne, at my direction, gathered a lot of old wood, punk, and grass, and gave it a good smoking. The object of this was to darken the timbers, and to give them an oldish smell. He then took a quarter of the elk meat, and, tying it to the saddle with a lariat, dragged it a considerable distance around the trap, so as to leave a strong scent upon the ground. Then baiting the trap, and nicely setting it, we packed our tools upon a mule, and, leaving everything in order, returned to camp. We now had three good traps, and reposed, with excellent hopes of success in a short time.

CHAPTER VIII.

BEAR EDUCATION.

The Philosophy of Education. My Black Bear Cubs. Experiment with the Cubs. I become a *Pater Familias.* The Grizzly Cubs. Lady Washington. First Lesson to Lady Washington. Its Effect. Second Lesson to Lady Washington. Jackson's Obstinacy. A Lesson to him. His Submission. The Science of Physiognomy. Educational Capabilities of Bears.

THE high state of training to which several of my bears were brought, will form an interesting part of my story; and, as they subsequently became my constant companions in all my wanderings and upon many of my hunts, the manner in which they were educated deserves careful and particular mention. It is with bears as it is with children, — although much allowance is to be made for the stock from which they spring, yet, if the right course be taken, their natural characters may be modified and improved to such a degree as to be a subject of wonder. Taking, for example, my own case: — with all my natural inclinations for the wild and adventurous life of the forest, I am satisfied that training might have made me a peaceful and contented burgher all the days of my life. This, my belief, is strengthened by what is to be seen in the world every day; and more so, because, with much less capable pupils than human beings, I myself have changed savage and ferocious natures to affection and gentleness.

My pets now amounted to four: the black cubs, which had been caught on our way through Oregon, and the grizzlies, lately taken. The former, which were quite young, and which were by nature of much milder disposition than the grizzly cubs, were already tame enough to follow us about camp, almost like dogs. They were frequently allowed to run perfectly free, and would play around us without the slightest desire to leave. On the contrary, they became so much attached to our persons that it was difficult to prevent them following wherever we went. If we moved but a short distance, they would jump up and pursue; and such was their watchfulness, that it was almost impossible to escape their vigilance. Many a time, when, apparently worn out with their gambols, they seemed to be asleep, did I endeavor to steal away unobserved; but never did they fail in a short time to discover my absence, and then they would run searching to find where I had gone.

One night I resolved to try a new experiment with the black cubs; this was to have them sleep by me. Upon spreading my blanket to retire, I drove a stake near my feet, and tied them to it. Making them lie down side by side, I then spread a corner of the blanket over them, and felt as responsible and proud as any *pater familias* in the abodes of civilization. During the night, my fondlings were a little troublesome, and required me to rise several times; but, with a little judicious boxing of their ears, they lay still at last, and we all passed a reasonably comfortable night.

With the grizzlies there was much more difficulty; not only on account of their natural ferocity, but because they were more than a year old. From the day on which they were captured, we were compelled to keep them chained; and, although they became by degrees more familiar, they did not show any disposition whatever to acknowledge a master. Lady Washington, whom I had treated with the greatest kindness, was particularly violent, and invariably would jump and snap at me, whenever within her reach. On one occasion, when she had nearly injured me seriously, I came to the determination to give her a castigation that would make her recollect me; and I called my comrades to witness, and, if necessary, assist me in, this first lesson of subjection.

I stepped back into a ravine, cut a good stout cudgel, and, approaching with it in my hand, began vigorously warming her jacket. This made her furious; it would, indeed, be difficult to describe her violence, the snarls she uttered, and the frothing anger she exhibited, — not that she was hurt, but she was so dreadfully aroused. My comrades, in view of the danger, cautioned me to desist; but, notwithstanding their fears and remonstrances, I continued trouncing her back, until finally she acknowledged herself well corrected, and lay down exhausted. It is, beyond question, a cruel spectacle to see a man thus taking an animal and whipping it into subjection; but when a bear has once grown up, untutored, as large as the Lady was, this is the only way to lay the foundation of an education, — and the result proved the judiciousness of my course. In a short time afterward I patted her shaggy coat; and she gradually assumed a milder aspect, which satisfied me that the lesson had been beneficial, and that she would not soon forget it. As she became calmer, I gave her a greater length of chain; and, upon feeding her, she ate kindly and heartily, and gave good promise of what she afterward became, — a most faithful and affectionate servant.

A week or two after this, I resumed the training of Lady Washington, being determined that her education should not suffer for want of tuition. Every day she had been taught a little; but this was rather to keep her in mind of the first lesson, than to give her a new one. On this latter occasion, having removed the chain and attached a lariat to her collar, I led her about the camp, and found her much more tractable than was to have been expected. A little stubbornness she indeed showed at first; but a few raps on her back reminded her of the duties she owed, and entirely removed the necessity of any more trouncing for the time being. Her education was as yet by no means complete; but, even in learning this much, she had made remarkable proficiency.

The male grizzly cub, which had been named Jackson, was even more difficult to be managed than Lady Washington. Upon an attempt being made to lead him, he would sit doggedly still, refusing to move, and growling defiantly. When his chain was pulled, he would place his paw upon it and bristle up, as much as to say, "At your peril!" Indeed, all my endeavors to do anything with him, peaceably, were ineffectual; and, as he seemed to be becoming fixed in his obstinacy, I determined to treat him also with the necessary severity. Accordingly, mounting a mule, having attached a lariat, one end to his collar and the other to the pommel of the saddle, I dragged him along by main force. After being pulled thus a short distance, he leaped at the mule's legs; but she kicked, and laid him sprawling on the grass. Being but little injured, however, he soon got up again; but was a sadder and a wiser bear than ever before; for, although he braced himself for a few minutes against my invitations to come along, he soon found it was of no use to resist the odds against him, and sulkily followed, wherever I was pleased to lead.

After leading him about, thus, for some time, I jumped down from my mule, took the lariat in my hand, and led him in that manner; feeling certain that his evil spirit was overcome, and that there was no danger in doing so. At one time, in a fit of returning obstinacy, he sat down and refused to move; but a few whacks over the haunches recalled him to his proper senses, and he again followed me. In fine, upon tying him to his tree, I felt safe in approaching, patting him upon the head, and scratching his neck, — actions which are grateful to the bear as well as to most other animals; and he received these favors with a pleasant countenance. It was easy to see that he might be considered as reclaimed.

Certain philosophers have taught a science, called

physiognomy, in which they profess to find an index to character in the form of the face. If character were an attribute of the face, there might be some plausibility in the science; but hardly otherwise. It is certain, however, that the face is frequently an index of the emotions; there seem to be certain muscles called into action by certain feelings; and an experienced eye will seldom misinterpret this language of the features. The repeated exercise of these muscles may give a cast to the face, indicative of the general character, and thus partially sustain the claims of physiognomy; and, so far, the science applies as well to beasts as men. When, therefore, I say that Jackson had a pleasant countenance, I mean that his face expressed a good and submissive spirit.

Such was the commencement of my bear taming; the subsequent steps, and an account of the various degrees of docility to which my pets arrived, are woven almost inseparably into my narrative. From all my experience, and from what has reached me in the way of unquestionable information, the conviction is pressed upon my mind that the grizzly bear possesses a nature which, if taken in time and carefully improved, may be made the perfection of animal goodness. At birth, like the dog and the cat tribe, his eyes are closed; but in the course of a week or ten days, when they open, he is as good-humored, and even more playful, than they. From this period, if left in a state of wildness, with his ferocious dam to watch over and instruct him, he becomes gradually more and more savage, until he roams the forest, an untamable and dreaded despot. But if, on the contrary, he be taken at that early age, his playfulness fostered, accustomed to the sight and sedulous attentions of his master, and managed with a firm, but at the same time, gentle hand, he grows up a devoted friend, exhibiting such remarkable qualities of domestication as almost to lead one to suppose that he was intended, as well as the dog, for the companionship of man.

CHAPTER IX.

A DAY AND NIGHT'S ADVENTURES.

Search for Antelopes. The Meaning of Tack-Ship. A Nibble at a Trap. Discovery of a Pack of Wolves. Philosophy of a Rifle's Sights. Attack upon the Wolves. Its Effect. Pursuit. A severe Bite. Mountain Water-Cure. An inconsiderate Scouting Trip. Adventure with a Coyote. Lost. A Panther's Scream. My Alarm. Character of the Panther. Withdrawal of the Panther. My Situation. Rule of Camp. The Glimmer of the Camp Fire. My Prostration. More of Mountain Water-Cure. The Philosophy of Curing Wounds.

In a few days after the completion of our traps we devoted ourselves to the hunt again; and, in a short time, abundantly replenished our diminished stores. One day the boys succeeded in finding a large band of antelopes, of which they killed four; and the next morning I took Tuolumne and the mules, and followed in the direction the animals had gone, with hopes of overtaking them. We rode four or five miles without seeing any traces of them, and at last I remarked that we had better tack-ship and put about. Here was another expression, which the Indian boy did not understand, and wished to have explained. I replied that "tack-ship" was a sea-phrase, which meant to turn off at an angle from one's course and go in another direction. We accordingly altered our route, and hunted towards other quarters, but still without success.

One of the traps being not far distant from our
position, upon giving up the morning hunt we proceeded to it, and discovered the tracks of a wolf
about it. The animal had evidently been on the
inside of the structure and taken a portion of the
bait, and it was a mystery why he had not been
caught; but this was explained on further inspection;
for the trap had been so unskilfully set that it would
not spring. The fault being remedied, I remarked
that we would surely have a wolf the next morning.
"How do you know that?" Tuolumne asked. I answered that it was to be inferred from the nature of
the wolf that the visitor of the previous night would
return.

It being now nearly noon, when no game was likely
to stir abroad, we lay down under the shade of a
tree and remained until the heat of the day was
somewhat over; then, mounting again, we started
off over the hills in a direction we had never before
been. We travelled five or six miles beyond the
trap, and came upon a gang of large black wolves.
My first thought, upon seeing them, was not to fire,
as they might be the wolves that visited the trap; but,
upon second thought, I concluded that, being so far
distant, they might not be the same, and, at any rate,
it was best to secure their hides at once, and run the
chances of others at the trap. I had their value for
lobos leggings before my eyes, and, accordingly, determined upon an attack.

The wolves were in a deep ravine and we on a high
precipice, almost directly over them, — a situation

unfavorable for shooting, for the reason that a rifle's sights are arranged to make allowance for the fall of the ball when discharged upon a level. Upon shooting directly downward or directly upward, there is no fall of this kind, and, therefore, the gun must not be aimed directly at the object. On this account, I directed Tuolumne to single out a wolf and aim at his knees, while I would do the same with another; and, upon firing, my wolf fell. The rest of the gang immediately huddled around it, having neither seen us nor heard the report of my rifle, owing to the hill upon which we were; this being often the case, that a noise on a height is not heard in a confined valley below. Tuolumne's piece having only snapped, I took it now, and, handing him mine to reload, made another shot, and this ball passed through the spine of a second wolf into the shoulder of a third. Tuolumne then handed me my own rifle reloaded, but the wolves, by this time, had become alarmed and made off; all, with the exception of two, which lay dead upon the ground, and a third, which was hopping away with a broken shoulder.

Having no thought of any difficulty, I dropped my rifle, drew my knife, climbed down the precipice, and gave the wounded wolf chase. Upon overtaking, I seized him by the tail and threw him upon the ground, with the object of stabbing him; but, by an unexpected turn, he snapped at my right fore arm and completely penetrated it with his fangs, and so potent was the bite that the knife dropped from my unnerved hand. For a few moments the pain was excessive;

but when the first paroxysm was a little over, I drew my revolver, and finished the beast by a shot in the heart. Upon turning up my buckskin sleeve, the blood flowed profusely, and the wound showed itself to be severe. One of much less severity, received from a coyote bite since my return from the wilderness, and the help of three surgeons, kept my arm in a sling eight months, and came near costing me my hand.

But, in the mountains, I acted as my own doctor, and practised the water-cure system with great success. I therefore merely directed Tuolumne, when he had loaded his rifle and came up, to wet my handkerchief in cold water and wrap it tightly about the wound. In civilized life, when an injury of this kind is received, it is poulticed and bandaged; sometimes probed and lanced; and, frequently, very bad work indeed is the result; but experience has taught me that cold water and nature are apt to be better than salves and doctors; and I would undertake to cure almost any bite, not poisonous, by simply dressing it with cold water. A simple cut of the finger by nature heals rapidly, but, if plastered up, remains sore many days.

Feeling comfortable after the water-dressing, I directed Tuolumne to pack the bodies of the wolves upon the mules, and proceed to camp, while I would scout around and examine the country which we had not yet visited. He asked what I would do with my lame arm if attacked. I replied, that there was nothing to fear. It did not occur to me that there could be any danger; but my over-great confidence betrayed me and brought me into confusion, as will be seen.

At first, I walked a considerable distance without meeting anything worthy of attention; when, suddenly, an animal bounded furiously from behind a clump of brush and startled me. It had by this time become dusky; and, if a dangerous beast should have attacked me, my situation would have been perilous; but, upon turning to face the assailant, what was my disgust to find nothing but a saucy coyote, not worth a charge of powder. I disdained to notice him, and passed on; but the whelp, imagining, probably, that my contempt was fear, followed, barking and howling, keeping just far enough behind that a kick would not reach him. Such conduct, even in a brute, provoked me; and, drawing my revolver, I cried, "Die, base beast, unworthy the boon of life; take the reward of your audacity." A shot felled him; when, placing my foot upon his neck and plunging my knife through his heart, I exclaimed, "Die, coward of the wilderness!" — and kicked the body from me.

Resuming my road, but not being familiar with the landmarks in the darkness which now lowered over the landscape, I steered for a distant hill. I judged from the stars, the chief guides of the hunter in moonless nights, that it lay in the direction of camp; but, upon reaching it, the country still continued to be strange; and at last the consciousness flashed across my mind that I was lost. Here was a dilemma:

which way to turn, I knew not, and I could only
stand looking about me and reflecting upon what was
best to be done. I had lost much blood, felt tired
and weak, and would have sat down, but I was suddenly aroused and again startled by the scream of a
panther in dreadfully close proximity, — so close, that
it seemed to be but a few yards behind me. I cannot
tell what might have been my fate if attacked by the
panther at such a disadvantage in the night, but I
thought that if it were possible to catch the glisten
of his eyes, I might plant a bullet between them. To
make an effort at least, and sell my life dearly, I
raised my rifle and waited for him. Even to this
day, the remembrance of the feelings with which I
stood there, beyond the reach of help, in utter darkness, with a lame arm, weak and hungry, and with a
bloodthirsty beast upon my track, is distinct.

The panther, notwithstanding the many stories related of his daring, has always appeared to me a very
cowardly animal. He never dares to meet an adversary face to face; and when he attacks, it is always
by springing from a covert, with the advantage all on
his own side. He seeks his prey by night: chooses
lurking-places in trees, rocks, bushes, and other spots;
and springs only when the victim is unprepared to
defend itself. Such being the character of the animal, I feared only an ambush, and strained my eyes
to discover him crouched for a spring; and this was
the only time in my life that I thought I needed four
eyes to look out for my own preservation. Under
ordinary circumstances, a brave man, with pistol and

knife, can protect himself against any panther; but with a lame arm, and weak from hunger and fatigue, I might have been badly injured, perhaps killed.

While considering matters in this light, the panther screamed a second time, apparently as close as before, but on the other side. I thought he was hunting out a favorable place for an attack; but again it seemed to me that, if such were the case, he would not give notice of his presence by screaming. My vigilance, however, was none the less active, and my finger kept its place upon the trigger of my rifle until the beast screamed the third time. This, by good fortune, was at a distance to windward; and it was evident, from this circumstance, that he had passed on some other trail; and I felt very much relieved.

Being thus free from apprehensions of the panther, I had leisure to consider where I was. The stars continued to point out the direction of camp, but could tell me nothing more, and none of the trees or rocks around were familiar. There happened to be a small pine-tree, with low limbs, not far distant; and, in my uncertainty, I climbed it to get a wider view, and, if possible, to catch the reflection of the brilliant camp fire which it is the rule of hunters to make when a comrade is out at night. While peering into the darkness, I heard the panther scream for the fourth and last time, at a great distance, showing that he was leaving the neighborhood, and, as is often the case with this animal when travelling at night, uttering his characteristic scream or shriek at short intervals of ten or fifteen minutes.

Meanwhile a faint glimmer flickered in the sky, and by degrees lightened up, assuring me that it came from camp, and that my comrades were stirring up the blaze for my benefit. With a cheerful heart, I now slipped down from the tree and hastened in the direction; but a hill and ravine, which were rough and difficult to pass, still separated me from camp. However, I pressed forward on my way, blundering and stumbling over the brush and stones which obstructed my path at every step. The nearer I approached, the greater became my weakness; at one moment, I would stumble and roll over with scarcely power to rise again; at another, I felt an almost uncontrollable desire to sleep, but still managed to drag my tired limbs along till within hailing distance, when I hallooed and sank down exhausted. My comrades fortunately heard the faint shout and came to my assistance, but it was impossible to answer their curiosity and alarm. I could only say, as they half led and half carried me to the fire, "Give me water; give me food!" A delicious drink revived my sunken powers almost instantaneously; and after eating heartily of roast venison, which awaited my coming, I felt like a new man. It was thirst and hunger, rather than fatigue, which had enfeebled me.

Before turning into my blankets that night, I removed the bandages from my arm, and directed Tuolumne to pour a stream of cold water upon my wounds. Used thus, the water at first feels very cold, but by degrees becomes apparently more moderate; when it feels warm, it is proper to desist and replace the bandages, which should be moistened again. Such was the course now taken, — the arm being bound tightly from the shoulder to the fingers. This mountain surgery was very effective, — or, to say the worst of it, did no harm. The next morning, the soreness was gone, and the arm much better than I anticipated. Sykesey thought such a bite would have laid a person up for a week; but that, I replied, depended much upon the person bitten. A wound, to be rapidly cured, requires a healthy, healing blood, — the result of an active and temperate life, — and also careful attention; but it is not to be expected that everybody and every wound can be cured in the same way.

CHAPTER X.

CAMP LIFE.

In the previous pages when I have spoken of "camp," the reader may have supposed that reference was had to some regular fortification, a cabin, or at least a tent. It was nothing of the kind. My camp consisted merely of a convenient spot where wood, water, and herbage were near at hand. There we would unpack our mules, turn them out to graze, and build a large fire, which was seldom allowed to go down. In the day, this fire served for culinary purposes; at night, for warmth and protection. I slept invariably in my blankets, upon the ground; never in any house, or within any inclosure, unless the weather was rainy, when a few boughs, disposed into a kind of booth, would constitute all my shelter from the elements. On a few occasions, a blanket was spread to keep off the rain or dampness; but, as a general rule, my bed was entirely exposed.

KENNASKET'S PRESENT.

My comrades were accustomed to crowd about the
fire, and lie with their feet fairly toasting at the
coals. It was my practice, on the contrary, to remove a short distance, and sleep in the dark, so that,
in case of attack I might have a better view of in-
truders, and myself not be seen. My bed consisted
of coarse and heavy blankets, with a bag full of dried
grass, by way of pillow; and, as there was always
danger of being waked by wild beasts or thieves, my
rifle was kept constantly wrapped with me in the
blankets, — thus protected from the dew, as well as
being always ready for use at an instant's warning.
My other weapons were likewise kept about me, ever
ready for any occasion of peril which might arise.
Nor was my sleep any the more troubled on account
of this hard bed and this liability to disturbance.
Rarely did I pass a night that the howls of wolves
and coyotes, or the shrieks of panthers, did not lull
me to slumber; but never was my sleep sounder or
more refreshing. The active life I led, early rising,
a generous flow of animal spirits, and a simple and
temperate diet, made my rest at night sweet and
grateful, beyond all the capabilities of feather-beds
and spring mattresses.

I was an early riser; seldom did the morning star
see me asleep; often before the sun rose from his
crimson couch was I out upon the hunt. My usual
practice, after rising, was to rouse my companions,
and put one of them to making breakfast, while another attended the mules. In the meantime, I proceeded to my pets, and spent the interval before

breakfast in feeding, watering, and training them. They were chained to trees near the spring, and not far from where I slept, so that, it might be said, we all camped together.

Breakfast consisted, generally, of fresh meat broiled upon the coals, or roasted on spits before the fire; and we drank only water, except sometimes, when not in a hurry for a hunt, when coffee or tea was made, if we had them; if we did not have them, roasted acorns or other seeds served as a substitute for coffee, and different sorts of fragrant herbs for tea. A few kettles and pots of civilized manufacture we used, when necessary for our cooking, but for general purposes Indian utensils. One of these, which was of great service, was a pail made of solid wood, in form like a washbowl, with a flat bottom, and capable of holding about two gallons. The natives made it by heating an end of a long stone redhot, wrapping the other end in bark, so as to hold it in the hands, and grinding and rubbing with it in the wood, until the pail was burnt out. Bowls, and dishes likewise, they make in the same way, and value highly — it requiring much time, care, trouble, and skill to fashion them.

As the day was generally spent away from camp, we carried lunch along with us on our excursions, and this consisted of strips of meat dried in the sun. While at work upon a trap or other structure requiring time, we kept a bag of this meat, suspended in a tree near the scene of labor, from which we used, as required, — occasionally roasting it, to render it

more edible and palatable. Fresh meat, at camp
and indeed wherever we had it, was invariably
swung in trees, being tied to a lariat, which was
passed over a limb, and hoisted up; it was thus kept
out of the reach of prowling beasts until needed,
when it was easily lowered.

Dinner was our chief meal; but the time at which
we enjoyed it was irregular, depending upon many
circumstances; being sometimes delayed until the
middle of the night, though usually taking place
shortly after sundown. This meal rarely wanted an
excellent roast, and good drink of its kind; also
such cakes and bread as we could make, and many
little delicacies which nature threw with lavish hand
before us. Plums, cherries, berries of various kinds,
small game of all varieties which the region afforded,
and a thousand little titbits which our experience
taught, or our ingenuity devised, graced our board
at this meal. Frequently have I dined at the Astor
House, in New York, and at first-class hotels in various parts of the Union, and have eaten as splendid dinners as the best cooks in the country ever
spread; but for real good relish, give me a camp-
dinner in the mountains. A mountain appetite is
more savory than the richest dish ever conceived by
a French gourmand.

It depended upon the time of our reaching camp
from our daily labors, whether we played with our
pets in the evening. If early, it was my practice
to spend several hours feeding, and, when occasion
served, training them. On other occasions, but not

often, after finishing dinner, I would get out my old pipe and smoke. A little of the tobacco of commerce generally constituted a part of my stores; but, if not, the wild tobacco, which grows plenteously in the mountains of California, Oregon, and Washington, and, in places also on the plains, served as a tolerable substitute.

The social part of our camp life was in the evening, before bedtime. After finishing the labors of the day, we would heap large logs of wood upon our fire, such as would last till morning, and gathering about the cheerful blaze, sit, sometimes hour after hour, discussing the events of our campaign, or telling stories. Many a strange adventure was told at my fire; and sometimes, when other hunters spent the night with me, as they occasionally did, have I heard narratives calculated to draw forth the deepest emotions. The scene around us, the howls of wild beasts in the distance, the flickering light, the strange figures which we ourselves made in our uncouth dresses, and the graphic words and gestures which the woodsman and hunter learns to call to his aid, all conspired to make those evenings as varied and entertaining as the most eventful chapters of Eastern romance. I have thus heard tales rivalling the Spanish novels in richness, and narratives that would have put Gulliver or Munchausen to the blush.

Upon first entering the mountains in California, I carried all my cares as well as all my property with me, taking no thought of others, having only myself and my oxen to provide for. In plain terms, I was a misanthrope, and looked down from the mountain crest upon the green plains and busy settlements below, with the disdainful spirit of an eagle from an inaccessible eyry. But with a change in my circumstances, my feelings also changed. As my little camp increased, I began to know again that I had duties and obligations to fulfil towards others; as responsibility rested heavier and heavier upon my shoulders, I gradually threw aside my indifference, and instead of entirely following the narrow maxim of "mind your own business," I gradually learned the lesson of enlightened minds, that one's own business embraces the business of others too. Upon leading my little company up into Washington, far removed, as it were, from the laws and jurisdiction of government, quite a burden of responsibility rested upon me, absolutely requiring at my hands participation and interest in everything that went forward. To all intents and purposes, indeed, I was a kind of sovereign, amenable in that remote quarter to no laws except those of God and nature; but so well was I imbued with the spirit of my country's free institutions, that no right was violated and no liberty infringed, to my knowledge.

Such being the condition of the domestic affairs of my camp, it may not be amiss to say a word of my foreign relations, if this phrase can be used with reference to the independent Indian establishment in my neighborhood. It had become evident to me, shortly after reaching the country, that these Indians would have to be conciliated; particularly if any favors were to be asked; and I therefore now paid more attention to the philosophy of diplomacy and the arts of political intercourse than ever in my life before. My advances to the Indians, when contracting for their horses, had been well received, and, fortunately, the friendly and intimate relations, then commenced, lasted during my stay in the region. Notwithstanding the suspicion entertained by Kennasket of the faith of hunters in general, I had certainly found favor in his eyes; and I determined, for the purpose of nurturing the good understanding so auspiciously inaugurated, to pay a visit of state on the first opportunity, promptly settle off the score due, and thus, by fair dealing, keep in his good graces.

A day or two after my wolf hunt, accordingly, taking the mules well packed, Tuolumne and I proceeded to the Indian village. Upon approaching it, we halted; and Tuolumne went forward with a white flag to announce my arrival. I had learned that the Indians were fond of ceremony, and that it was both easy and comfortable to humor their fancies. To this embassy Kennasket returned answer, that Gray Beard was always welcome to his lodge; and I at once drove the mules to his door and delivered their burdens of meat to his squaws. As the choice pieces were unpacked, the Chief seemed well satisfied, and volunteered the loan of his horses again; to which I replied, that the Old Hunter was glad to keep his promises, and the red man could find no cause of complaint; and we proceeded thereupon to compliment each other for a full half hour upon our respective virtues.

Having at last finished my business, I was about to withdraw, but Kennasket stayed me. He wished, he said, to make the white man a present, and he hoped the white man would keep it carefully as long as he lived, in memory of the Great Chief. The Great Chief's present should be sacred, I replied; and he withdrew to procure it. For some time, now, my mind was filled with visions of splendid calumets, necklaces of bears' claws, Indian badges of honor, wampum belts, ornaments of bead-work, and all the wardrobe of barbaric finery; but what was my surprise to see the old fellow return with only a puppy in his arms, and that as black as any coal! I could see Tuolumne snickering, and it was with difficulty that I restrained my own risibility; but, nevertheless, with an effort of philosophy, I managed to assume a look of great interest. The Great Chief meanwhile approached, knelt down before me, and, lifting his eyes and arms towards Heaven, muttered some almost inaudible words, and then presented the scrub as a great treasure. I received it with the most scrupulous ceremony, and, kneeling down in the same manner as the giver had done, deposited it in my bosom, and took care, until out of sight on my return to camp, to show nothing but the liveliest pleasure in the possession of his present. Little as was to have been expected then, I have kept my word with the Chief; and still possess his remembrancer, which has grown scarcely any since puppyhood.

CHAPTER XI.

THE ART OF TRAPPING.

Race between Antelopes and Mules. A Wolf and two Whelps entrapped. Tuolumne's Caution. The Bonds of Nature. Savage
Affection. The Philosophy of the Prophetic Art. The Requirements of a good Hunter. A Black Wolf entrapped. Treatment of captured Animals. Capture and Slaying of an old Grizzly.
Hanging up his Meat. Banquet of baked Bear's Head. Skin
Curing. Practical Value of Science. How Traps ought to appear. Notions about Trapping. True Philosophy of the Art of
Trapping.

THE day after our visit to Kennasket, Tuolumne
and I proceeded to the trap in which we had seen the
wolf-tracks. On the road, as we were travelling leisurely along, we came upon a small band of antelopes,
and, in a spirit of frolic, gave them chase. They
flew like the wind; but being disposed to test the
speed of our mules, we put them to the stretch in
pursuit. The result was a race, which would have
amused any one to see; we, who rode it, had to
laugh at the ridiculous spectacle each presented to
the other. I soon came to the conclusion that mules
are very good things in their places; but their stiff-
kneed gallop, in comparison with the well-oiled and
graceful speed of an antelope, — the swiftest of animals, — is a mere snail's pace. We saw the game
disappear like a speck in the distance, and, turning
about, proceeded on our legitimate road.

Upon reaching the trap, we saw that the doors were sprung, and that we had caught a large black wolf with two small whelps. She was very savage, and rushed ferociously towards where we looked in; but her rage, of course, was futile, worrying only herself. I directly took a strong rope, and making a noose, lowered it into the trap through a hole in the top, while Tuolumne kept her attention engaged by poking sticks through the cracks. While she expended her fury biting at the sticks, the noose was suddenly whipped over her head, and she was secured sufficiently well to enable us to put on a collar and attach a lariat to her.

The whelps, also, were very furious; and I noticed, as we were about to open the trap, that Tuolumne had armed himself with a large club, to protect himself against them. This made me laugh, but Tuolumne protested that he only wished to prevent them running off. I replied, that there were other bonds besides those of iron and rope; that, while we had the mother, the whelps were as securely ours as if they were bound with chains. The truth of this saying was soon apparent, for, upon leading the dam captive, the whelps, though at first they ran into the brush, soon came out and followed. On the way to camp, as I had several times to dismount and arrange the lariats with which the dam was led, invariably as she snarled and snapped, the whelps dashed at my leggings. Their savage affection for their mother was indeed so interesting that I did not pretend to drive them away; and Tuolumne, who had at first been scared, by degrees became so delighted with their harmless rage that he teased them purposely, until I made him desist.

On our arrival at camp, our comrades were astonished with our success, and admired to the last degree the wolf and her whelps; but, more than all, they wondered at the verification of my predictions, and gave me credit for being a sort of prophet. This strange idea of theirs occasioned a great many still stranger ideas in me. Mine, of course, was no gift of prophecy; but common sense enabled me to reason out a result in the future, from facts which already existed, much better than they could; and this gave me a superiority over them which, had such been my disposition, might, perhaps, have been turned to my advantage. Indeed, I persuaded myself that, had my lot been cast among a numerous people, much my inferiors in intellect, it would have been easy to set up and sustain a reputation as a prophet. I believe that all the prophetic powers ever possessed by Mahomet, the first Inca, and others of this class, so far as concerned foresight, consisted only in their superior sagacity.

That evening, during our usual talk around the camp fire, Sykesey was inquisitive about the manner of putting the rope on the wolf's neck; and, upon my giving the explanation, declared that he should never have thought of such a plan. "To be a good hunter," said I, "you must be a thousand things besides a good shot;"— and this is a good saying, which can be repeated and recommended.

In a few days after this, we found a splendid black wolf in one of the other traps, and managed him in much the same manner as the last. When brought to camp, he was chained to a tree near the others, thus making the fourth of his species in our collection. This method of chaining up to trees was, indeed, the disposition of all the animals entrapped, except coyotes, which were shot and thrown away; and old bears, which, being exceedingly difficult to tame, we generally destroyed for their skins and meat, — as happened not long afterwards, when one night we captured an old grizzly.

This bear was so violent as to gnaw entirely through some of the floor timbers of the trap. It was almost a pity to kill the noble old fellow, but there was no help for it; and, accordingly, inserting the muzzle of my rifle through a crack, I put a half-ounce ball through his heart. Upon the reception of the fatal missile, he uttered a tremendous roar of pain and rage, and tore about with such fury that I feared he would break out. I indeed drew my knife and pistol to meet him, should the structure give way; but in a few minutes he began to weaken, his rage softened, his head declined, he sank down, and gradually his life passed away. He was one of the largest of his class in this region, weighing nearly a thousand pounds; so large that, upon hoisting the trap doors, we were unable to budge him, and were compelled to hitch the mules to drag him out. His hams and shoulders were so brawny and fat, that we could with difficulty lift them; and when, according to our usual custom, we came to hang them up in trees out of the reach of wolves and coyotes, it was necessary to divide them again, thus making eight pieces: and a beautiful sight it was to see the meat hanging among the green leaves, like choice cuts in a market-stall at Christmas.

With the head of this bear we made a repast as splendid as it was strange. A hole large enough to receive the mass was dug in the ground, and a large brush fire built over it. When the fire had burnt to coals and ashes, the head was rolled in a cloth, placed in the hot hole, more brush piled on, and a fire kept up for several hours, when the head was entirely cooked; and delicious eating it made.

Subsequently to these successes, we caught many other animals in the traps, from time to time; making it a special business to visit and attend to them almost every day, keeping them baited with fresh meat, and disposing of the captured animals according to their value. Thus, besides a large number of living prizes, we accumulated, by degrees, a number of skins of various kinds, which were cured in much the same method in practice among the Indians. For instance: when wolves were taken, the skins were spread upon the fleshy sides with the brains, — sometimes, also, with salt and alum, — and then rolled up for a short time. Afterwards, they were worked in the hands until quite soft, and then subjected to a thorough smoking. It gave us much trouble, at first, to make a smoke-house; but subsequently we found a hollow tree, which answered the purpose excellently.

The art of trapping requires some knowledge of the science of natural history, just as any other art requires some intimacy with the science with which it stands in connection. As every man who reasons knows something of the science of reasoning, though he may be totally unacquainted with the name of logic, so the trapper must have a practical acquaintance with the nature and habits of the game which he seeks to ensnare; and the more intimate his knowledge, the more successful is he likely to be. When he builds his traps, he ought to know where his animals prowl, by what path they go forth, and by what they return. It is necessary to find out the places where they pass when hungry; for, when sated, it is not likely that they will turn aside for a bait. He must also know the kinds of food they prefer; as some will touch nothing but living food, while others can be beguiled best with carrion.

The next matter of great importance, and which at first gave me much trouble, after the suitable location of the traps, was the proper appearance of them. Wild beasts, as a usual thing, are very cautious and, if there be anything about a trap to excite their suspicions, will avoid it. Should it be too new, or show too plainly the marks of tools, or retain too strongly the human smell, or be too much smeared with blood, a sagacious animal will quickly suspect something wrong, and keep at a safe distance. Most of these difficulties, I afterwards learned to remedy, by building a small fire in the traps before setting them, and thus not only removing any scent that might pervade them, but darkening and giving an oldish appearance to the timbers. Indeed, upon becoming more skilled in the art, it was my invariable practice to carefully clear away all marks of labor, remove all the chips, and replace the logs or stones which had been removed, so as to give the spot as natural and wild an aspect as before. And even after all these precautions, it was not an unusual thing to find tracks of animals leading to the traps, and then away again, showing that beasts, wiser than ordinary, had approached, inspected the snares, made up very correct opinions, and left without troubling them. Instances of this character were always regarded by me as unfortunate, as animals, in some way or other, have a method of communicating their thoughts to each other; and I therefore made it a rule, upon finding a trap thus suspected, to do something or other, either by re-smoking, or throwing something near it, to give it the natural appearance it ought to have. I also avoided as much as possible, the killing of animals in the neighborhood, and, in general, took all care to remove from the vicinity of the snares everything that could, by any possibility, indicate to animals the purposes for which they were intended.

On some occasions, when a trap did not seem to attract animals, I caused haunches of meat to be dragged over the ground for some distance around, for the purpose of leaving the scent, and thus leading them up. As to the efficacy of plans and contrivances of this kind, however, there may be consid-

erable doubt, for if an animal will not of its own
accord approach and enter a trap, it is not likely
that he can thus be enticed to do so. Some hunters
also suppose that drugs of a peculiar smell will aid
in attracting animals; and some have various super-
stitions, and foolish notions, which are not worth notice.

There is but one good rule for the trapping of animals, — a plain and universal one, and, like almost all
other good rules in any department of human knowledge, the dictate of common sense. This is, that
the animal to be enticed to eat, must be met where
and when he is hungry; and the most palatable bait,
— which is also, generally speaking, his natural and
usual food, — must be offered, and offered in such a
way as not to alarm his fears or excite his suspicions. To accomplish these objects in a better or
worse degree, exhibits the more or less consummate
skill of the trapper. In a country perfectly wild,
there is not so much necessity for care; but where
there is much hunting, and animals have become very
wild, the art is one of great nicety, and all the knowledge of science, so far at least as relates to the subject, cannot be too well known.

CHAPTER XII.

THE INDIANS.

ONE morning very early, as we were all sleeping about the camp fire, I was aroused by an Indian yell; and, supposing an attack, I jumped up, with my rifle in my hand, ready to fire. An evil result might have come from this manner of entering my camp; but the well-known appearance of Old Pompey and two of his Indian friends, who stood before me, in a moment dissipated all cause of alarm. They came, so they informed me, from their Chief, Kennasket, who proposed giving a great feast, and desired me to furnish as much game as possible for the occasion, as it was some great anniversary in their tribe. The feast, they said, was to take place on *lunar* day, — referring probably to some change in the moon, which would be two days ahead; and, as a distinguished honor, I was especially invited to be present. • In accordance with my general principles of intercourse with the Indians, I readily consented to all that was asked, but required the Indians to remain and assist me.

It was desirable, in view of the feast, and of the large number of participants which I was given to understand would be present, to collect a very large quantity of game; and I therefore made two parties, — despatching Sykesey, Tuolumne, and one of the Indians in one direction, while I with Pompey and the third Indian, took another. We each took a mule, and started out for a general hunt. After separating, my party proceeded until we came to a dense thicket; when, seeing tracks, I asked the Indians whether they liked bear meat. They replied that they liked it much; but when I pointed out a fresh track, they seemed much frightened, and very little in the spirit of following it up. Their alarm, however, subsided when I proposed to pursue the trail alone, and when, after a long and tedious search in the chaparral, I succeeded in finding and killing a bear, which was a black one, they pronounced the Old Hunter *mucho bravo*, or something to that effect.

Proceeding ahead, we fell in with two black-tailed deer, a buck and doe, feeding in a little valley. These fine animals usually stand long enough before flying to enable a hunter to obtain good aim, and, therefore, they make a pretty mark. It is also frequent, when a buck and doe are together, and the buck is slain, that the doe remains; and, on this account, it was always my rule to kill the buck first. This noble fellow I soon brought to his knees; but, before my piece was reloaded, the doe took the alarm and escaped. Further on, the Indians pointed out a solitary doe, which was nibbling the bushes a short distance off, without appearing to take much notice of us. I shot her; but, upon examination, found her to be only a poor, little, lame thing, which had evidently been attacked and injured in the shoulder by some wild animal; and, being thus disabled, had been eking out an inadequate existence in the brush. I was sorry I had killed her; but the Indians exclaimed, "White man muchee goodee; killee muchee *muck-a-muck.*" I replied, "*Muck-a-muck* no good;" but they pronounced the doe very first rate, and we packed the body on top of the bear and buck. These constituted our success this day; but Sykesey and his party brought in several small deer, an antelope, and a quantity of small game.

The next morning, as we determined to hunt towards the Indian village, we took all the game killed the previous day; and as Stanislaus, who usually remained, desired to attend the feast, though it was much against my will, I consented to leave the camp entirely unguarded. Sykesey, indeed, who supposed himself not included in the invitation to the feast, would willingly have remained; but we overruled him, and, therefore, the camp was left totally alone. We, however, put everything to rights; and dividing into two parties, as on the day before, we started in different directions, intending to meet at the village in the evening.

During this day I did nothing worthy of particular notice, but had an exhibition of the skill of the Indians, which, considering the admiration they expressed for my hunting, surprised me. We discovered a doe and two fawns, feeding on a grassy spot in a plain; and the Indians asked to be allowed to try their powers for once. I was curious to see their method of stalking, and how they worked their bows and arrows; and, therefore, not only consented, but to stimulate them to greater care, offered a good price for the fawns, if taken alive. The Indians, thereupon, crept to a position about three hundred yards from the animals; and pulling out their knives and cutting a quantity of grass, they wove large caps, resembling growing bunches of green, and placed them on their heads. Thus disguised, they crept within a hundred and fifty yards of the deer; and then, falling flat upon their abdomens, they crept, like snakes in the grass, within twenty or thirty yards of them. Both then suddenly sprang upon their knees, with their bows drawn, — fired as one man, — and the doe fell, transfixed with two shafts. They then jumped upon their feet, and, after cutting her throat, pursued the fawns which ran towards the brush. The whole affair was conducted more skilfully than anything else I have ever seen done by Indians, and pleased me so much that I directly went to measure the distances. While wondering at their abilities, they returned, bearing the fawns, and I pronounced them great hunters. At my commendation, their eyes flashed with pleas-

ure. "You excel the White Hunter," said I; but
they replied, "The White Hunter is a hunter of
bears!"

After this, we proceeded till within a few hundred
yards of the village of Kennasket, when an Indian
went forward to announce my arrival. In a short
time afterwards, one of the chief's wives came out
with a wreath of wild flowers, which she placed upon
my head, and then conducted me to the lodge, where
Kennasket, his wives, and chief men had assembled
to receive me. As I entered, the company knelt,
and the chief made a speech calling me friend and
brother; after which, a circle was made around me,
and, while I in turn knelt, they all placed their hands
upon my head and danced and sang, repeating the
words of the chief, "Good is the White Hunter, who
comes with much game from the east. No thief is
he, but friend and brother of the Red Man. He is
welcome."

Much the same ceremony was performed over
Sykesey, when he and his party arrived, which
was not long afterwards. As he approached, a
squaw advanced and placed a wreath of vine leaves
upon his head. Now Sykesey, though he had lived
much in Indian countries, knew little of Indian cus-
toms, however much he pretended to know; and,
therefore, out of curiosity, I watched him as he entered the lodge. He was already alarmed regarding
the crown about his head, not knowing what to make
of it; and, as I seized an opportunity to tell him
when to kneel, he supposed that he was being led

like a victim to martyrdom. His eyes stared wide; and he replied that he would not kneel, that he had never done so in his life. "But," said I, "you can surely kneel to say your prayers." At this, he was still more alarmed; but, added I, "Pluck up your courage and die like a man." For some reason or other, I felt a kind of wicked pleasure in witnessing his imaginary terrors. More like a ghost than solid flesh, did he stand there, and, had he fainted, it would not have surprised me. However, he got through the ceremony safely, and managed to fall upon his knees at the proper time; yet when the women placed their hands upon his head and danced in a circle around him, he appeared really more dead than alive.

This curious ceremony of reception being over, I had a laugh with Sykesey about his fright. We then unpacked our mules, and spread forth the game, which made a goodly display, — there being a bear, deer, antelopes, a badger, rabbits, squirrels, and birds; in all, about forty bodies. Kennasket, who stood by, was much pleased with the show, ordered our mules to be put out to good pasture, and invited us to amuse ourselves; and "this night," said he, "you shall sleep in my lodge." "The White Hunter," I replied, "never sleeps under cover, nor ever where women sleep." At this answer, the old fellow laughed heartily, and replied, that the women would not hurt anybody, but that the white man should please himself. He then pointed to some beautiful mats which hung in his lodge, and gave me to understand that they

were at my service; but I replied, "No; the White
Hunter prefers his blankets and the ground."

When supper was announced, we sat down to one of
the most curious meals it was ever the fortune of white
man to partake of. Two large wooden tureens were
placed upon the ground, containing a kind of mush,
which was made by mixing grass seed, meal, and
water in the tureen, and then throwing in hot stones,
till it was cooked. At the side of these, were heaps
of roasted meat, piled upon flat stones; and around
these aboriginal dishes we sat flat upon the ground,—
and a curious sight we made. But however strange
the spreading of the board, much more strange was
the etiquette which governed at table. The chief
gave us to understand that we must not be backward;
and, as he did so, he scooped up three fingers full of
mush, which he transferred from the common bowl
to his mouth, with remarkable agility. The other Indians followed his example, each dipping for himself;
for of such things as spoons, these fellows seemed to
have no idea. Now, I am as free from prejudices as
almost any man, but, I confess, this method of eating
mush rather staggered my tastes, and made me con-
fine myself to the meat exclusively. Although the
chief repeatedly urged me to try the mush, commend-
ing it with a hearty smack of the lips at every mouth-
ful, I assured him that I never ate mush, but that the
meat was superb. The meal lasted till all the provisions were exhausted; when at a nod all knelt, and the
chief muttered over a prayer to the great Spirit, en-
treating him to be propitious to the feast of the mor-

row; after which we all rose, and soon afterwards retired.

Meanwhile, as it commenced to grow dark, I began to think of camp and the poor pets. I feared they could not fare well alone, and I could not bear the idea of remaining away, though such had at first been my intention. Therefore, I requested of the chief one of his best horses, to ride back, promising to return early in the morning. He replied, that if I were determined to go, I should take his fleetest animal; but if I did not return in time, to beware of his displeasure. He need not fear, I answered; and mounting a splendid courser, galloped off; and in a short time, after looking to the pets, I turned into my blankets, under my own tree, in my own camp.

The next morning, I rose before dawn, and mounting my horse, rode back to the village, where I arrived at daybreak. All was still and quiet; not a watcher waked; and even the makers of the approaching festival continued to slumber. I thought to rouse the sleepers, and usher in the day with sport; and, accordingly, spurring my horse, and rushing furiously through the village, I cried with all my might, "*Chawawi! chawawi!*" which is an Indian note of alarm. The whole people rallied, and rushed out of their lodges, with their hair on end, and their eyes distended with surprise. As soon as they collected, I informed them that they need not be alarmed; the White Hunter had only taken this method of announcing his arrival, and his heart was merry.

Upon passing through the village, I found that it consisted of forty or fifty lodges, and about four hundred people. The chief's dwelling, which was situated in the centre of all, was a round structure, made of long poles stuck into the ground and running up in a conical form to a smoke-hole in the top. The poles were interlaced with boughs and small sticks, over which was plastered a composition of clay and mud, which, when dry, would turn the rain well. A deal of care had been taken in building this lodge, which was by far the best in the village; the others, however, were built in the same general manner, except that some were oval; and all appeared tight and warm, and were doubtless comfortable in the winter time. On examining the lodges, I found a few scalps, but they were all of Indians; and I was assured that no white scalps were in the village, and that none had ever been taken. The tribe was one of those who flatten the heads of their children, — a custom common to various nations, — but I am at a loss whether to call them Nez Percees, Pend Oreilles, or some other name.

After rousing the rancheria, I proceeded to where my comrades had taken up their quarters, and roused them also; and soon afterwards, the chief invited me to examine with him the ground where he intended to celebrate the day. We walked together three or four hundred yards, to a level and grassy spot, with here and there a noble oak spreading out its ample branches and promising the most grateful shade. All the stones and dry limbs had been removed from the ground, and four or five circles, the size of circus rings, the largest in the middle, had been staked off, evidently for dancing. There was also places fixed in various spots for roasting meats; and everything appeared ready to begin the ceremonies. The chief explained to me the purposes of all which we saw; and I, following out the line of policy previously adopted, admired everything. In one respect, however, I came near breaking through the rule; — when breakfast was announced, remembering the mush, I begged to be excused: but Kennasket shook his head, and said the White Hunter must eat with him. This "must" was sufficient, and I went into the lodge and took breakfast; but, fortunately, mush did not constitute a portion of the bill of fare this time.

As soon as breakfast was finished, preparations were made for the celebration. The meats were carried to the places assigned for them, the fires were kindled, the cooks were stationed; and in a short time barbecues gave forth their pleasant flavors on every side. When the grateful smells ascended, as from altars to the Great Spirit, the chief and his household made their appearance, decked and painted in all the splendor of barbaric display; and, following in the train, came the whole people and their guests, about eight hundred persons, all in the costume of Indian festivity. It was, indeed, a great sight to see them in their finery, with their beads, feathers, and painted bark, their furs and woven garments, and themselves painted; to watch their stately and solemn steps, as they marched into the circles; and to behold

their wild and curious dances, so full of meaning and
character, when seen in their native places. The
music of these dances was a kind of chant kept up
by several of the Indians who stood outside the
circles.

About the middle of the afternoon, the chief announced dinner; after which, would take place the
great club dance. The meats, — which consisted of
bear, deer, antelope, and many other kinds, in all
about two hundred animals of various sorts and sizes,
— were now spread forth on pieces of bark and flat
stones, in a large circle upon the ground. There
were also about a dozen large tureens of mush, made
in the same way, and intended to be eaten in the
same manner as that of which I had had previous
experience. There were also buckets or large bowls
of water in abundance; but no liquor. Around these
viands the feasters were arranged in circles; some
sitting, some standing, and all with ravenous appe-
tites. The feast began at a signal from the chief;
and such a destruction of food as then took place
was astonishing to all my ideas of human capacity.
But the banquet progressed well; great enjoyment
prevailed; the bucks became lively, and shouted,
hallooed, and whooped, as if mad, and the Governor
himself could barely restrain his enthusiasm; but,
suddenly, in the midst of the merriment, he jumped
up, and, commanding silence, harangued the people
upon the great deeds of his younger days, the glory
of his tribe, and the greatness of his nation. Others
followed, discanting upon the same fruitful topics.

After dining, the warriors returned to the circles, and the club-dance began. This remarkable ceremony consisted of a dance of braves, with war-clubs in their hands. It took the form of a battle; each warrior flourishing his club against his neighbor. It seemed as if forty skulls would certainly be broken every instant; but such was the dexterity shown in the dance that not a blow was given. It was, indeed, a great spectacle. After the club-dance, other dances began, in some of which the squaws participated; and great was the pleasure with which they entered into the spirit of the scene. At the same time, exercises in archery took place in another portion of the green, and great skill was shown. These Indians are wonderfully correct with their arrows; I repeatedly saw small balls of wood pierced at thirty yards distance; and, on several occasions, an Indian would hold a nail in his hand and allow others to shoot at it.

Towards evening, the archery ceased, and all crowded into the dance. Large fires were lighted about the field; and, as the night grew darker, the scene became romantic. The forms of the plumed and painted Indians, as they passed to and fro in the ruddy glare of the night fires; the dark shadows and the flickering lights on every side, presented a spectacle which will remain indelibly impressed upon my memory. About midnight, the dancers resorted again to the viands, and cleared the abundant supply to the last fibre; then, again, they took up the dance, and continued, doubtless, until morning warned the revellers that the day and night of celebration were past. As for myself and companions, we withdrew shortly after midnight; and, returning to our camp, tired and weary, turned into our blankets and slept out the short remainder of the night.

THE FRIGHTENED GRIZZLY.

CHAPTER XIII.

PROGRESS OF LADY WASHINGTON'S EDUCATION.

The Effect of the Feast. A Sleepy Hunt.   Tuolumne's Yankee Trick.
Passage of Words with Sykesey.   A Lesson in Pack-carrying to
Lady Washington.   The Lady my Companion.   Discovery of
Deer.   A Grizzly Bear.   Situation of Myself and the Lady.   The
Devil in the Wilderness.   My Affection for the Lady.   A Surprise.
Robbery of Camp.   Suspicions.   The Lady on Guard.   Clean-
liness of the Grizzly Bear.   An Antelope Hunt and Slaughter.
Our Return to Camp at Night.   Pursued by Wolves.   Sykesey's
Fright.   Attack by a Panther.   The Panther a Sneak.

IT was late the next morning when we awaked,
still drowsy and sleepy from the effects of the feast.
Sykesey complained of indisposition, and Stanislaus
had gorged himself; so that it fell upon Tuolumne
and me to go upon the hunt and provide fresh meat,
of which there was not a particle about camp. We
accordingly mounted the mules and rode forth; but,
for a long time, could see nothing. Suddenly we
came upon four deer, and dismounting, managed by
cautious working to approach within ninety yards;
when one of the band happened to espy us, snorted
the note of alarm, and all began staring about, pre-
paratory to starting on the run. At this instant,
however, I ordered Tuolumne to fire; and, doing the
same myself, we killed two; with the bodies of which,
as soon as they could be packed, I sent Tuolumne
ahead, ordering him to stop and await me at a cer-

tain hill, while I would make a circuit and try to kill something more. But, either because I was too drowsy to see, or because game was scarce, I could find nothing; and, soon giving up the hunt, proceeded to the appointed hill.

I found that Tuolumne was indeed waiting for me; but as he sat on a shady bank, holding the lariats of the mules in his hands, he had fallen fast asleep! Thinking to have fun out of this circumstance, I tried to get the lariats out of his grasp; but he had wound them so tightly about his arm as to render this impossible. He suddenly waked, and cried that he had learned the Yankee's trick of sleeping with an eye open. We then proceeded on our way, and arrived at camp early in the afternoon; so early, indeed, that Sykesey expressed surprise; "for," said he, "this is the best time of the day to hunt." "Yes," I replied; "but you are not the only man whose flesh and blood tire and sleep."

The next day, I resolved to remain at camp and train my pets, and particularly Lady Washington, who had now become tame enough to follow me without leading. The thought struck me of teaching her to carry a pack; and getting an old flour-bag, and filling it with sand, I lashed it upon her shaggy back. It was barely bound on, however, before she threw her head around, seized it with her teeth and tore a great hole, and the sand ran out. I talked to her, tried to make her understand what was wanted, and reproved her with a stick, but it was of no use; she grew angry, and I found that it was not prudent to carry the affair any further that day, so I busied myself with Jackson, the wolves, and the little black bears, all of which improved rapidly.

A few days after this, an adventure occurred in which the Lady played an important part. Having determined to build another trap, we all set forth to the spot selected, which was about four miles distant. Being anxious all the time to accustom the Lady to my companionship, I allowed her to follow me. It was a little hazardous, perhaps, to take her so great a distance, but so firm was my confidence in her training as to overrule all objection. She followed like a dog, and during the whole day remained at my side, partaking of my lunch at noon.

Towards evening, as we got ready to start home. I gave my rifle to Stanislaus, and directed him, with Sykesey and Tuolumne, to make a circuit and kill what game they could, while I would go direct to camp with the Lady. They went off in one direction, and I started in another, with nothing to defend myself except my pistol and bowie-knife. I had not gone far before several deer, grazing on a hill-side, attracted my attention; and though it was foolish to attempt to shoot them with a pistol, my ambition was such that I could not think of allowing the opportunity to pass without an attempt. Accordingly, I tried to creep around to a spot from which to fire with advantage; and, coming to a thicket, commenced crawling through the brush, the Lady following in my wake. But before advancing more than a hundred yards, I felt that my position was dangerous; there certainly were bears about, and if one should attack me, being without a rifle, I would have but a poor chance. The deer, it is true, still remained grazing, and this was the first time the Old Hunter ever refused an opportunity of killing a deer when he was in need of provision; but the risks seemed too great, and the chance of success too small, and, finally, I turned around and began backing out. Suddenly, Lady Washington gave a snort and chattered her teeth. I wheeled around at this, and directly behind the Lady, full in sight, standing upon his hind legs and wickedly surveying us, stood a savage old grizzly. That he had hostile intentions, all his actions clearly showed; and there I was, almost without arms, and with the Lady as well as myself to take care of.

In this emergency, I seized the chain with which the Lady was usually tied, and which was now wrapped about her neck, and unwound it as noiselessly as possible. I was then about to move to a tree which stood near, when the enemy dropped upon his all fours, came a little nearer, and rose again. Here was a dilemma. I knew from the nature of the beast that if I moved now, I was to expect him either to instantly attack or precipitately fly, — but the former much more probably than the latter. I did not wish to hasten an unforeseen determination on his part, however, and therefore stood stock-still, with my pistol in my hand; and thus we both, motionless as stone, eyed each other. It is difficult to tell how long the bear would have gazed without acting, — not long, probably; but seeing his indecision, I resolved to turn it to my advantage; and suddenly discharging the pistol, rattling the iron chain, and at the same time yelling with all my might, I had the gratification of seeing the enemy turn tail and run, as if frightened out of his wits. Not satisfied with this, I followed after him yelling and shouting, with the Lady growling and the chain clanking. It seemed as if a thousand devils had sprung up all at once in the wilderness, and the old bear tore through the bushes as if each particular one was after him.

Such was the first instance in which Lady Washington, my faithful friend and constant companion for years afterwards, stood side by side with me in the hour of danger and dire alarm; and from that time, I felt for her an affection which I have seldom given to any human being. The remainder of the way, I kept a watchful eye; but nothing further, worthy of mention, occurred, and we safely reached camp an hour after sundown. I gave notice of my approach, as usual after dark, by discharging a chamber of my pistol. Upon getting in, my comrades at first laughed at me for being lost again, as they supposed; but they opened their eyes wide, when I came to tell of the old grizzly, and the deadly fright which the rattling of the Lady's chain had given him.

The narrative of this adventure was curious enough; but my comrades replied that they had also surprising news for me; and when I asked what could be so wonderful, they told me to guess. I supposed that they had killed a large amount of game; but no, that was not it; I then guessed that they had had a fight with a bear or a panther, but neither was this it; a third time, I guessed that they had been frightened into camp, for they wore a scared look; but neither was this it. They then told me that, upon arriving at camp, they had noticed a bright fire burning, which showed plainly that some one had been there but a short time before. Not thinking much of this, they had proceeded to feed the pets, but found that the two little black bears were missing; and, shortly afterwards, that a portion of our stock of salt, a portion of our pepper, a portion of our powder and lead, and a sack of dried meat, were gone. All this surprised me indeed, and I reproached myself that my anxiety to finish the trap had betrayed me into such great carelessness as to leave my camp unguarded. However, I concluded, from the nature of the articles taken, that some neighboring hunters must have visited our stores and helped themselves to what they wanted; and, though not aware that any other hunters were within fifty miles, I felt confident of hearing of my bears again, and calmed the fears of my comrades with this trust.

As, however, the unknown visitors might be hostile, we took the precaution that night to remove our blankets from the fire, so as not to be exposed, in case of an attack. We were too much fatigued, nor was it at all necessary to place a watch; but a guard I did station at my side, in whose wakefulness and fidelity I already could place the greatest reliance. This was no other than Lady Washington; for the bear, notwithstanding its apparently drowsy and slumberous nature, is a wakeful animal; and, should anything approach during the night, I knew the Lady would be likely to observe and give me notice of it. Subsequently to this time, my bears often waked me, though but a coyote or a skunk approached my quarters; but, upon this occasion, nothing disturbed us, and the Lady remained perfectly quiet — except, indeed, in one instance, when, actuated by an innate love of cleanliness, she roused and removed to the end of her chain. My personal observations, made on this and other occasions, have convinced me that cleanliness is as much a natural virtue in the ursine, as in the feline race.

The next day, having resolved never to leave our camp unprotected again, we left Stanislaus in charge; and the rest of us proceeded to the new trap, which, by energetic work, we finished and baited early in the afternoon. We then set out to return, intending to hunt upon the way; and, for this purpose, made a circuit towards a ravine in the hills, into which, in the morning, we had driven a band of antelopes. As it was now towards evening, I expected these antelopes to be coming down from the hills to graze in the plain during the night, as was their habit; and, accordingly, Sykesey and I posted ourselves at the mouth of the ravine, while Tuolumne went over the hills to drive down all the game he should find. In a short time, a band of thirty or forty antelopes passed directly in front of our ambuscade; when Sykesey, who was concealed behind a tree, fired and wounded one. As they came to my concealment, which was a rock, they were all in a cluster; and, upon firing, I also brought one to the ground, and then, snatching my revolver, fired three additional shots into the band and wounded another. As the band rushed on, we mounted our mules to pursue the wounded ones, which we soon despatched; but the main band reached the plain and escaped.

It was now nearly night, and the road to camp long, but we packed the antelopes as quickly as possible; and, while Sykesey rode one mule and led the other, loaded, Tuolumne and I pioneered the way. Thus we proceeded about a mile and a half, when a gang of wolves opened upon our trail, and Sykesey became so frightened that he would not go behind with the meat any longer; for the meat, he said, was what they were after, and it ought to go in front. I replied, that all the wolves in the country were not very formidable; but, if he wished, he should go ahead, and we would follow. He accordingly changed to the van, and Tuolumne and I brought up the rear; and again we proceeded. The wolves, meanwhile, kept coming on howling behind us, drawing nearer and nearer, and more and more emboldened with their approaches; but we paid no attention to them, till at length we came to a thicket, through which we would have to pass and where they might, perhaps, attack us in disadvantageous straits. Here, therefore, I directed a halt, and we sat down and awaited the coming up of the pursuers; but the cowardly rascals were afraid to approach nearer than fifty yards, where they sat howling at us. It was

LADY WASHINGTON'S EDUCATION.   111

starlight; we could see their eyes; but they dared come no nearer; and, finally, nothing was left but to discharge our pieces very much at random into their midst. Whether any were killed or wounded, there was no means of knowing; but, certain it is, that the shots had a good effect, for the gang was frightened and left us.

We then entered the thicket, Tuolumne and I in front again, and Sykesey and the mules following; but, before we had gone far, Sykesey suddenly uttered an exclamation of terror, and the packed mule rushed wildly past us through the bushes. It was too dark to see what the difficulty was; but Sykesey soon explained, that some wild beast had sprung from the roadside upon the mule, though, missing its footing, it had fallen over and escaped. I asked, what he supposed it was; he replied he did not know, unless a lion. To satisfy myself, I pulled out a flint and steel, and, gathering some dry leaves, struck a fire; and, upon examination, we soon ascertained, by the prints which the animal had left in the ground, that it was a huge panther.

It is said of the African lion, that when he makes a spring and misses his prey, he makes no second attempt; and the same is said of the California lion, or, in other words, the panther. It is doubtful whether the remark is true in either case; but, if it be, we should not, from such a circumstance alone, conclude, as some have done, that there is any great magnanimity in their characters. They both belong to a genus, which I cannot better describe than by

calling them sneaks. We found where this sneak
had been lying in wait for prey, and whence it had
doubtless leaped. It was not far from a fountain
where animals congregated, thus affording a fine field
for treachery and assassination. Having thus satisfied ourselves, we proceeded on to camp, where the
runaway mule had arrived before us, with her pack in
order; and, but for a scratch or two, all safe and
sound.

CHAPTER XIV.

BUFFALO HUNTING.

WE were awakened the next morning, as we had been awakened once before, by the shouts of Indians; and jumping up, we found the same three braves as previously, who had come up from the village thus early so as to find us before we went out for the day. I had on several occasions spoken with Kennasket about purchasing two of his horses, and the braves proved to be his messengers, with answer that he would sell provided his price were paid, a portion of which must be my two wolf whelps. I answered that I would visit the chief the next day and settle the terms; and then, with the usual hospitality of a mountain camp, I invited my guests to breakfast. As we sat talking, they told me of other white hunters stationed a few miles on the other side of their village; and these hunters, they said, had two black bears exactly like mine. "If," said I, "they are exactly like mine, they must be mine."

After the Indians departed, we proceeded to our
traps, but found only two thievish coyotes, which I
soon despatched with my pistol. We then took a
wide circuit, intending to hunt around towards camp,
and travelled a long way, when, unexpectedly, we
discovered a few buffaloes grazing at a distance. It
is not usual to find buffaloes west of the Rocky Mountains, and especially so far west as where we now
were; but they sometimes stray from their general
haunts; and, before leaving the country, we had the
pleasure of several excellent buffalo hunts, as will be
seen.

Usually, buffalo hunting is conducted by direct and
open attacks upon extensive grassy plains, with not a
tree, rock, or other lurking-place in sight. The buffalo hunter, armed with light and handy weapons,
mounted on a hardy Indian horse skilled in the ways
of the battle and hungry for the combat, rushes into
the midst of a herd and fights a close conflict, not
without danger. It is a manly sport, not unworthy
the buckskin-coated heroes whose fame is handed
down on many a wampum belt and pictured rock.
For myself, I knew little of the sport as it is carried
on upon the slopes of the Platte and the Upper Missouri, nor was I prepared for such game; but having
a good rifle, and considerable experience in the general principles of hunting, I laid my plans according
to my circumstances. My comrades I sent to take
up an ambush beyond the game, while I ascended a
hill directly over where they grazed; and I was con-
gratulating myself upon my success so far, when the

buffaloes espied me, rolled up their tails, lifted their rumps into the air, and scampered off in the greatest consternation. Fortunately, they galloped directly past the spot where my comrades were concealed, who fired, and broke the leg of one of the cows; and this being the first buffalo blood drawn by our party, I cried, with great satisfaction, "Bravely done!" They shouted back, in great glee, that they had beaten the Old Hunter for once, and then ran after the crippled animal. I stood a moment watching the race, but seeing that the buffalo, though grievously wounded, would outstrip them. I hastily mounted a mule, and, with my rifle in one hand and a club in the other, galloped after them to assist at the death.

The boys had chased the buffalo into a wide plain, where several times they tried to approach within gunshot; but, at every endeavor, the wary animal started off with redoubled speed, and fled beyond their reach. Seeing this, I applied the club to the mule's back, and galloped like a madman, over hill and knoll, across valley and ravine, now seeing the game and again losing sight of it, until, after nearly a mile's hard riding, I caught up with the chase and stopped the pursuit. In a short time, as I had expected, the buffalo, weak with fatigue and loss of blood, lay down in a patch of tall grass; and, as soon as she did so, giving the mule to Tuolumne, Sykesey and I tied wreaths of grass about our heads, such as the Indians had used for deer hunting, and, by crawling upon our bellies, approached within sixty yards of our game. So perfect was our disguise, that the watchful animal, though glaring upon every side, did not observe us. It was, however, impossible to procure satisfactory aim in that position; and, therefore, determining to try my grizzly plan, I rose, with my rifle at my face, and gave a sharp whistle. This caused the buffalo to spring suddenly upon her feet, and, wheeling around, she gazed and gathered herself for a charge upon me. As she lowered her head, I fired, and heard the ball tell upon her forehead; but the animal only staggered, and would have still made her plunge, had not Sykesey, who was upon the flank, opportunely fired a ball behind the shoulder, and she fell. I jumped forward, drew my knife across her throat, and she soon poured out her life upon the plain. Her companions of the herd had already long disappeared over the farthest verge of the horizon.

We hastily disrobed our game, and packed it; but, before doing so, I examined the skull, and found that my ball had glanced from the bony forehead without penetrating it. Sykesey laughed, and claimed the credit of killing the first buffalo, — an honor which I joyfully accorded, as his shot was really excellent in itself, and excellently well timed. We then hurried to camp, which, being eight or ten miles distant, we did not reach till long after dark; but such noble buffalo steaks as we had for supper, and that violence of appetite which a deferred meal produces, fully compensated for the lateness of the hour. The anticipation of this meal, indeed, hastened our travel; so that, although antelopes and other game invited our attention on the way, we did not turn aside, and, upon reaching the camp fire, our first movement was to spit a number of choice cuts.

That evening, Stanislaus gave me an account of a white man who had visited camp during the day, professing to be a hunter from Texas, wishing to see me very much. He had come to California in the same company with me, — so he said, but the boy could not recollect his name. I recalled all my companions of that disastrous journey, but was unable to imagine who this could be. It seemed strange to me that destiny could have led any of them by a long, circuitous course, evidently widely different from mine, thus to meet me in the wilderness.

Before going to bed that evening, I placed the buffalo skin in pickle; and, although this was my first attempt to cure a skin of the kind, it turned out a beautiful robe. My method of preparing these hides was to take saltpetre, alum, and a little arsenic, well pulverized together, and rub them lightly over the fleshy side of the skin. These substances seemed to have the effect of preventing putrefaction, and, at the same time, preserving the hide soft and pliable. The skin was then doubled, bringing the raw parts together, rolled up, and left to lie for a day or two, when it was unrolled and the greasy parts scraped off. Next, a root which grows in all portions of the country, called soap-root, was pounded with water into a kind of paste and rubbed on the skin, which was then left to lie a day or two longer. This root had the effect of tanning and further softening the hide, or such was, at least, supposed to be its virtue. Next, the skin was placed upon some hard and smooth substance, and laboriously rubbed with a large, smooth stone, until perfectly soft and dry. It was then hung up and smoked, which gave it the finishing touch, when it assumed a light snuff color. The smoking also served to preserve it from bugs and other insects, which would otherwise have soon destroyed it. This was also the method in which many of the Indians cured their buffalo robes, with the exception that it was rare to find saltpetre, alum, or arsenic among them; but soap-root, or something equivalent, and smoke, they always used.

The next day, according to appointment, having loaded a mule with buffalo meat, and taking the two wolf whelps, Tuolumne and I went down to the village of Kennasket to drive a trade for horses. We found him awaiting us; and as soon as his eyes fell upon the "lobos," he was in raptures, and could not get enough of looking at and playing with them. His pleasure gave me much satisfaction; and, on coming to bargain, I found his valuation of the whelps was by no means niggardly; but we were interrupted in our bargaining by the squaws, who announced dinner, and we sat down to buffalo meat and tule bread.

This tule is a remarkable vegetable; and, considering the immense tracts of it in California, and, indeed, throughout the whole western country, it may, at some future period, assume an importance far beyond the imagination of the present day. To how many differ-

ent uses it will be applied, is not for me to prophecy;
but that it is not mere waste, fit only for the concealment of elks and the fuel of autumn fires, we may
be well assured. Civilization, so far as I know, has
not yet found a use for it, unless in a few places for
the pasturage of swine; but the Indians use the
reeds in large quantities for making hampers, baskets, and mats, and the roots for their bread, such as
was now placed before us. The squaws collect large
quantities of the roots in the marshes, where the reed
grows, and cutting off the exterior rind, retain only
the interior part, which is sweet. This they cut into
small pieces, about the size of chestnuts, and place in
the sun until thoroughly dried. When required for
use, they grind it between stones very fine and mix
it with grass or wild dock meal, usually in the proportion of two-thirds tule to one third grass or dock
meal; the object being not only to give the dough a
more positive taste, but also the proper consistency,
as the tule is rather crumbly, like corn meal, while
the others are pasty. The dough, so prepared, is
rolled into small loaves, which are placed in the ashes
and baked; and they make very healthy and palatable
bread.

Dinner being over, we proceeded with our bargaining, and effected a trade, by which I received two
horses for two wolf whelps, two sacks of dried venison, and a black bear. The horses were received,
and the wolves given over immediately; but I asked
time for the delivery of the venison and the bear;
to which, the chief, as soon as he heard of my

being robbed, readily assented. Tuolumne and I
then mounted our newly-purchased horses and rode
off towards the stranger camp, which was pointed out
to us a few miles distant.

CHAPTER XV.

TEXAN HUNTERS.

The Strangers. Kimball. A Reminiscence of the Colorado Desert. Hunter's "Sport." Comparison of Notes. Further Bargaining with Kennasket. His Valuation of Bears. The Plague of Wealth. Guarding our Horses. Dried Meat. Elk Late. Slaying Elks in the Tules. Return to Camp. Lost by the Carelessness of Comrades. Second Visit to the Lake. Tuolumne's Horseback Feat. Visit to the Traps. Coyotes. Bears. Stones in living Hearts. Vitality of Animals. Reception of Kimball and his Comrades.

THE strangers proved to be three Texan hunters, one of whom I immediately recognized and called his name, — Mr. Kimball. I asked what could have brought him into these wild regions. "Well," said he, "to tell the truth, Mr. Adams, I never would have got so far, had it not been for that canteen of water which you gave me on the Colorado desert." He was, indeed, a fellow traveller with me over the ninety mile desert in 1849, when several of us, being worn out and incapable of further travel, were left by the remainder of the company to get along as best we could. I happened to have a canteen of water, which I shared between Kimball and a companion of his; and ever afterwards, Kimball declared that that canteen had saved his life, — and there may have been truth in this declaration; for the third man, notwithstanding our assistance, soon after died of fatigue and exhaustion.

We talked a considerable time over this matter, when Kimball broke out into a loud laugh, and remarking that one favor deserved another, said that he had been at my camp a number of times; but, being never able to find me, he had finally taken my bears and a portion of my stores, supposing that I would, of course, hunt them up, and we would certainly meet. It was a little difficult to see the wit of bringing about a meeting in this way; but, as it would, among hunters generally, be considered legitimate sport thus to help one's self, I could make no complaint, and accepted Kimball's invitation to remain over night. Soon afterwards we all sat down to supper; after which, Kimball and I recommenced our conversation, and related over our respective histories, from the time when we crossed the desert together till the time of our strange meeting. It appeared from his story, that he and his companions, who were named Foster and Partridge, had come up into the northern territories for the purpose of making a settlement; but being all hunters, they had stopped for a week or two to hunt. My story was a longer one than his; and we sat talking together by the camp fire long after all the rest were slumbering.

In the morning, Tuolumne and I mounted our horses, and, bidding adieu to the Texans, took our bears and proceeded back to the village of Kennasket. As the chief had acted liberally, I gave him the choice of the bears; but he found it so difficult to choose between them that he at last proposed a third horse for the second bear, which, of course, was readily accepted. We thereupon returned to our camp in great good spirits, having accomplished, by our journey, a great deal more than was anticipated.

It is not unpleasant to possess valuable property, for it makes a man feel, so far, rich; but in many cases, by so much the more valuable that a thing is, just so much the more trouble and anxiety does it require to watch and preserve it. There are many rich men, who lead miserable lives on account of their riches, being bothered almost to distraction with acres to which the poorer man is a stranger. Thus it now became a plague to us to have valuable horses, because we had to watch them. While there was nothing but mules about our camp, which no man cared to steal, we slept soundly, but with our horses we had to keep a watch every night; and from this period, it became a new regulation in camp, that there should be a constant guard, — sometimes one, sometimes two of us relieved at midnight.

The season got by this time to be pretty well advanced, and we began to think of our return to California, and of laying in a stock of dried meat for the support of ourselves and our animals on the journey. While at the village, the Indians had told me of a lake, some twenty-five miles distant, in a northeast direction, where they said there were elks in abundance; and, having now good horses, I determined to visit it. The next day, accordingly, Tuolumne and I mounted the two best horses, and set out in the direction indicated.

After riding hard for several hours, we came in

sight of a considerable body of water, the shores of
which were low, and covered for miles with tule
rushes, — making a sight which was beautiful to look
at. For a time, as I cast my eyes over the prospect,
my errand in visiting it was forgotten; but upon our
approaching nearer and nearer, a number of elks
feeding in the tule, recalled me to my business, and
I set about making a slaughter among them. We
determined to creep upon them; and as the tule was
tall and thick, and the animals busy feeding, we were
enabled, after dismounting, to approach close; and,
fairer mark could not have been desired than I had
at one noble buck, which at my first fire dropped
in his tracks. The next moment, Tuolumne's rifle
cracked, and immediately we both reloaded as quickly
as possible. The elks had probably not been hunted
before, for they did not run, but tramped around in
bewilderment; so that I had an opportunity to fire
again, and broke the neck of another, which also
dropped. Tuolumne likewise fired a second shot,
but in doing so, he incautiously exposed himself, and
the elks, observing him, broke for the higher grounds,
and away they went. By the four shots we killed
two, and wounded another, which I pursued, and
finally also brought to the ground. Thus, three large
bodies lay before us, — more than our horses could
carry; and I was sorry, upon taking a survey, that
we had not brought the mules. We however did the
best we could, which was to pack three quarters of
an elk upon each horse; and then after dragging
the rest together, and covering them with tules, and

hoisting a flag to keep off the wild beasts, we started with our loads towards camp, intending the next day to return for the balance.

It was so late and dark before we got half the distance to camp, that we missed our course, and for several hours stumbled through gullies and ravines, without knowing where we were. We must have wandered several hours; but in no direction was there any light to be seen, nor could we recognize any landmarks, though they seemed familiar. At last we determined to fire off a shot as a signal; and, sure enough, it was answered; but, upon getting in, we found that Sykesey and Stanislaus had been careless, and allowed the fire to grow low; so it was for this reason that we could not tell our position in the darkness, approaching from an unusual direction. It is of so much importance on such occasions to have a beacon, that there was no other way than to reprove them for their neglect, though of course, their watching over the horses half of the previous night, pleaded to some extent in their justification.

The next day I would willingly have rested, but as Sykesey was not disposed to go out after the elk meat at the lake, which he thought he could never find, I took the two boys, the three horses, and the two mules, and made a second trip. As we approached the lake valley this time, a band of elks was feeding on the plain. and thinking to procure more meat as well as to try the speed of our horses, Tuolumne and I gave them chase, and ran several miles, when Tuolumne managed to shoot one from horseback, — which

was a very skilful feat. This was a fine buck, which
weighed about six hundred pounds, and with what had
been left the day before, made fair loads for both
horses and mules. After packing them, we returned
to camp, which we reached in good season.

We made the round of the traps the next day,
and in one found two coyotes, which I shot with my
revolver, considering them not worth the bother of
keeping; but this caused me regret afterwards, for
they proved to be of a kind none of us had ever
before seen, being large and finely haired. It was
however too late to help the matter; and whipping
off their hides, we swathed their carcasses in bark,
and tied them in a tree. We did this because we
had no tools to bury them, and did not wish them
lying about near the traps, as they might have
prevented other animals from entering. As we were
returning to camp, towards dusk, we observed four
or five grizzly bears. We tied our mules, and ascended a hill to view the valley, which intervened
between us; but finding we could not reach them
except by making a large circuit, we determined for
once to pass on. I was loth to lose any chance for
my favorite game, but allowed myself to be overruled, and we proceeded to camp.

During this day, Sykesey had been busy at camp,
jerking up the bountiful supply of elk meat so as to
dry it; and in the evening, upon my return from the
traps, he told me a story which it was a little difficult
at first to credit. He said, that in cutting up the
heart of one of the elks, he had found the stone-tip

of an Indian arrow imbedded in its substance; making
it appear that the weapon had been shot, and broken
off some time before, and that the wound had afterwards healed, surrounding the stone with matter which
was hard and callous. He had kept the heart, and
now showed it to me; and, sure enough, there it was,
with the stone imbedded.   Without this positive proof,
it would have been hard to make me believe that any
animal could have lived with such a stone in its heart;
but two years afterwards I killed a deer in Corral
Hollow in California, and found a small bullet in its
heart, incased in very much the same manner as this
stone was.   So, from these two instances, it is certain
that animals will sometimes live and get well, with
wounded hearts.

The next day, which was the fifth after our visit
to Kimball's camp, he and his friends were to make
us a visit; and therefore we remained at home, expecting them.   It was not long before they hove in sight,
each on his own horse; seeing which, I directed
Stanislaus to stir up what flour we had, and bake
bread, as a token of our most hospitable welcome.
At dinner, they appreciated the delicacy, and we sat
and talked over our old travels and adventures all the
afternoon, and until bedtime.   When I came to speak
of the lake, and the elks, the Texans wished to go
there with us, and it was soon agreed that we should
all hunt in that direction the next day.

CHAPTER XVI.

ELK HUNTING.

THE lake appeared still more beautiful and romantic upon the third visit than it had upon either the first or second. The landscape about it was composed of hills covered with trees, and plains rolling in green luxuriance. On one side, in the low marshy ground skirting the water, was a heavy growth of tules, several miles in length and a half mile in width; and it was among these that bands of elks, in the dry season, loved to congregate. It is a habit of elks, as of many other wild ruminants, to graze in the open plains principally in the evening, at night, and in the morning. During the warmer portions of the day, they retire to shady thickets like deer; or, if there are tules in the neighborhood, these they seem to prefer, and among them they stand almost up to the knees in mud and water, stamping about to keep cool and drive off the tormenting flies until evening, when they again sally forth into the plains.

As we approached the lake, several hours before sunset, we rode down to a small wooded stream near its shore; where, hitching our horses, saddled as they were, we made preparations for an immediate hunt. That we would find game in the tules at that time, I was well satisfied, and, therefore, directed the party to spread out and make a clean sweep through the rushes, so as to assure ourselves of starting any that might be there.

Accordingly, we spread out and began beating through the tules; when, presently, we heard the whistle of a buck in front. Upon this warning, we advanced more cautiously; and, in a few hundred yards further, we heard the whistle again, and knew, by the distinctness of the sound, that there was a band of elks not far off. We soon came in sight of them, and I directed each man to single out one, and all fire as nearly at once as possible; then each to reload and remain comparatively motionless till another opportunity occurred, and then all fire again. In accordance with these directions, we acted in concert. At the first fire, the elks were astounded, and kept tramping around till we reloaded and fired a second shot, when they took the alarm and started off. There was a great rushing through the tules, which sounded as if there were a hundred elks; but the tules were too high to enable us to see the actual number.

We had anticipated a considerable slaughter; but,

upon going up to the spot, found that the band had left only three of its number behind. This we all thought very strange, and followed the trail several hundred yards, in the expectation of finding wounded ones; but not another elk, or even a sprinkle of blood, was to be seen; and, being thus satisfied that all the wounded had fallen, we returned and dressed the three bodies. We then endeavored to bring the horses to where they lay; but the ground was so soft that it was impossible to do so, and thereupon we cut poles in a thicket near the lake, and, slinging a quarter elk on each, carried them out on our shoulders to firmer ground, where they were packed on the horses and borne to where we had stopped, in the timber, on the banks of the creek. As usual, we hauled the meat up into trees; all but a choice piece, of which we made our evening meal. A rousing fire was built, and we devoured a hearty supper of elk meat, all enjoying it to a great degree; and then, drawing forth our pipes and smoking, we listened to the shrill piping of the frogs in the low grounds and the occasional hoot of the owl; or told stories of hunting and adventure, till the sinking flames of our fire warned us to replenish it and retire.

We were afoot the next morning again with the dawn, wishing to kill game enough to load all our horses; but we had to go several miles from the lake before coming up with the elks, which, at this time, were grazing on the plains. We found them in an excellent situation to be surrounded; and, as there was a very good number in our party to accomplish this manœuvre, I sent Tuolumne and a Texan around behind them, while the rest of us spread apart, and all advanced. The elks, seeing riders upon every side, became bewildered, and stood staring wildly about, giving us a chance to shoot them down as we pleased. There were about twenty of them, and we might, perhaps, have killed half; but, after the first fire, which brought down three, we stopped and allowed the rest to escape, knowing that it would be impossible to carry away more; nor, indeed, could we carry all the six we had, for each, when dressed, made a good load for a horse. The hides and one of the bodies we left hanging in the trees, intending to return for them at another time; and then, each leading a loaded horse, we returned on foot to our camp, which we reached about sundown, having been absent two days.

Upon unpacking, we heaped the meat against the butt of a tree, and the pile, together with that which hung in the branches around, reminded me of a place familiar to my eyes in old times, — that is to say, the old Boston market; but there was a wide differemce between the strict old city and the wild scenery here. As it grew dark, wolves and coyotes began howling and yelping on every side, and we soon found that the meat would have to be watched all night. After supper, accordingly, sending a Texan and one of the boys to keep guard over the horses, Kimball and I took our places by the meat. We soon got into conversation, and, in the course of the evening, he told me that when he was at Portland, in Oregon, there was a vessel lying there, bound for Boston, which would sail in the latter part of September. Upon learning this, a thought struck me which had not entered my head before; this was, to take my animals to Portland and make a shipment of them by this vessel from there, instead of from California, as at first intended. I spoke to Kimball of this, and proposed that he and his companions should hunt with me, catch all we could, procure all the peltry and bear-oil possible, and ship them. He immediately replied, that, as for himself, he was perfectly willing to hunt a month for me, as he owed me more than a month's work at any rate. I answered, that it was nonsense to talk in such a manner, for he owed me nothing; but if he and his party would remain and aid me to get the shipment off, I would pay them what was reasonable. After talking the matter over by themselves, Kimball and his companions determined to remain and have a glorious hunt for a month; and, at the end of that period, we were all to set out together for Portland.

Early the next morning, accordingly, the Texans started off after their effects; Sykesey and Tuolumne at the same time went off with a horse and the two mules for the elk and elk hides left at the lake, and I to make the rounds of the traps. In one of them I found a wild-cat, but had to leave it till next day, when Tuolumne and I went out and made a sugar-pine cage, in which we packed it on one of our mules. On our way to camp, this second day, I made an excellent shot at a gray fox, which was eating a bird on a hill-side quite a hundred yards distant; and Tuolumne also shot a wild-cat out of a tree. We packed the skins of both; and going on till we came near camp, we met two wolves on the run, which we shot at, but missed. Afterwards we learned from Sykesey and Stanislaus, who had remained cutting up the meat, that two wolves had been prowling about camp nearly all day; and, as it was probable that they would be back in the night, I made arrangements to give them a couple of ounces of lead to fill their hungry bellies.

The Texans, meanwhile, had arrived; and during the evening we laid our plans for the month, resolving to build two more traps, and agreeing to divide into two parties, each to build one. After thus arranging our plans, we took our places near the meat that still remained unjerked, in expectation of a visit from the wolves, which kept up a great howling at a distance. A short time after midnight, a large pack burst upon us with a terrific howl; but, there being no light except what was shed by the stars, we could not see them distinctly, and were compelled, for the purpose of getting a fire, to allow them to approach the meat, which they soon attacked with ravenous ferocity. There were so many that they seemed like an army; but, after three of us had fired into their midst, and they put off, there was only one left killed. They must have been very hungry, for these were the first wolves that ever dared to come into camp; and the great quantity of meat there, which they snuffed afar off, must have proved too great a temptation for the exercise of prudence.

The next morning we separated into parties, the
Texans going in one direction, and my party in another, and commenced our new traps, at which we
worked steadily two days; by which time we had
completed ours, though the Texans were not done
with theirs. While they went out on the third day
to finish, Tuolumne and I started upon an excursion
for fresh meat. We rode four or five miles; when,
coming upon three deer, I fired from horseback, — this
being my first attempt of the kind from the horse I
now rode. The flash, or the report of the rifle, so
frightened the horse, that he suddenly sprang from
under me, and I fell flat upon the ground; but, jumping up and brushing the dust out of my eyes, I found
myself but little hurt, and soon commenced looking
for the deer. As was to have been expected, however, they had fled unharmed. Proceeding further,
we perceived a few antelopes grazing in a valley.
Tuolumne made a circuit, and fired at them, but
missed; seeing which, I galloped forward, and, running them into a ravine, made a second attempt at
firing from horseback. The horse was by no means
vicious, and I had learned from the fall before how
to accommodate my centre of gravity to his motions;
so that this shot was successful, and brought down an
antelope, the flesh of which afterwards served to bait
both the old and the new traps, — the one built by the
Texans being finished just as we arrived at it in the
evening.

When the baiting was finished, we all, five in number, mounted our horses, and, in great good spirits,

started for camp; but, on our way, we suddenly heard a bear snort; and the horses pricked up their ears, and pranced in alarm. I stopped and looked around in every direction, and at last espied the bear in a bunch of bushes only twenty yards off. It was by this time too dark to procure correct aim, but, giving directions that all should fire at once, I blazed away; and Kimball and Tuolumne did the same, but at random, not seeing the bear, which gave a snort, and away he went, probably untouched. The Texans were anxious to pursue; but I replied, No, it was too dark, and there was too much brush in that direction. They rejoined that they were very anxious to kill a bear; to which I answered, that they should only wait a few days, and I would take them to a part of the country where they could have their fill of bear killing.

As we proceeded thence very leisurely to camp, Tuolumne proposed that we should frighten Stanislaus by pretending to be Indians; but this I would by no means listen to. I said that it was not right to deceive a messmate, nor good policy; for it would destroy all that feeling of confidence which ought to exist between hunters. It is true, I had deceived Tuolumne once by pretending to be a bear, but he deserved reproving; still the plan was not justifiable, as I am willing to confess. It would have been greatly wrong to have done anything of the kind on this occasion; for Stanislaus during the day had been working diligently at the meat, and had it all jerked and hung up. That which was already dry he had packed in sacks, made for the purpose, of antelope skins sewed together with thongs.

Having thus finished our traps and all the work before us, we discussed plans for the next day as we sat about the nightfire. I addressed the company, and said that we must now be industrious, and collect all the animals, hides, oil, and meat we could, for we had but a month to remain. The others replied that they were willing to do their best, but that I should act as chief, to direct the labor and point out the hunting-grounds. This position, as it naturally belonged to me, I willingly accepted; and I immediately directed that, in a few days, a party of us should proceed to a valley about forty miles to the east, where there was said to be plenty of buffaloes, and have a grand buffalo hunt before leaving the country. This speech met with great favor, and confirmed my authority with that best of sanctions, — general and willing consent.

ADAMS AND THE BUFFALO.

CHAPTER XVII.

MISHAPS.

THE hunting of the next month, the number and character of the animals captured, and the quantities of skins and provisions gathered together were astonishing. Every variety of animal which the country afforded fell in our way; our traps, during the entire time, brought us profit; our stores of curiosities increased with a remarkable rapidity; and indeed the most sanguine expectations could hardly have exceeded the good fortune which attended all our efforts. So numerous were our prizes, and so crowded and varied the incidents of this month, that a detailed narrative of them would only perplex the story; I propose, therefore, to group the adventures in such a manner as to avoid the confusion of too great a multiplicity of minutiæ.

As the time for our departure from the country

was fixed, we had constantly before our minds the
necessity of laying in a large supply of dry meat, for
the sustenance not only of ourselves but also of our
animals upon the march to Portland. We looked for
these supplies principally to the bands of elks which
grazed about the lake, and to the buffaloes which
roamed over the plains to the east; and a large portion of our time was therefore devoted to hunting in
those regions. The day after finishing the last trap,
four of us proceeded to the lake, and, driving a band
of elks into the tules, we dismounted, and, pursuing
upon foot, killed three fine ones, which we packed
home the same evening.

On the second day, in accordance with previous arrangement, Kimball, Foster, Tuolumne, and I started
on a buffalo hunt, and took with us the six horses
and two mules. We road hard all day, and arrived
at the border of the valley, spoken of by the Indians,
about sundown. We camped under the trees, in a
ravine among the hills, from which we could look
down over the plains below, and see the grassy undu-
lations rolling gently away as far as the eye could
reach. It was a beautiful spot, destined some day to
present as splendid a domestic picture as now a wild
one; and, as my eyes dwelt delighted upon it, I could
not help thinking of a time when millions of stock
shall crop the herbage there, and the now wild landscape be studded with the farms and villages of a
numberless and thriving population. This will only
be, thought I, when these old bones of mine shall
have crumbled into dust, and when the memory of

the present inhabitants shall be preserved only in
old stories. Such were my thoughts as I lay in my
blankets, with my rifle by my side; and, when sleep
came, with its fantasies, my imagination enlarged
upon these musings of the evening, and presented a
scene such as is familiar in the agricultural valleys in
the east, but will not be, here, perhaps for many
years.

We were up in the morning before the sun; and,
looking down upon the plains, we beheld eight or ten
dark objects moving slowly about at a distance, which
were at once recognized as buffaloes. We mounted
our horses and road towards them. Upon approaching, supposing the others to be in their proper places,
I fired, and brought one of the animals to his knees
by a ball in his shoulder; and the next moment a shot
by a comrade brought another to the ground; but
the surround had not been complete, and the rest of
the band soon broke away and escaped us. The two
which were killed, however, furnished work for the
day, as the meat had not only to be carried to our
rendezvous, but also cut into strips and hung upon
the drying-poles, and the hides to be spread with
saltpetre and other articles for preservation. In the
evening, again, we mounted our horses, and, taking
the direction in which the band had escaped, came
upon them at a distance of six or eight miles, near a
creek, the banks of which were beautifully timbered.
They were grazing on the further side. We dismounted, and, tying our horses, got into the worn, but
now almost dry, channel of the stream, and without

difficulty crept upon and killed three mighty bulls at
first shots. Thus, in one day, we secured five buffaloes.

This large quantity of fresh meat, as was to have
been expected, attracted many prowlers; and, during
the whole night, the screams of panthers, wolves, and
coyotes, were heard all around. By dint of close
watching, however, we worked through the night, and
preserved our meat intact, with the exception of one
quarter, which was seized by a bold coyote; but the
thief paid dearly for his temerity, for I gave him such
a lick with a club as broke his back. In the morning
we found him endeavoring to drag his paralyzed hind
parts off the field, but soon put a period to his thiev-
ing existence.

The second day we also made a morning and an
evening hunt, and killed three buffaloes, five deer,
and four foxes. The skins of all we preserved, and
the meat of all, save the foxes. Again, the next afternoon, we started out for buffaloes, and soon came upon
a large band. They ran towards a timbered marsh,
into which we followed, and killed three, which we
packed to our stopping-place in the ravine.

This marsh was an excellent place to kill these
unwieldy animals; for, once in it, they mired, and fell
almost as easy a prey as when, on the upper waters
of the Missouri, an unlucky band becomes entangled
in a deep snow-drift, and the Blackfoot warriors are in
need of meat. The next day, again on the hunt, we
attempted to drive a band into the same marsh; but
the animals, probably aware of their danger, broke

off sidewise, and thundered along towards a part of our semicircle which was guarded by Foster. This unfortunate man had always been anxious to distinguish himself, but yet knew little of that prudence and caution which characterize the true hunter, and, as the band approached, rashly threw himself in front, and was overthrown. Buffaloes rarely turn aside from their direction, and it is almost impossible to head them off when in full course. I have known them run against trees which stood in their way; and more than once, upon the great plains, have they been known to run over men, horses, and sometimes over emigrant teams. Nor did poor Foster fare better; for he and his horse were not only overthrown, but the band passed over them. Buffaloes either carry their heads too low to see well, or their momentum becomes unmanageable, or they rush purposely upon obstructions, or — and this is the most probable explanation of their conduct — all three of these reasons combine to drive them headlong forward.

Upon rushing to Foster's assistance, we found him badly hurt, though not seriously. I recommended the water-cure, which had availed so well in my own case when bitten by the wolf; and, as his injuries consisted of bruises principally upon the back, we tore a blanket into strips, and wound them, dripping with cold water, about his body, from the armpits to the hips; and in a few days, such was the virtue of the remedy, he was able to accompany us upon the hunt again.

The same afternoon, leaving Foster at the ravine,

Kimball, Tuolumne, and I pursued a small band of buffaloes for a long distance; but at last they began to labor, and their tongues hung out almost as long as a man's arm. Encouraged by this sign of fatigue, we struck our heels into our horses' sides, and yelled and hallooed, as jockeys do by way of incitement, and finally overtook them. As we passed, I wheeled and fired at the forehead of one; but the ball glanced off, without penetrating. The suddenness of the action, however, or the flash of the gun, amazed the band for a moment; and, in this nick of time, my comrades wounded two, which we soon killed. We packed the bodies to the ravine, as before, and the next day devoted ourselves to jerking meat and curing hides.

On the fifth day of the hunt I had one of those dangerous adventures into which too great a confidence in one's own powers sometimes betrays a person. We had risen early, and soon discovered a large band of buffaloes, and gave chase. We pursued several miles, till they came to a precipitous bank of a creek, down which they plunged fifteen feet, and crossed over into the marsh that extended for miles beyond. Seeing them fairly in the mud, we sought low places in the bank, and rode after them; but, as the soil grew less and less firm, we soon dismounted, and pursued on foot. The animals plunged deeper and deeper, and, being hampered with their great bodies, completely mired; so that we easily reached them, and in a few minutes slaughtered four. There was one lying in the mud a little further

distant, and, as my rifle was discharged, I resolved
to kill him with my bowie-knife. I was actuated
in this, I confess, by a foolish desire of exhibiting
my bravery, and approached without sufficient caution; for, upon getting close with my knife drawn
ready to plunge into his neck, he suddenly made a
mighty effort, lunged against me, and laid me sprawling before him. He then, with his crooked horns,
butted against my prostrate form, and pressed me
deeply into the mire; so that I was in great danger
of being drowned. The mud was soft and yielding,
and my body sank deeply; but this turned out to be
a fortunate circumstance; for, had the ground been
harder, I should certainly have been ground to pieces.
While thus going down into what threatened to be my
grave, Kimball ran up, and, just as I was disappear-
ing, sent a ball into the bull's body, which made him
throw up his head. In this moment, I sprang to
my feet, with the knife still in my hand, and stabbed
the beast to the heart, and he soon expired. Foster
and Tuolumne meanwhile killed two more, — thus
making six, in all, for this day.

During the next two days we spent most of the
time in drying the meat and curing the hides of the
last killed buffaloes. One more hunt, indeed, we took,
and killed three animals, but preserved only the skins.
The next, or eighth day of the hunt, we prepared for
our journey to head-quarters by placing all the dried
meat in sacks, which we made, as usual, of deer and
antelope skins and bark. There being six horses
and two mules, we filled sixteen sacks, two for each

animal; and the next morning, having packed them, and distributed the skins, — consisting of twenty buffalo, six or eight deer, ten antelope, and twelve or sixteen valuable fox skins, — among the loads, we started for camp. Much dried meat we of course left behind; but there was no other way, it being impracticable at that time to remove it.

Upon getting back to camp we found that our comrades had succeeded well in hunting and trapping, having taken two black bear cubs, three black wolves, and a large grizzly bear, the latter of which they had killed. They had also killed eighteen deer, six antelopes, four gray foxes, and three raccoons; the skins of which they had preserved, as also the meat of the deer and antelopes. That evening we sat about our camp fire and narrated our adventures, as usual; but when I came to tell of the buffalo fight in the mud, it exceeded in interest all the other stories which were told. During the next two days we caught another huge grizzly bear, which we killed and skinned, and three black foxes. We also killed, upon the hunt, five antelopes and five gray and black foxes, which were so wild that we had to shoot them upon the run; also several silver-gray foxes, which are the most valuable of the species for their magnificent fur.

The next day we all made another visit to the lake; and, in the evening, killed three elks, which we hung in the trees, and then camped. In the course of the night we were awakened by a grizzly bear, which approached; but, upon my jumping up and firing, the animal made off with a tremendous growl. This adventure excited the whole camp, and particularly Foster, who was of a chivalrous and impulsive character, and wished to go after the beast, even in the darkness. Such madness I would, by no means, allow; but, in the morning, we had hardly started upon the hunt, when we came upon a large grizzly with two large cubs. She was probably the visitor of the previous night; and Foster was almost beside himself for a shot. I cautioned him to go around with the rest of us to a wooded knoll beyond the animals; but he thought he could kill a bear as easily as a buck, and determined to advance from where he was.

Seeing that he was bent upon his self-willed resolution, we exacted only a promise that he would not fire until we reached the knoll; but, before getting upon the top of it, we were startled by the report of his rifle, and, at the same time, one of those terrific roars which the grizzly makes when it rushes for a man. I knew, in an instant, there was danger, and sprang forward; but only in time to witness poor Foster's death. He had wounded the brute, and then ran for a tree; but, before he could climb out of reach, the bear seized his feet in her mouth, and dragged him to the ground.

Time and again had I cautioned Foster, as also the others of my comrades, if ever they fell in the power of a grizzly bear, to lie perfectly still and show no signs of life, however severely scratched and bitten they might be. This is a simple but valuable rule,

for it seems that no variety of the animal will wreak
its vengeance upon a body which shows no indications of vitality; a trait which appears to have been
known in the remotest times, for the old fabulist
founded one of his stories upon it. I myself have
tried the efficacy of feigning death; and there have
been cases where a bear would leave a pretended
dead man perfectly unharmed, but return and exhibit
the greatest fury upon his attempt to move. It is
therefore no more than prudence, in such cases, to
remain perfectly passive and quiet until the animal
is beyond sight and hearing. But poor Foster, in
his extremity, forgot these injunctions, and not only
shrieked for help but struggled to get away. I immediately drew my knife and rushed towards him,
with the object of attracting the brute's attention;
but, before I could approach, the bear, with one
tearing grasp, ripped through his breast, and drew
out the heart, liver, stomach, and intestines, — presenting to my gaze one of the most awful sights that
ever my eyes beheld.

The bear pawed and snuffed at the poor man's
entrails, and in a few minutes was joined by her
cubs, which no sooner smelt the blood than they became almost frantic with fury. I was much agitated,
but ran to a tree, and, taking as deliberate an aim as
was possible under the circumstances, pierced the old
bear behind the shoulder. She fell, but in a few
moments got up and tried to rush towards me; when
a second shot, at the butt of the ear, penetrated her
brain, and put an end to her existence. I again

reloaded; and Kimball, Partridge, Sykesey, and Tuolumne coming up, we all fired together upon the cubs,
one of which fell; but the second, though wounded,
showed fight, and, being a year and a half old, made
an assailant which could not be despised. As our
rifles were discharged, we threw them aside and
awaited the attack with our knives. The beast came
up, nothing daunted, and made his first pass at Tuolumne, whom he struck to the ground. We leaped
forward at this, and Kimball and I, at the same time,
from opposite sides, plunged our knives into the bear's
vitals, so that he soon expired. Tuolumne was considerably bitten and scratched, but not seriously injured; and we turned our attention directly to our
deceased companion.

Having neither pickaxe nor shovel at the lake, we
despatched Partridge and Sykesey to head-quarters
for them. The rest of us then laid out the remains
as decently as we could, and began our watch over
them, which, as the tools did not arrive till the next
evening, lasted two days and two nights. On the
third morning, we dug a grave four or five feet deep
under an oak-tree; but, before consigning the body
to its final resting-place, I requested Kimball to make
a prayer to that Great Being whose presence per-
vades the wilderness as well as temples built with
hands; and he made an untutored appeal, praying
Heaven to witness the last sad rites due the dead, — to
which I fervently replied, Amen. We then lowered
the body, which was wrapped in a blanket; and,
placing sticks over it, threw in leaves, and then earth,

which we heaped up into a small mound. Two smoothed pieces of wood were placed, one at the head and the other at the foot of the grave; and, upon the side of the tree immediately above, we carved the name of William Foster, and the date and manner of his death.

Having thus done all in our power for our deceased comrade, we gathered our tools and started for camp. It was a solemn hour that we thus had to leave one of our companions behind; and deep and lasting was the impression it made upon us. Poor Foster! He was an unfortunate but brave-hearted and willing-handed man, and we had all begun to love him. May he rest peacefully in the lonely grave to which our rough but friendly hands consigned him!

CHAPTER XVIII.

IN THE CHAPARRAL AGAIN.

OUR hunting in Washington lasted a few weeks
longer, and, during this time, we had severable notable
adventures; but for several days after the death and
burial of Foster, inspired with the solemn feelings
which that sad event occasioned, we had little heart
to hunt, and busied ourselves about camp, overhauling
our dried meats, curing our peltries, and attending
the traps, which continued to yield prize after prize.
We entrapped, in succession, from this period till our
final departure from the country, two black foxes; two
black bear cubs; a white wolf, the first of the kind we
had ever caught; two small animals called fishers,
which occupy a position in natural history between
the raccoon and the mink; a brown bear and cub;
two panthers, an old and young one; a large grizzly,
which we killed in the trap; a black wolf; two other

fishers; two other black foxes; another black wolf; and another white wolf, apparently the mate of the one caught previously. All the larger animals thus caught we took to our camp with lassos; the smaller ones, including the panther, we caged, and packed in upon our mules. During the same time we killed many deer, antelopes and foxes, and also caught a number of fawns.

In caging the bear cubs last mentioned, Kimball and I wrapped the lower part of our arms up to the elbows with bark, and, while our comrades hoisted the trap-door for a moment, we entered, seized the captives, bound them, and, without difficulty or scratch, placed them in the cage.

Whenever we wished to hunt a particular species of animal, we knew where it would most likely be found; as various animals prefer particular kinds of country. Buffaloes love grassy plains; elks, moist ground; panthers, heavy timber; and so on with other animals. A rugged and brushy part of the country was prolific in foxes; and another, a dry, airy plain, was a favorite place for antelopes; but all these animals roamed in different directions, and upon some expeditions we would meet with almost every variety in the same quarter. Our camp was, so to speak, a centre, where different ranges of animals merged into each other. In one direction was a hilly country, sparsely timbered, but covered with dense chaparral, and this was the bear ground. It was here that my other principal adventures in Washington occurred.

On the fifth day after Foster's burial, we proceeded to the bear ground, and reached it towards evening. We soon descried four bears, two old ones and two nearly full-grown, digging on a hill-side, and close together. I turned to Kimball and Partridge, and exacted a promise that they would follow my injunctions implicitly, which they agreed to do; and I then gave the necessary instructions, directing all to get upon the hill above the bears, fire upon them, and, if pursued, each man take an oblique direction, around and up the hill, — such as the bear finds it difficult to follow, — and, if necessary, climb one of the trees which here and there stood upon the eminence. All acted according to this plan; and upon the first fire both the young bears were wounded. The old ones, however, immediately observed and rushed towards us, when I directed the whole party to climb; and we were soon seated in the boughs of trees.

Full-grown grizzly bears rarely climb, and rarely attempt to do so; but, sometimes, if they see the object of their pursuit climbing, they will attempt to follow. In this case we had time to locate ourselves before the bears approached; and, upon coming up, they merely ran from tree to tree, looking at us, and growling, but without attempting to climb. As we had carried up our rifles, I soon reloaded, and fired at the old female, which was under my tree; and at the same time Kimball fired at the old male, which was under his; when both, badly wounded, made a tremendous howling, and went off together towards their cubs. We immediately reloaded, and, following,

found them making a great ado about one of the cubs,
which lay dead; but the other cub was nowhere to be
seen. We crept as near as we safely could, and
fired another volley; but, owing either to our excitement, to the growing darkness, or to the distance at
which we fired, our shots had apparently no effect,
except that the old bears, leaving the dead cub,
escaped into a thicket of chaparral. We pursued
a short distance, tracking them by frequent blood-
stains; but, finding the chaparral very thick, we resolved to wait until morning, and took up our night-
quarters where we were.

There was a moon for several hours that night, and
we kept a strict watch, expecting the old bears to
return; but they came not, nor gave any signs of
their whereabouts. From this circumstance, as well
as from the quantities of blood staining the trail, I
concluded that they had been badly wounded, and
determined to penetrate the thicket after them; but
my comrades, when I announced my determination,
regarded it as madness, and demurred. I placed the
butt of my rifle on the ground, and asked, "Gentlemen, was it bears you came out to hunt?" They
said it was. "Well then," said I, "I am astonished
to see you falter. We have lost a companion, it is
true; but that is no reason why bears cannot be
hunted with safety. Here we have several fine ones
wounded, and, without a doubt, disabled; and we can
find them without much search. It is safer and
easier to follow these than to hunt up others; and
besides, it is cowardly to falter at this stage of the

business." These reasons seemed to have weight; and my comrades replied that they were ready to follow. Accordingly we crawled in under the interlaced thicket, and followed the bloody trail.

We proceeded four or five hundred yards, and came to the bed of a creek, dry at that season of the year, with banks four or five feet high, all densely overgrown with chaparral. We halted there, and held counsel for a few moments; and then proceeded on, down the bed of the creek, as the trail led us. In the course of a few hundred yards further, I discovered the old she bear lying on her side, and knew from her position that she was dead. Being several yards in advance of the company, I hastily jumped upon the body, and, placing myself in an attitude as if holding her down, shouted for my comrades, who were just coming around a bend in the creek; and, seeing me in that position, they started back; but I soon showed them there was no danger, and we all had a hearty laugh. Upon examining the body, we found that it was shot through the head, heart, and bowels; and that several balls had struck her in the sides, but had not gone through the fat.

After a further consultation, we determined to proceed, and followed the trail a long distance further down the creek. There was now not so much blood; but we could see the tracks of bears in the sand, and occasionally a few red stains. I think we proceeded as much as a mile from where the body of the female lay, when we discovered a den, and the two remaining bears lying in it; and, judging from their position, I knew that both of them were alive. Without the loss of a moment, I directed my comrades to stand ready to fire; and myself creeping to a bush within ten yards of the den, laying off my cap, and steadying my nerves, I raised my rifle, and, aiming at the old bear's breast, sent a ball through his heart. He lay with his head upon his paws, but, upon the fire, he rolled over, uttered a growl, and died. The cub, at the same time, tried to rise, but had been too badly wounded the previous evening, and my comrades soon finished him. After cutting up, we packed the skins of all four bears, and the meat of the last two, and proceeded to camp.

In a few days after these adventures, we proceeded to the bear ground again; and, towards evening, came to a small valley covered with wild oats, where we discovered three bears, an old female and two small cubs. I climbed a tree to reconnoitre; and, observing their positions, directed my comrades to make circuits, while I would proceed directly forward, and he who should have the best opportunity was to fire first. After waiting long enough for them to pass around, I advanced, and was crawling up among the oats, when suddenly I heard the report of one of their guns. I rose at once, and, looking over the tops of the oats, saw the old bear running towards Sykesey, who was reloading. I cried out to him to climb a tree; but immediately Kimball fired from the other side, and the old bear, being struck in the buttock, suddenly turned around, and, seeing the new assailant, rushed at him. Kimball was a considerable

distance from any tree; and, fearing that he would be
in danger, I rushed forward to his assistance; but he
managed to reach and climb an oak, and I popped
behind a bush before the bear saw me.

In his haste, Kimball had dropped his rifle, and,
having no weapons but his pistol and knife, could
scarcely have contended against the furious beast, if
she should have reached him. I saw that she was
about to climb, and therefore fired; but my shot,
which struck her in the neck, only served to enrage;
and while I hastily reloaded, not having observed me,
she made a leap at the tree, and clasped it. Kimball
fired his revolver, charge after charge, at her, but
without apparent effect; and up she went, while he
climbed out towards the extremity of a limb. Seeing
that he was badly frightened, I shouted to him to
have courage, and ply his knife like a man, if she
reached him; and at the same time, rushing up with
my rifle and getting nearly under her as she was
climbing, I planted a ball under her fore leg. She
rolled over on the limb, and in a few moments, fell
heavily to the ground, which she no sooner reached
than I sprang upon her, and plunged my knife to her
heart several times.

As soon as she was dead, I looked up for Kimball,
and found that he had gone into the very top of the
tree. I hinted that he would have shown a properer
spirit had he come down instead of gone up, so as
to have assisted me if it had been necessary; but
he excused himself on the plea that he thought only
of his own safety, and did not know that I was in

danger. We had barely got done talking about this matter, when Sykesey, who had also consulted his own safety more than my danger, came up; and we then consulted as to the best mode of securing the cubs, which were running about yelping and bawling. They had annoyed me considerably by flying at my legs, while approaching the old bear; but I had kicked them off, knowing that it would be impossible to secure them while the dam lived.

By this time it was dusk; but, as there was a good moon, we proceeded to cut a large number of poles and green boughs, and built a brush house around and over the body of the dead bear, leaving only a door for the cubs to enter. We then retired a short distance, and, lying down, watched the motions of the cubs; but it was several hours before they approached the corral. When they did so, they hopped upon the brush, and then off again, and smelt around, as if very suspicious, for a considerable time. Finally, however, one of them ventured in, and was soon followed by the other; both vainly expecting to find there that protection, which, had their mother been alive, she would have afforded to the last drop of her blood.

The cubs being thus both encaged, I sprang to the door of the corral, and, seizing one by the tuft of the head, held, while my comrades tied him. With the other, however, we had more trouble; he was the stronger and more savage of the two, and retired to the farthest corner, so that I had to creep in after him. The place was only a few feet high, and six or

eight feet in diameter, and very dark. At first I
could only hear him growling; but presently could
see his eyes glisten. As I got quite close, he flew
at my face and eyes; but, being ready for this, I
seized and secured him, with but a few unimportant
scratches, which made me quite bloody, it is true, but
did no serious injury. Thus we added two more fine
specimens to our stock of living wild animals. In
the morning, we packed the meat and hide of the
old bear, and carried our prizes to camp.

The time that we had appointed to leave for Portland now approached; and, setting apart a day, I
went down to the Indian village for the purpose of
engaging the necessary horses and men to aid me
in the conveyance of my animals. I explained my
wants to Kennasket, and said that my business was
to make a great bargain; but at the word "bargain"
he smiled in a significant manner, and held out his
arm, which was bandaged from wrist to elbow. What
this meant I did not understand; but he soon told
me that one of the black bears which he had purchased of me had bitten him badly. "White man,"
said he, "very good; but white man's bargains —
very bad!" I replied that if the bears were so bad,
I would buy them back. He asked whether I would
return the horses, but I took care to change the
subject of conversation as quickly as possible; and,
after an extended circumlocution, we came to business, which was the hiring of thirty horses and six
Indians, to go to Portland, which was nearly three
hundred miles distant. Kennasket did not like to

trust the horses among the pale faces of Portland, but he finally consented; and we agreed that I was to have the horses and men at the rate of two sacks of dried meat for every horse, and six fawns and one young elk for the men. Saddles and trappings for the horses I was to find at my own expense.

The next day, we made a last expedition to the buffalo valley, to procure as much meat as possible, for the purpose of defraying our indebtedness to the Indians; and, in a hunt of several days, killed seven buffaloes, six antelopes, and four or five foxes, which we packed in. The succeeding three days, we busied ourselves arranging for our journey. We made saddles of boughs fastened together with wooden pins and a few nails, and covered with elk-skin; also girths and straps, as many as were needed. We also prepared and arranged the packs, marking and numbering them; so that our camp, in a short time, resembled a sort of bazaar, where the packages of a caravan are displayed.

As soon as all was ready, we sent to the village all the meat, fawns, and the young elk, which constituted the payment for horses and men; and the same day six Indians arrived with thirty horses, making our party now consist of twelve persons, thirty-six horses and two mules, in addition to the wild animals, which formed quite a menagerie. The next morning, we arose early, packed our horses, and collected our animals; but there was much besides to be attended to, and it was, therefore, not until nearly noon that we finally broke up camp and got under way. All our animals which could not be driven or led, we packed in boxes upon our horses or mules; also the skins, dried meat, tools, and in fact everything worth taking; and a strange looking cavalcade it was, as we moved off in column.

CHAPTER XIX

OUR CARAVAN.

IT produces a feeling of melancholy in the mind to leave forever a spot where much pleasure has been experienced, and about which cling many delightful associations. For this reason, notwithstanding the rudeness of our accommodations, the wildness of the country, and the character of wanderers which we had assumed, it was not without regret that we looked for the last time upon the noble trees, the rocks, the green lawns, and the beautiful, clear spring of our sojourning-place in Washington. But, in my mind, the feeling of regret was soon superseded by that of care for my caravan, to see that every member fulfilled his duty. This, in a short time, withdrew my attention from the retrospect; and, after a single backward glance, I left the place, looking only forward to the requirements of the journey, and the many exigencies which would necessarily arise upon it.

We proceeded in good style and comfort the first day as far as the residence of Kennasket, where we unpacked, and encamped overnight. During the evening I made the chief a farewell visit; and he and I talked a long time upon various subjects of mutual interest, and, among others, about the bears which I had sold him. He evidently wished to be rid of them; and, after some bargaining, I purchased them back for six sacks of dried meat and four wolf skins. He asked about the puppy he had given me, and when I replied that it was in my caravan, he seemed much gratified, regarding my care of the whelp as a compliment to himself. After some further conversation, he asked what I was going to present him as a remembrancer of the great White Hunter. I replied that I had only wild beasts, but if he would accept one of them he should be welcome. He answered that he would like a white wolf; and I gave him one.

The next day, we again got ready to start; but, even after we were drawn up in column, there were many little matters with the chief and with other Indians to be arranged, and delay after delay took up much time. Besides, there were difficulties in putting the caravan in motion; for of all heterogeneous compositions, it was one of the most curious. It was, indeed, a strange assemblage. In the first place, there were five horses packed with buffalo robes, of which we had about thirty-five; next, four horses

packed with bear skins, and several large bear skulls;
then, two packed with deer skins; two with antelope
skins; one with fox and other small skins; seven
with dried meat for the use of the animals on the
journey, and, in part, on their intended voyage;
one with boxes containing the young bear cubs last
caught; two with boxes containing wolves, untamed;
a mule with foxes and fishers in baskets; and a
mule with tools, blankets, and camp luggage. Almost all the horses, besides the seven specially
devoted to the purpose, carried more or less dried
meat, — even those we rode. But the most remarkable portion of the train consisted of the animals
which we drove along in a small herd; these were
six bears, four wolves, four deer, four antelopes, two
elks, and the Indian dog.

In the disposition of the caravan, two Indians, who
served as guides, rode foremost; next followed the
packed horses, with four Indians to attend and govern
them; and next myself, with the animals. Kimball,
Partridge, Sykesey, Tuolumne, and Stanislaus, brought
up the rear. This order, however, was sometimes
varied; from time to time, Kimball and I would ride
at the head of the column; but, as neither of us
knew much of the route, we could give but little aid
to the guides, and were compelled to leave much to
their discretion.

As we started forward in the presence of the
assembled inhabitants of the Indian village, Kennasket invoked the blessing of Heaven, and asked the
Great Spirit to have us in his special keeping; and

thus, with the prayers of the Chief for its success, the little caravan entered upon its fatiguing journey, which was to lead over mountains, across rivers, and through dangers and perils. We travelled that day until the middle of the afternoon, when the animals became weary, and I thought it high time to camp; but the guides assured me that in half a league further we would come to good springs, at a place called Little Rock, where we soon arrived, having travelled about twenty miles during the day.

At Little Rock, which was a ledge of stones at the bottom of a high hill, whence sprang the head waters of a stream flowing west, we unpacked our horses, and, arranging the packs in the form of an inclosure, mounted a guard of two men, and prepared to pass the night. One, at least, of my own men was always on watch, for it was not impossible that the Indians might be treacherous; not that they really were unreliable, but, considering the circumstances and peculiar dangers of my situation, there was much to make me distrustful and anxious at first. The night, however, passed over without a difficulty, and the next morning we resumed our journey.

We travelled the next day until noon; when, finding some of the animals foot-sore, we halted until the third day in a small valley, where there was plenty of grass, though but little water. The fourth day we proceeded, and travelled till the middle of the afternoon, and then camped as before. We should have hurried on the succeeding day, but found the backs of the horses too much chafed and swollen to proceed, and had to lie over a few days, during which the sores were washed, and doctored with soap-root.

We should have remained there longer than we did, but the deficiency of water, and our exposure to the attacks of bears, panthers, wolves, and other beasts, during two nights, induced us, the second morning, to proceed, notwithstanding the still sore and swollen condition of our horses' backs; and we moved on five miles further to Yellow Rock, where there was excellent grass and water. Upon reaching that spot, we were all much delighted. It was a vale richly covered with grass, and the high hills about it with oak, pine, cedar, and other forest trees. A little stream meandered through it, exposing, here and there, a yellowish colored rock, from which the place received its name. We remained three days, and provided ourselves with fresh venison in abundance, by hunting in the neighborhood.

At the end of this time, leaving Yellow Rock early in the morning, we travelled till afternoon, when we were suddenly thrown into consternation by the appearance of a band of fifteen or twenty horses rushing furiously down a valley in the hills, and making a straight direction for our caravan. At first, I supposed them to be wild horses; but soon found that they belonged to Indians, who were chasing them. There was not a moment to be lost; but, dashing forward, swinging my lariat, and whooping with all my might, I managed to break the course of the band, turned them to the right, and thus, doubtless, prevented a disastrous stampede in my train.

It is necessary for those having numbers of horses
under their charge to guard against stampedes with
much care, particularly in wild countries, where they
are most likely to occur, and where there is the greatest danger in them. When horses get into one of
these panics, they frequently ruin, sometimes kill
themselves; and it is always difficult to recover them
at all. An old horse, which otherwise could hardly
be whipped along, will sometimes, in a stampede,
dash off so furiously as not to be possibly overtaken.
It is, indeed, a notable fact, that the increased
strength as well as the recklessness of great excitement which are sometimes observed in panics among
men have their counterparts among animals. For
instance, when upon a crowded ocean steamer the
cry of fire is raised, and men plunge madly into the
devouring waves, instead of coolly applying their energies to extinguishing the flames, in what do they show
more of the reasoning faculties of mind than horses,
when, frightened with some sudden terror, they plunge
over precipices?

Those in pursuit of the horses were three mounted
Indians, who would have passed on; but, upon my
beckoning, they stopped and came up. I had a short
conversation, and learned from them that there was
a large rancheria of Indians about twenty-five miles
ahead, — a camp on a large fishing-stream. I also
asked about the country and trail towards Portland,
and gave them to understand that my party was a
portion of a great nation of white people, and that
we were bound, on particular business, to the white

settlements at Portland and along the river. The
intention was, to impress them with the idea that they
could not attack us without drawing the vengeance
of our government upon their heads; but I added
that the white people would use them well if they
allowed us to pass undisturbed. At the same time, I
gave them each a package of dried meat and a piece
of fresh venison. They replied that the red men
would not trouble the white people; and then, breaking up the interview, they proceeded upon their way
after the horses, which by this time were far in the
distance. After this interruption, we travelled on
until evening, when we encamped, and placed a
strong guard as a matter of precaution, knowing the
Indians to be in our neighborhood; but nothing occurred during the night to disturb us.

The next day we journeyed on, bearing off to the
right so as to avoid the rancheria. I should have
liked, on my own account, to visit this place; but
considered it better, for the safety of my caravan, to
keep at a distance. Had we gone there, and found
the Indians as exacting as is usual with them, we
should have had to part with a large portion of our
stores. We therefore passed, and pushed on through
a hilly country, densely covered with oak, pine, cedar,
and other large trees, until at last we descended into
the valley of the Upper Columbia, and encamped
upon its bank.

Here we were brought to a stand, to know how to
cross the river; but, as there was only one way to
proceed, I threw off my coat, and, taking a long pole,

mounted my horse and plunged in, for the purpose
of testing its character. My horse was almost immediately beyond his depth, and commenced swimming;
but I could touch the bottom with my pole until near
the middle, where the water was very deep. On the
opposite side, it became shallower, and the bottom
sloped regularly to the bank. After ascertaining
these facts, I rode up along the bank several miles
and crossed back again; but, finding no more favorable spot than the first for a passage, I returned to
camp, convinced that it would be necessary to build
a raft.

During my brief absence, the boys had been an-
gling, and caught some beautiful fish of the perch species. They obtained sufficient for a good supper,
which we fried upon flat stones heated in the fire,
using bear's oil instead of butter, — and a choice
meal they made. After supper, we consulted about
the manner of our passage of the river, and decided
upon commencing the construction of a raft the first
thing in the morning.

In the morning, accordingly, we all went diligently
to work, and by night had our raft completed. It
consisted of pine logs, and was about twenty feet
long by ten wide. A floor of split cedar planks was
pinned upon it, making, in all, a complete raft, capable of carrying about one third of our luggage at a
trip. We should have crossed immediately, but, it
being already sundown, we determined to wait until
the next day.

We had hitherto, fortunately, not been molested by

the Indians of the neighborhood; but this night several blundered into camp. We hurried them off as soon as possible, and, knowing that we should be completely surrounded in the morning, immediately prepared to cross, night as it was. For this purpose, leaving the loading of the raft to my comrades, I took a number of lariats, tied to one another, and, fastening one end to a tree on the bank, taking the coil on my arm and mounting my horse, plunged into the stream and crossed to the opposite bank, where I fastened the other end of the rope to another tree. Having secured it, I plunged again into the water, and, crossing back, ordered the passage to commence.

It required eight men to work the raft,— some pulling at the sweeps, others attending to the ropes; after arranging whom, I placed myself at the bow, with a due feeling of importance, being, for the first time in my life, captain of a water-craft. The float was then shoved off, and we moved forwards as gently as could be desired,— the men working well, speaking scarcely a word on the passage; and we landed on the opposite side, in a short time, with complete success. We unloaded, and placed the luggage on the bank; then recrossed, took a second load, which was ferried over with like success; and then returned for a third and last load, consisting of the animals and the remaining portion of the baggage.

As we were about to push off for the third time, daylight began to appear. We had experienced great delay in arranging the animals on the raft;

and, even then, it was a matter of impossibility to keep them quiet, so that I was compelled to leave my place as captain of the craft, and take a position among the bears, which were very restive; but the more I endeavored to quiet them, the worse they grew. In the midst of the uproar, the raft being about two-thirds of the way across the river, the guide-rope broke; and our craft, being set adrift, commenced floating down stream. The confusion became almost indescribable; the men were wild, and two of the animals, Lady Washington and a black cub, plunged overboard; but, being good swimmers, they followed the raft. It was difficult to restore order; but finally the men took to the sweeps, and we managed to strike the shore about a quarter of a mile below where the guide-rope would have taken us had it not broken.

All would have been well now, but the horses still remained upon the opposite side. I had intended to ferry them over too; but, after the breaking of the rope, this was impracticable; and there was no other way but to swim them. The Indians, meanwhile, were collecting in large numbers, and, as delay might be dangerous, I jumped into the stream and swam over to where they were; and, directing Tuolumne to take the lead, I mounted my horse, and, with the Indians of my party remaining on that side of the river, drove the other horses after him. We got them easily into the water, and drove them, swimming, across, — all but two, which, being unable to keep their noses up, soon strangled and floated down.

We gathered our animals and luggage together, but could not get ahead that day, and accordingly camped; but the next morning, early, we started off, and travelled all day. In the evening, when it was time to stop, the guides thought we would find water in a league or two, and we pushed on; but these expectations proved to be entirely delusive. We travelled several hours longer without the least indications of water, and finally were compelled to stop, almost completely worn out with exhaustion and fatigue. To make the matter still worse, I found that the guides had lost the way, and did not know in what direction to proceed. Here again was a dilemma; for, besides the want of water, the dismal prospect of a long and difficult search for the trail caused anything but pleasant anticipations.

The next morning, early, Kimball and I started out with the double object of searching for water and for the lost trail. I rode fifteen or twenty miles, without having success in either particular; but Kimball, though he could not find the trail, managed to discover water, to which the caravan directly moved; and there it had to remain until we could find the trail. As soon as we had refreshed ourselves, Kimball and I and the guides started out again, but were compelled to return at nightfall, as unsucessful as before. I felt provoked at the carelessness of the guides; but, as the matter could not be helped in that manner, I could only resolve to make more strenuous endeavors the next day.

CHAPTER XX.

THE ROAD TO PORTLAND.

Character of the Trail. Wood-craft. Plan to find the Trail. Discovery of it. Progress. The Humpback. View from the Humpback. A Night Stampede. Traces of a Panther. Search for the Horses. Progress. The Country. Sight of the Lower Columbia. Strike the Columbia. Notable Quarrel with Hall, the Ferryman. Passage. Down the River Bank. We attract great Attention. Arrival at Portland. Shipment of the Animals. Their Attendant and Provision. Final Separation of our Party. The Character of my Writing. Account of the Animals shipped. Spread of Information. Lady Washington. The Journey homewards. The Cascade Mountains and Sierra Nevada Foot Hills.

THE reader will better understand the difficulties to which we were now reduced, when it is stated that the road we were travelling was a trail, used only by Indians in their periodical journeys to and from the fishing-grounds of the Columbia. There was no regular road, in the civilized sense of the term, nor were there even landmarks; but the guides were expected to know the way by the general appearance of the country, the direction of the hills, and such other signs as are cognizable in Indian science. Place a good woodsman in an unknown wilderness, and he will soon master it. As he goes through, he notices every hill, every rock, everything, indeed, of peculiarity, so as to know it on returning, and be able to recognize it again, even after a long period of intervening time; and the same is to be expected of Indians, to whom, usually, this sort of wood-craft is a necessary accomplishment.

The recovery of the lost trail, however, was not as easy as was to have been expected; for, though we searched several days, it was all in vain. I at last determined to send Kimball and one of the guides back to the river to follow it up from there, directing them to blaze their way upon the trees; but, as fortune willed, they struck the trail at a distance of fifteen miles. Their discovery spread satisfaction throughout camp, and we all rested easy that night, and the next morning early were again on our way, pushing towards the southwest.

The country became more and more wild and rugged as we advanced, until it seemed as if we would be intercepted by a certain mountain, to which the Indians gave the name of the Humpback. It was quite a mile in steep ascent, and difficult to surmount, but we reached the top at last. Looking from the elevation over the country, we saw that it was all a wilderness; but the view of the white peaks of the mountains St. Helen's and Rainier made us forget our fatigue; and, after sufficiently enjoying the prospect, we struck down through a rocky, barren, scrub-oak country, to a stream of water, which we followed a few miles, and camped in a grassy cañon.

At this camp, about midnight, we were thrown into great confusion by the report of a stampede among the horses, caused, we supposed, by an attack of Indians. At any rate, the horses had broken from

their pickets, and gone off. I seized my rifle, and
ran out to the place, but, upon inquiring particularly
of the guards about the circumstances of the stampede, concluded that some wild beast had disturbed
us, and not Indians. The next morning, at dawn,
upon examining the ground, we were convinced of
the correctness of the conclusion by finding tracks
of a panther, and also traces of blood; by following
which the distance of about a mile, we came upon
the carcass of a dead horse, the neck of which had
been gnawed. We were satisfied, on minuter examination, that a panther had sprung upon this horse,
and retained his hold until he had killed him.

From the finding of this carcass, we were able to
conclude positively that it was not Indians that had
made the attack; and we therefore expected to find
the horses in some ravine, it being impossible for
them to proceed far alone in that rough country, even
in a stampede. We accordingly divided into small
parties, and, proceeding in different directions, soon
discovered and collected them, losing only two. Returning, we packed up and proceeded down the
stream until night, and camped again.

The next day, we crossed over a mountainous
country, covered with rocks and scrubby trees, and
camped at night in a comfortless place, where our
horses suffered from the want of water and grass.
The next morning early we were on our road again,
and travelled till the middle of the afternoon, when
we came in view of a beautiful valley, down which
we hastened, and camped in a grassy spot which pre-

sented a welcome contrast to the rocky and rough
country we had passed over in the higher lands.
During the next two days, we crossed over hills and
ravines, well timbered, and, on the third morning,
came in sight of the great valley of the lower Columbia, which all hailed with pleasure; and, descending
into it, we camped, with good grass and water.

The point at which we struck the Columbia was
near the Cascades, a few miles below a ferry, to
which, after a brief stoppage, we proceeded. At this
place, I had a notable quarrel with the ferryman, a
most unconscionable fellow from Pennsylvania, named
Hall. He possessed a good boat of hewn timber, but
demanded so large a toll that, had I acceded, the ferriage of my train would have cost over a hundred
dollars. I offered to pay a reasonable price in dried
meat, or peltry, or animals; but he would not listen
to any such thing, though I had no money whatever.
I then endeavored to induce him to take one of my
horses; but neither would he do this. Finally, finding I could do nothing with him in the usual manner,
I gave him notice that I was determined to cross at
any rate, and, as he was not disposed to do what was
right between man and man, I would take his boat in
spite of him. He swore that I should not; I per-
sisted that I would. Words grew loud, and he started
towards his cabin, as if going for a weapon; but I
took my rifle from my shoulder, and told him to stop;
and, seeing me to be in earnest, he did so. We now
had more hard talk, when the fellow offered to ferry
us over for the best horse in the train; but I would

not allow this. "There," said I, "stands a horse worth seventy-five dollars in any market; if you like to take him, good and well; if not, it cannot be helped." "I suppose," he replied, "if I do not take him, I will get nothing?" "I know," rejoined I, "that you will get nothing!" A little more grumbling, and Hall illnaturedly prepared his boat, and we crossed over in two divisions.

From the ferry, we travelled down the river till evening, when we camped, and the next day proceeded through a well-settled country. Along the road we attracted much attention, as may easily be imagined. The people who saw us gazed with wonder, for such a caravan had never been seen before in those regions. They asked many questions, too, about whence we came, whither we were going, and who we were; but we did not stop to answer them. Pushing on, we arrived towards evening within a few miles of Portland, and camped in a grove of beautiful trees, which we made our headquarters during our stay there.

Thus we arrived at our place of destination, in full time for the sailing of the vessel, which proved to be the bark *Mary Ann*, bound for Boston. Within a few days after our arrival, I made all the necessary arrangements for the shipment, and placed all the animals, skins, oil, and curiosities, which I had collected during the summer, on board, — all except my favorite, Lady Washington, to whom I was so attached that I could not think of parting with her. The other animals were placed in charge of a competent person, employed to feed them during the voyage. For their sustenance, meat and other provision in abundance was shipped; and indeed the salmon which constituted a portion of the cargo of the vessel would have served, and did afterwards serve, as food for most of them. In the meantime, I obtained an advance on the credit of my brother, and settled with Sykesey, Kimball, and Partridge, and made presents to all the Indians. These matters being all attended to, on the appointed day of breaking up, we separated, and each party took a different direction. The Indians, with their horses, started out on their return to the eastern part of Washington; Kimball and Partridge determined to remain in Oregon, and Sykesey with them; and I and the Indian boys, Tuolumne and Stanislaus, with two horses, two mules, Lady Washington, and my dog, took the road up the Willamette River, on our return to California.

Such were the adventures of my first season's hunting. I have endeavored to relate them truthfully and plainly. In some instances, memory may have failed, and mistakes have occurred, — no work is free from faults. But two things will be borne in mind: first, that I kept no notes, and speak only from memory; and, secondly, that I make no pretensions to do more than I perform. Doubtless, the story might have been told in a more interesting and lively manner; but, surely, I have done my best; and this must suffice.

It may be here added, that the animals shipped at Portland reached Boston in due time, and were disposed of to advantage by my brother William. They were sold to different persons, — some placed in museums, others carried about the country,— all contributing more or less, to spread a knowledge of the natural history of the Pacific Coast of the United States. As for Lady Washington, whom I retained, she became my constant companion; and, as will be seen in the sequel of the narrative, travelled with me the next year to the Rocky Mountains, and the subsequent year to the Kern River and Tejon countries.

Nothing worthy of special mention occurred on the road from the valley of Willamette to California, except, perhaps, the passage of the Mountains in the snow. We had been cautioned against the attempt; but the previous winter in the Sierra Nevada had given me such experience of snow and snow travelling that we hastened on, without heeding the cautions, and accomplished the task without any great difficulty. Thence we crossed over to the Yreka Valley, and travelled southward along the foot-hills of the Sierra, in the same manner that, in the spring, we had advanced northward.

PART SECOND

CHAPTER I.

OUR CAMP IN THE SIERRA NEVADA.

My old Camping-ground. Condition of my Wigwam. Predominance of the destructive Faculties. Repairs. Preparations for Winter. A Visit to Howard's Ranch. Furlough of Tuolumne and Stanislaus. My Solitude. Occupations. Lady Washington. Her Disposition. A Hunt at Bell's Meadows. Experiment of packing the Lady. Conduct of the Lady. An old Grizzly entrapped. The Lady and I on Watch. A Grizzly Dam and two Cubs entrapped. Disposition of them. Return of Tuolumne and Stanislaus. Adventure with a Bear at Strawberry Ranch. Attacked by Coyotes. My Castle. Advance of Winter. Our Excursions. The Snow. Tuolumne's Feet frostbitten. Treatment of them. Stanislaus and I overtaken in a Snow-storm. Our Shelter. Lady Washington my Bedfellow. Snow-shoes. Sledges. Lady Washington as a draught Animal. Selected Passages of my Adventures.

Upon reaching the old camping-ground near the head waters of the Tuolumne River, I found that my wigwam, in its untenanted and uncared-for condition during the summer, had become dilapidated. Not that the elements had done much to demolish it; its substantial construction would have successfully resisted all attacks of the weather; wild beasts would not have troubled it, and the Indians would, for my sake, have respected it; but my brother white man, it seems, could not forego his destructive inclinations, and on every side there were evidences of his devastating visits. The doors, which I had made with much trouble, were broken down; the clay plastering

178

ADAMS AND BEN FRANKLIN.

of the walls was peeled; many of the poles which made a part of its frame were displaced; and the marks of the hatchet were to be seen all about it. Just as, in the settled world, every man feels it incumbent upon him to fling a stone at, or kick off a board from, a deserted shanty, so, in the mountains, a hunter or a miner can rarely pass a vacated cabin without hacking into it or pulling apart its timbers. Curiosity, or a hope of finding hidden treasure, might, perhaps, instigate this desolation; but the more probable cause is the mere spirit of wanton destruction which characterizes a large class of men, and particularly the greatest rovers.

Fortunately, my tools amd all my small valuable property, left in California, I had concealed in a cave; and, as those had escaped, there was but little to be lost, even though my cabin had been entirely destroyed. At any rate, the labor of a few days, with Tuolumne and Stanislaus to assist, placed things in a better condition than before; and I soon found myself completely prepared to meet the winter, which was rapidly approaching. We made a comfortable home for ourselves, a good stable for such of the horses or mules as we might wish to keep about us, and put up several stacks of dried grass for horse-feed, when the mountains should be buried in the deep mantle of frost.

In a few days after thus arranging camp, I made a visit to Howard's Ranch, where I had left my wagon; and, finding that it had been well taken care of during my absence, made a further agreement with Howard to retain it, and also to take charge of my mules till I should require them the next spring; for I had already projected a visit to the Rocky Mountains, and wished them to recruit for the service by an entire winter of ease and good pasturage. Upon this visit, I passed a village of Indians, who proved to be the tribe to which my boys belonged; and their chief wished to know of me what had become of them for so long a period. I replied that he should see them in a few days; and, upon getting back to camp, I presented Tuolumne and Stanislaus with new suits of buckskin, and, giving them one of my horses to dispose of as they pleased, started them off on a visit to their people. They were highly delighted with the permit, as well as with the presents, and bade me good-bye in high spirits, promising to return before the spring, and accompany me upon any expedition, wherever I should choose to lead them.

When they had gone, I was, of course, again left alone in the mountains, far from my fellows, far from what are usually considered the pleasures and comforts of society, with none to think of but myself, my horse, my bear Lady Washington, and my little dog, the gift of my friend, the Indian chief, Kennasket. For a few days, after being thus left, I felt lonely indeed. It seemed as if I had lost everything in the world, and I knew not what to do; but, by degrees, the burden of solitude grew lighter, and, in the course of a week, I was as busy and contented as during the solitary months of the previous winter.

The old cave in the rocks, which served as a hiding-place for my tools, had preserved them well, and I was soon at work, repairing and getting traps ready for every prize which chance might throw in their way.

Lady Washington was now a constant companion of all my little excursions. She accompanied me to the scenes of my labors, stayed by me while I worked, and followed me when I hunted. The kind and gentle disposition she had begun to exhibit in Washington Territory improved with time and care, and she was now as faithful and devoted, I was going to say, as it was possible for any animal to be; but, in making this assertion, my noble California grizzly, Ben Franklin, that most excellent of all beasts, must be excepted. But for Ben, the history of whose magnanimous traits of character will adorn the following pages, the Lady could truly be pronounced second to none of all the creatures over which the Creator appointed man to be the lord and master.

One day, when hunting with the Lady at Bell's Meadows, four or five miles from camp, I killed a fat buck, and attempted to carry it home upon my shoulders; but soon found it more than I was either willing or able to bear. The idea here struck me, of making the Lady carry half of it; and no sooner thought than done. She had been taught to carry small burdens in Washington, as has heretofore been related; but never before had her power been applied to a practical purpose. I accordingly split the deer in two parts, and bound one upon her back, — not, indeed, without an expectation that she would roll upon and render it useless; but it would still serve for her own food or bait for the traps, and would, consequently, not be a matter of much loss. Having bound the burden as firmly as possible, I took the remaining meat upon my shoulder, and with my rifle started ahead.

During all the time of the packing the Lady stood very still, only sometimes looking up in my face with an expression indicating that she would rather eat than carry the load; but, as soon as I started ahead, she looked around at the load and the lashings, then raised first one paw, and then the other, and endeavored to pull them off. Each time she did so, I exclaimed at her, and she made a step forward; but presently she fairly turned around, caught a portion of the pack in her teeth, and would have torn it off had I not picked up a stout cudgel and given her several raps, on the receipt of which she growled, but desisted. I then started ahead rapidly, calling her along, and she jumped up and followed. We advanced, however, only a short distance, when she lay down and commenced rolling, trying in this manner to get the burden off; but again I gave her a few cuffs. On starting forward a second time, she again followed a short distance, then lay down and rolled as before; but at last, finding that resistance to my authority was vain, she acquiesced in her task, and finally, after a troublesome and hard afternoon's work, we arrived at camp. Such was the first packing of the Lady, who afterwards, on more than one occasion, bore my camp equipage and other heavy burdens with willingness, and even alacrity.

In a few days after this, I entrapped a large grizzly, which was so violent that it was necessary to watch to prevent his breaking out of the structure. On this occasion, for the first time, I packed the Lady with my blankets; and she carried them without dissent, thus affording me the satisfaction of foreseeing of what great assistance she would be. She remained with me at the trap all night; lay peacefully by the rousing fire which I built; and for several nights, indeed until a secure cage was made and the new prize safely transferred to it, she kept me company in my exposed vigils.

A week or two subsequently, I caught a female grizzly and two yearling cubs, which, together with the old grizzly above mentioned, I soon afterwards carried down to Sonora, and disposed of at good rates, laying in and bringing back with me a stock of necessaries for the winter. Just previous to starting on this trip, the Indian boys, Tuolumne and Stanislaus, returned according to their promises; and my camp was therefore in good hands during my absence.

On my return, when within a mile of Strawberry Ranch, late in the afternoon, I shot a fat buck; I was, however, too much fatigued to pack the body, and left it lying, while I rode on to a vacant log-hut, intending to go back for it after refreshing and resting myself. Upon returning about sundown, I perceived that a grizzly bear had taken possession of the meat, and was busily making his supper; which audacious intermeddling of his, after I had made up my mouth for a good roast that evening, was as unpleasant as it was unexpected. I determined to punish the fellow with proper spirit; and, accordingly, crawling around without being perceived, I got behind a huge pine-tree, from which, taking a deliberate aim, I fired at him. Owing, however, to the duskiness of the hour, my aim was not as good as could have been wished, and the ball must have glanced, for the bear, after uttering a tremendous growl, rose upon his feet and looked around for the disturber; but, not discovering me, he soon dropped upon all-fours again, and ran off with a speed which did credit to the locomotive powers of the species. After he had disappeared, I ventured down to the deer; but found that the bear had got his full share, for he had eaten nearly half. He had, as is the general habit of bears, commenced operations at the breast, consumed the vitals, and then attacked the foreparts. I shouldered what he had left, and started off; but must acknowledge that every rustle and stir for a while produced anything but a pleasant effect upon my nerves, and more than once I supposed that now the real battle would come.

The bear, however, had got enough; but in a short time three saucy coyotes came up behind me, and disputed the title to the venison. They ran around, barked and snapped at the meat, and endeavored to seize it; and, it being too dark to procure aim with my rifle, the only way left to defend the booty was to take my bowie-knife to them. The cowardly knaves seemed to understand the virtues of the cold steel, and kept at a respectable distance; till at length I reached the hut, and built up a large fire, which effectually scared them off, though they afterwards returned with an accession of forces, and barked and yelped about the neighborhood all night. After roasting and eating my supper, I carried the remainder of the meat with me into the cabin, and, bolting the door, lay down and had a comfortable night of sleep, to which my fatigue had disposed me.

The next day, I reached camp and found everything in good order, as was to have been expected under the care of my faithful boys. From this time, for the next month or two, we continued in our mountain camp, making short excursions in search of game only as we required it. Meanwhile the winter advanced; first the rains fell, and by degrees the snows came more and more frequently, until at length the regular snow-line descended from the higher peaks far below us; and at last the entire mountain-side was enveloped for the season in a glittering white mantle. As the snow-line descended, the game, as usual, preceded it; so that it was only occasionally that our traps procured us a stray wolf or bear, and all our hunting had to be done in the more moderate climates of the foot-hills below. In our trips up and down the mountains, we were at first much incommoded by the snow; but presently, after a few thaws and frosts, the crust became sufficiently hard to bear us well, and we travelled upon it with comparative ease.

Upon one of these trips, Tuolumne complained about his feet; and, on examination, I ascertained that they were frostbitten. I immediately directed him to bathe them in very cold water, then anoint them with panther's oil, and wrap them up in cotton cloths. After doing this, he was put to bed and required to remain at camp for several days, by which time he fully recovered.

One of these days, Stanislaus and I went out on a short hunt, but were overtaken by a dreadful storm, and compelled to take shelter for the night under a pine-tree. We built a rousing fire, and lay down to sleep; but in the course of the night I awoke, and finding the weather very severe and Stanislaus suffering from cold, I made him take my blanket in addition to his own. As for myself, I coaxed Lady Washington, who accompanied us, as near the fire as possible, and then lay down next her, having her shaggy coat on one side and the fire on the other. It was my first experiment of this kind, and I felt a little fearful for a while of having a troublesome bedfellow; but, being very sleepy, I soon forgot my anxiety in slumber. Once only she rose and withdrew for a few minutes, but soon came back, lapped my hands a moment, and again nestled down in her former position, apparently with the object of getting as close to me as I wished to get to her. It was late the next morning before I waked, when I found my shaggy companion still sleeping, and as calmly and peacefully as could have been desired.

In the early part of the winter we also made ourselves snow-shoes, by bending tough pieces of green wood into large bows, and weaving over them strips of green hide. These we fastened to the bottom of our moccasins with straps of buckskin; and, having thus wide foundations, we were able to walk easily upon the surface of the snow, even when it was very soft; and they were of great service on many occasions. We also constructed sledges to transport our game through the snow; and sometimes hitched up Lady Washington, and made her draw them. She was slow in learning her duty at this kind of service, and required watching and correction some time before she took to the work with proper spirit; but, by degrees, she learnt the lesson well, and was thus of great value, not only as a beast of burden, but also as a draught animal.

But a detailed account of our wintering in the mountains of California, where there were so many objects to attract and engage attention, would furnish in itself ample matter for a large volume. I must remember that I have an almost interminable subject before me, and am therefore compelled to compress and abridge with an unsparing hand; and sometimes pass over much time in a few words. I must remember that, now and here, I can only select the more important passages of my adventures, and present them to the reader in as brief, plain, and unadorned terms as possible.

CHAPTER II.

YOSEMITE.

Arrival of Solon. Resolution to visit the Yosemite Valley with him.
Our Contract. Our Start. The Road. First Impressions of the
Valley. Splendors of the Scene. The View from the Foot of the
Cliffs. General Hunting. Birth of Rambler. Ben Franklin.
Discovery of a Grizzly's Den. My one Idea. My Resolution.
My Preparations. The Ravine. Chaparral. Reconnoitring.
The Position and Appearance of the Den. Provision for my Mule.
A Night-watch. Report of the Rifle among the Hills. Subter-
ranean Sounds. A Day-watch. A Sight of the Grizzly Dam.
Change of Position. Preparation for a Combat. Sleep. A
Panther's Scream. Alarm. Reflection. My Determination. The
Grizzly Yell. The Response. Appearance of the Bear. Our
relative Positions. My Attack. A desperate Effort. Death of
the Bear. My Feelings.

As the spring of 1854 approached, and the snow
line moved higher and higher towards the summits of
the mountains, and the grass began to spring upon
slope and shelf, and the game to follow, and the hunters to come up, we had occasional visits from the rovers of the countries below. One of these was Mr.
Solon, of Sonora, who stopped on his way to the famous Yosemite Valley, that most sublime region of
California, and perhaps of the world. He came, he
told me, having heard of my hunting, to persuade
me to go upon a general hunt in the great valley;
and it was not long before we projected a trip, which
was to last about a month. The agreement between
us was, that, in consideration of my furnishing a

horse, two mules, and the assistance of Tuolumne, I was to receive two thirds of the prizes and profits of the expedition. We immediately proceeded to make arrangements for the hunt; and, at the end of a few days, after bringing up the mules from Howard's, and laying in a stock of provisions for the subsistence of Stanislaus during our absence, we started off over the mountains southeastward, taking with us, besides the horse and mules, my bear Lady Washington, and a greyhound which I had purchased on my last visit to Howard's, and brought up with me.

Our road was rough and difficult; but, after travelling three days, we arrived upon the brink of the great valley. The first view of this sublime scenery was so impressive that we were delayed a long time, as if spellbound, looking down from the mountain upon the magnificent landscape far below. It is vain to attempt to convey the effect produced by those giant and picturesque cliffs three thousand feet high, that romantic valley-bottom with its green carpet and silvery stream, and those groves of trees, which are formed and placed as if a skilful artist had disposed them to portray the essence of romance. It is vain to attempt with words alone, to convey the impressions produced upon the mind by such an enchanting sight; magnitude may be imagined, beauty may be conceived, but the breadth and scope of these rocks, the tempered tints of these distances, the influence of these sublime forms, inclosing within their compass lawns and groves and grassy banks, presenting at every turn new and unimagined splendors, — all these must be seen and felt, to be fully comprehended.

But, however grand the valley looked from above, it was not until the next day, when we descended into it and looked upward, that we obtained the grandest views; just as, at Niagara, the most awe-inspiring sight is from the foot of the falls, looking up at the waters, pouring, as it were, out of heaven. There is a fall here, too, thousands instead of hundreds of feet in height; but it was not the fall, so much as the scenery below and around, that ravished my eyes, and produced impressions upon my mind that are ineffaceable. Who could ever forget those stupendous cliffs, with their fit associates, the tapering evergreens? or the greenswards, and oak and cotton-wood groves of the valley, with such surroundings?—and Flora adorns the carpet underneath, as brightly as the rainbows paint the spray above. We spent the entire day visiting interesting points, and searching out the varied beauties of this inexhaustible valley.

The next morning, we moved about ten miles above the falls, and pitched our camp in a grassy glen, where for several days we hunted with great success, slaying deer and bears. In this camp, the greyhound unexpectedly presented me with a litter of puppies, one of which grew up to be Rambler, the companion of Ben, and, as such companion, a sharer in my affection for that noble animal.

My next adventure, and the most fortunate of all my career, was the capture of Ben Franklin, the flower of his race, my firmest friend, the boon companion of my after-years. Upon reviewing the adventure now, it seems that an inexplicable influence was at work within me, foreshadowing the singular good-fortune in store, and attracting me, with an irresistible impulse, to brave the dangers and fatigues of besieging, day after day, and night after night, the stronghold of his ferocious dam, slaying her in the very portals of her den, and seizing her offspring by fighting my way over her body.

We had moved to the head waters of the Merced River. On the first hunt there, I discovered a grizzly's den, and no sooner had my eyes fallen upon it, than I forgot all other hunting; I thought and dreamed of nothing else but how to take it;—this, at once, became all my ambition. Deer, panthers, wolves, and other bears there were, in plenty, about me; it seemed, too, that they crossed my path more frequently than ever; but they were unheeded; all my mind was taken up with the one sole idea of what proved to be the greatest of my achievements. Fired with this single thought, I determined to separate from my companions, leaving them to employ themselves as their inclinations pleased; as for myself, I had chosen my post, and would station myself at it, to succeed in my undertaking or die in the attempt.

Having thus resolved, I cleaned my rifle and pistol, sharpened my knives, prepared muzzles and strings, furnished myself with provisions, and, packing my blankets upon a mule, started off for the scene of my labors. It was a cañon-like ravine between two hills, densely covered with thickets of chaparral, with here and there a bunch of juniper bushes, a scrubby pine, or a cedar. A heap of fresh dirt in the thicket on one side, indicated the site of the den. It resembled the earth which a miner wheels out and dumps at the opening of a tunnel; and in size was as much as about fifty car-loads. The chaparral around it contained some thorn bushes, but could still be penetrated. Like almost all the California chaparral, it was thornier than that found in Washington; but not so much so as that of Mexico, which cannot be safely entered, unless a man be clothed in leather.

In a short time after arriving, which was late in the afternoon, I climbed a tree, and reconnoitred the entire ravine. From that position, I observed and chose a spot for concealment in a bunch of junipers, on the opposite side of the cañon, and about a hundred yards distant from the den; and, upon cautiously crawling up, found, as I had anticipated, that it afforded a fair view of its mouth at the same time that it screened me entirely from observation. Though it was impossible to see far into the den, I soon ascertained its character to be similar to that usually dug by the California grizzly;—in form something like an oven, having an entrance three or four feet in diameter and six or ten feet long, with a larger space, or den proper, rounded out at the extremity, intended for the lying-in place of the dam and the bedding of the cubs. A number of such dens I had seen in the Sierra, varying only according to their position and the quality of the ground in which they were excavated. The ravine here was rugged and narrow; and the den penetrated its steep, bushy side, about fifty feet above the bed of the stream, at this time dry, which formed the bottom of the cañon.

After making these observations, and satisfying myself that my position was the most judicious possible, being convinced that there were cubs in the place, I went back to the mule, built up a little fire for her protection, and then, leaving her to herself, I took my blankets, returned to my post in the juniper bushes, and commenced my watch, which I kept up unremittingly till morning. It was an uncomfortable vigil; the ground was so steep that there was no level place to lie down, and the night was very cold. I thought several times in the course of it that I could hear the barking of cubs in the direction of the den; but, with this exception, every thing in the ravine was silent and dreary. Other wild beasts had evidently been driven away from the region by the fear of the savage tenant, who made all a desert in her neighborhood; so that even the lugubrious howls of the wolf and coyote, which custom had made music to my ears, were inaudible; and for the very want of melancholy noises, I was more than usually melancholy.

As the light of dawn began to peep, the thought struck me to discharge my rifle for two reasons: first, to see what effect it would have; and, again, to put in a fresh charge. Upon doing so, the report echoed off among the hills, as if they were playing with the unaccustomed sound. It had barely died away, when there seemed to be a snuffing underground, very faint at first, but growing louder and louder, until there was no mistaking it for the growl of a bear. I climbed a small tree, and looked and listened attentively, in hopes of seeing her; but the sound died away in a few minutes, and again all was silent. Descending to my place in the bushes, I continued the watch, now peeping into the den, and then looking at the vultures and buzzards sailing high overhead, till the sun rose, which, in that narrow gorge, was not until nearly noon. I then returned to the mule, moved her to a new pasture, and provided myself with a meal of dried venison, which I ate with excessive relish, and washed down with water from a spring at the foot of the ravine. After satisfying myself, feeling much refreshed, I cautiously returned to the juniper bushes, resumed my watch, and sat most of the afternoon with my arms ready for action; — but there were no signs of bears, and no noises save the chirping of a few birds among the chaparral. Shortly after mid-day I got a short nap, and in the evening went back and built a fire near the mule; but before dark I was at my post again, and there I remained, shivering, till morning.

About daybreak there was again a noise in the den, and I thought the old bear might be stirring, and prepared for her reception; but it was a vain expectation; for in a short time all was quiet, and it seemed as if she never would show herself. As the morning advanced, however, I discharged my rifle again, and was gratified, not only with a snuff in the den, but also with the sight of the occupant's head and paws, as she came to the mouth of her stronghold; but the most gratifying circumstance was the yelping of cubs, which could now be distinctly heard. Being thus convinced, beyond the possibility of a doubt, of the presence of what I sought, I directly made arrangements for an encounter with the dam.

For an attack, my position, chosen for an outlook, was too far distant; and, besides, a rugged, deep hollow intervened; so that, even had a ball wounded the animal, I would not be near enough to improve the advantage. Accordingly, after attending to the wants of my mule and eating my lonely meal, I moved my position across the ravine to a point about forty yards above the den, from which I could easily see the bank of excavated dirt, though not the entrance. To reach this point, I had to move through the bushes very circumspectly, and, therefore, slowly; in many places it was necessary to use my knife in cutting my way; and much noise would inevitably have brought the ferocious brute upon me, while unprepared. Upon reaching the position at last, there appeared to be nothing to disturb my view, except several twigs which stuck up a few yards in front; these I found it necessary to remove; and, for this purpose, laying aside my rifle for the first time in two days, and crawling forwards under the brush, I rose, cut the twigs with my knife, laid them aside, and, creeping back to my position, as cautiously as if in an Indian ambush, again felt safe in the companionship of my rifle.

As the third evening approached, I visited the mule as before, but neglected to make a fire; and, hurriedly returning, took up my post for the night. Up to this time excitement had kept me wakeful, but tired nature now called for rest; and, as I sat with my blankets drawn closely round me, and my rifle between my knees, I unwittingly fell asleep, and for many hours was totally unconcious of my purposes in that wild and savage glen, and the dangers which surrounded me. It was nearly morning when I was suddenly aroused and dreadfully startled by the screech of a panther on the hill above me. For a moment my very bones quaked with terror; but I soon reasoned myself calm. What a fool, thought I, to be thus startled by the cry of a panther, a cowardly brute, which dare not stand face to face and fight with a man; while here I am, inviting a combat with a grizzly bear, the savagest beast that ranges the forest! With this comfortable reflection, I worked up my courage, and, being greatly refreshed with my sleep, felt bold enough to face almost any odds; — but the panther did not approach; and in less than twenty minutes a distant scream notified me that he was already far beyond my reach.

Daylight came, but the bear still remained housed, and I began to think she would not make her appearance. My watching was now becoming very irksome, and, feeling much like bringing the adventure to an issue, I determined to rouse her. There was some danger in this; for my plan would probably attract her directly to me, and, as sure as she should see me,

I knew she would give no time to draw an aim. Before putting my plan into execution, therefore, I stuck my cap full of green twigs, and stationed myself in such a manner in the bushes that it would take a nice eye to discern my form, even though looking directly towards me. Having thus disposed myself, cocking and drawing my rifle, I uttered one of those terrific yells with which I have so often started the grizzly to his feet. It echoed like the roar of a lion up the cañon; and in a moment afterwards there was a booming in the den like the puffing and snorting of an engine in a tunnel, and the enraged animal rushed out, growling and snuffing, as if she could belch forth the fire of a volcano. She rose upon her hind feet, and exhibited a monster form,— limbs of terrible strength. She looked around in every direction; but in a few moments, seeing nothing to attack, she sat down upon her haunches, with her back towards me and her face towards the opposite side of the cañon, as if her enemy were there.

During these few minutes I stood as motionless as a statue, hardly breathing, waiting and watching an opportunity to fire. Had I met such an animal unawares, in an unexpected place, her ferocity would have made me tremble; but after my long watch I was anxious to commence the attack, and felt as steady as a piece of ordnance upon a battery. As I watched, I saw her turn her head towards the den; and, fearing she would retire, I gave a low, sharp whistle, which brought her to her feet again, with her breast fronting directly towards me. It was then, having my rifle already drawn, that I fired; and in an instant, dropping the rifle, I drew my pistol in one hand and my knife in the other. The bear, as the ball slapped loudly in the fat of her breast, staggered and fell backwards, and began pawing and biting the ground, — a sure sign of a deadly hurt. Copious streams of crimson blood also gushed from her breast, and I knew that they came from the fountainhead. The work was, indeed, nearly done; but so anxious was I to complete it at once, that I commenced leaping over the bushes to plunge my knife in her dying heart; when, gathering her savage strength, she rose, and, with one last, desperate effort, sprang towards me. The distance between us was only thirty feet, but, fortunately, full of brush, and she soon weakened with the prodigious energy requisite to tear her way through it. I discharged the six shots of my revolver, the last of which struck under the left ear, and laid her still for a moment; when, leaping forwards, I plunged my knife to her vitals. Again she endeavored to rise, but was so choked with blood that she could not. I drew my knife across her throat, and after a few convulsive struggles she expired.

My feelings, as she thus lay dead at my feet, it would be difficult to describe. I looked at the hills around, to see if any eye had beheld my success; but all was silence. I looked to the heavens; but all was quiet, only a vulture was circling like a speck in the distant ether. I was alone in the gorge, and, as I looked upon the dead monster, felt like Alexander sated with victory and wishing another foe to engage, worthy of my prowess.

ADAMS AND THE WOLF.

CHAPTER III.

BEN FRANKLIN.

Pleasurable Recollections of the Mariposa Adventure. Determination to enter the Den. My Caution. My Preparations. Torches. Construction of the Den. Seizure of the Cubs. Retreat. My Joy. Disappearance of the Mule, "Betz." Trace of the Panther. Return to Camp. Solon's Wonder. Christening of the Cubs. Revisit the Den. Reëntry of the Den. Discovery of a Wolf. Adventure with the Wolf. Solon's Fright. Manufacture of Milk. A new Idea. The Hound a Foster-mother of the Cubs. Buckskin Mittens. Thriving of the Cubs. Solon's trading Trips to the Mines. Lady Washington as a Pack-animal. Hunting with the Lady. A gray Wolf. Capture of Wolf Whelps. Deer's Eyes by the Nightfire. Mountain Sheep. Slay a Ram. Solon and I on the Hunt. Solon attacked by a Panther. His Peril. My Attack. Solon's Story. Solon's Forethought. Reflections. Solon's Wounds. The Water-cure. The Philosophy of the Water-cure. Mountain Surgery in Earnest. Search for the Panther. Discovery of the Beast and her Kittens. Our Attack. Slaying of the Dam. Seizure of the Kittens. Solon's Satisfaction. Characteristics of Mountain Sheep. Our Family. Lady Washington with the Kittens on her Back. Return to Camp. Presents to Tuolumne and Stanislaus. Their Devotion.

IT is with pleasure that I dwell upon this part of my story, and I would fain distinguish it with living words. In all the after-course of my career, I could look back upon it with peculiar satisfaction; and rarely, in the following years, did I pat the shaggy coat of my noble Ben, but I recurred to my fatiguing and solitary vigils in the Mariposa cañon, my combat with the monster grizzly, my entry in her den, and seizure of her offspring. The whole adventure is impressed

upon my memory, as if it had occurred but yesterday.

No sooner was the dam dead, than I turned towards
the den, and determined to enter it without delay.
Approaching its mouth, accordingly, I knelt, and tried
to peer in; but all was dark, silent, and ominous.
What dangers might lurk in that mysterious gloom, it
was impossible to tell; nor was it without a tremor
that I prepared to explore its depths. I trembled for
a moment at the thought of another old bear in the
den; but on second thought I assured myself of the
folly of such an idea; for an occurrence of this kind
would have been against all experience. But in such a
situation, a man imagines many things, and fears much
at which he afterwards laughs; and therefore, though
there was really no difficulty to anticipate, I carefully
loaded my rifle and pistol, and carried my arms as if,
the next instant, I was to be called upon to fight for
life. Being thus prepared, I took from my pocket a
small torch made of pine splinters, lighted it, and,
placing my rifle in the mouth of the den, with the
torch in my left and the pistol in my right hand, I
dropped upon my knees and began to crawl in.

The entrance consisted of a rough hole, three feet
wide and four feet high. It extended inwards nearly
horizontally, and almost without a turn, for six feet,
where there was a chamber, six or eight feet in diameter and five feet high, giving me room to rise upon my
knees, but not to stand up; — and its entire floor was
thickly carpeted with leaves and grass. On the first
look, I could see no animals, and felt grievously disap-

pointed; but, as I crawled around, there was a rus-
tling in the leaves; and, bending down with my torch,
I discovered two beautiful little cubs, which could not
have been over a week old, as their eyes, which open
in eight or ten days, were still closed. I took the little sprawlers, one after the other, by the nape of the
neck, lifted them up to the light, and found them very
lively. They were both males; a circumstance which
gave me reason to presume there might be a third
cub, for it is frequent that a litter consists of three,
and I looked carefully; but no other was to be found.
I concluded, therefore, that if there had been a third,
the dam had devoured it,— a thing she often, and if
a cub dies, or be deformed, she always, does. Satisfying myself that there were no others, I took the two,
and, placing them in my bosom, between my buckskin
and woollen shirt, once more emerged into daylight.

The possession of the prizes delighted me so much
that I almost danced my way down through the
bushes and over the uneven ground to the spot
where my mule had been left; but, upon arriving
there, it gave me great concern to find that she was
gone. At first, I thought surely she had been
stolen; but, as my bag of dried venison remained
undisturbed upon the tree, and much more as the
tracks of a panther were to be seen in the neighborhood, I became convinced that she had been attacked
by my disturber of the previous night, and had broken
away. Indeed, upon further examination, I found
her track, leading off through the chaparral; and,
following it over a hill and through another cañon, at

length found her grazing in a grassy valley. She
seemed much frightened at first upon seeing me,
but when I called her "Betz," she stopped, turned
around, looked, and then came up, apparently glad
to meet me again. Her haunches bore several deep
and fresh scratches, which were still more convinc-
ing evidences to my mind that the panther had
sprung upon her, but that she had broken loose and
escaped.

Mounting the mule, I returned to the dead bear,
and, cutting her up, packed a portion of her meat;
the remainder I left in the mouth of the den; and,
turning my face out of the ravine, I proceeded in
excellent spirits, bearing the cubs still in my bosom,
towards the camp of my companions. Upon reaching there, shortly after dark, I showed Solon what I
had accomplished; and, placing the cubs before him,
chose one for my own and presented him with the
other. He thought that this was more than his share;
but I insisted upon his receiving it, and he did so
with a thankful heart. He asked me the story of the
capture, and I told it, from the moment of my leaving camp to my return. He wondered much at my
patient watching in the juniper bushes, and said he
would not have done it, but still he wished he had
been with me; — and thus we went on talking, till the
dying embers admonished us of the lateness of the
hour. Before retiring, Solon christened his cub General Jackson; I remarked that General Jackson was
a great man in his way, but I would call my bear
Ben Franklin, — a greater name. Such was the man-

ner that, in one and the same day, I captured and christened my noble Ben.

The next morning, Solon expressed a desire to see the den, and we hunted in that direction. Upon arriving at the spot, we found that the bear-meat, which I had left at its mouth the previous day, was torn to pieces and almost entirely eaten. What had done this we did not know, and conjectured vultures; but, as our supply of meat was already ample, the loss gave us no concern, and we thought nothing more of the matter; and, as we had brought with us several torches, I told Solon to light one if he wished to examine the den, and go in. He, however, seemed backward about venturing, and finally I seized the torch myself, and prepared to lead the way. As I did so, the leaves in the den rustled in a singular manner, and, upon getting in nearly to the chamber, I heard a jump and a growl. This startled me for a moment; but, having my pistol in my hand, I kept my ground, and, holding the torch over my head and looking keenly before me, soon perceived the dark outlines of a wolf, sitting upon his haunches close up against the further side of the den, and grinning at me with a most ferocious expression.

The wolf, notwithstanding his cowardly disposition, is an ugly fellow to deal with in close quarters, and many men in this situation would have been very willing to leave him alone; but I determined to give him fight, and called to Solon to stand ready, provided he should get past me. Then, sticking my torch in the ground, and drawing my knife in my left hand, having my revolver in my right, I fired at the growling brute, and would directly have fired a second shot, but, without giving me time to do so, the beast bounded past, in the endeavor to escape. As he did so, I seized his tail and struck with my knife; but this did not stay his progress, and he would have certainly escaped, but, fortunately, Solon was well prepared, and gave a blow which laid him cold, as he emerged.

Having thus cleared the den a second time, I handed the torch to Solon, and he stooped down and started in. He had crawled but a few feet, however, when, in a spirit of mischief, I cried out to him to beware of the other wolf; — and he suddenly backed out, so terribly frightened that I was sorry for him. He would have become angry about the matter, but I laughed the humor out of him, and after a while he entered the den. I followed; and after viewing the place to our complete satisfaction, we came out and returned to camp.

Having thus caught our cubs, it next became a matter of difficulty, which troubled me several days, how to feed them. In the morning, I had given them a mixture of water, flour, and sugar, which was the nearest approach to milk I could think of; but this substitute would hardly answer for any length of time. While thinking over the matter, however, an idea struck me; and, on being put in execution, it worked much better than could have been anticipated. This was no less than making the greyhound suckle them. To make room, we destroyed all the greyhound's litter except one, and foisted the cubs in their places. As was to be expected, the hound was at first a little ugly towards these strange foster-children, and would snap and bite them; but by degrees she admitted them freely, and would even lap and fondle them,— so that, in fine, they at last shared in her affection with her own offspring. To prevent the scratching of their paws, we made little buckskin mittens; and these were put on every time they sucked, — which continued for about three or four weeks. They were only a little heavier and clumsier than the puppy at first; but they grew fast, seeming to thrive well on the milk; and by degrees we taught them to eat bruised meat, and, finally, entirely weaned them.

Meanwhile we continued our hunting; and on several occasions Solon made trips down the mountains to the nearest mines, taking with him the horse and mules, packed with fresh and dried meat, which sold readily to the miners, and for a good profit. During these trips, Tuolumne and I, upon our excursions, took with us Lady Washington in place of a pack-animal; for, by this time, she had become so well trained that she answered every purpose. I had made a kind of saddle of green hide, resembling a Mexican *aparejo;* and with this we could pack upon her loads of two hundred pounds' weight, which she would cheerfully carry.

Our success in hunting exceeded our expectations, and various were the adventures we met with. One day I left camp with the Lady, and travelled over a

large extent of country without meeting anything
worthy of notice. In the evening, I came into the
midst of a region of large cliffs and shelving rocks,
full of holes and caves, and with many large cedar
and pine trees. It was too far distant to think of
reaching camp that night, and I therefore determined
to spend the night there; and, searching out a safe
spot near a spring of water, took up my station, having the Lady lying at my side. I had not been sitting
long, when a gray wolf, with two fine pups about a
month old, approached; and as it was not yet dark,
I easily killed her.

The pups gave me greater difficulty, having run
into a cleft in the rocks, from which it was only with
smoke that they could be dislodged. As they came
out, I seized them; but, catching the last by the tail
instead of the neck, it turned and bit my hand severely; however, I kept my hold and secured him.
I then built up a fire near the spring, and threw myself upon the grass, waiting for whatever might come.
In the course of half an hour, a band of deer approached, and it was not long before I saw half a
dozen pairs of glistening eyes looking curiously at the
fire. They presented a beautiful sight, and it was almost with sorrow that I fired at the foremost one,
which fell; but the rest scampered off. The remainder of the night, having first roasted and eaten a bit
of fresh venison, I endeavored to sleep, but was much
disturbed by wolves and panthers, which kept up a
dreadful howling and shrieking. In the morning very
early I mounted the cliffs, and reached a very rough

and barren region, higher up in the mountains than I usually went. Looking around, I soon discovered a flock of mountain sheep, in every respect similar to Rocky Mountain big-horns. I crept forward among the rocks very cautiously, till within sixty yards of the flock, but could procure aim only at an old ram which had a broken horn. I waited a considerable length of time, in hopes of seeing a better head; but at last, getting out of patience, fired at what there was. As the ball struck, the ram bounded, like a piece of India-rubber, high into the air, and fell dead, flat upon the rock; but the remainder of the flock ran up the cliffs, and before I could reload, had entirely disappeared. The ram, which weighed about seventy-five pounds, and the deer killed in the night, I packed upon the Lady, and, taking the wolf pups in a bag, travelled back to camp.

On another occasion, Solon and I started out very early; and, coming to a spot where two ravines came together, he started up one and I the other. I had not gone more than a quarter of a mile before I heard Solon cry out for help. I bounded up the ridge which separated us, and, upon reaching the top, saw him lying under a large tree in the other ravine, and a panther on top of him, apparently gnawing into his neck. I shouted to him to lie still, and, drawing my rifle, fired at the beast; but, in my anxiety to shoot wide of my comrade, I did not strike the panther fair, and he bounded off into the bushes, and escaped.

In answer to my inquiries in relation to this singu-

lar adventure, Solon told me that as he was walking
up the ravine, looking only forward, and paying no
attention to the trees overhead, the beast suddenly
leaped upon his back and struck him to the ground.
In the same moment that he fell, he cried out for me,
and pulled the cape of his buckskin coat over his
neck — and this evidently saved his life. How he
came to have such forethought was strange; some
others might have done so, but most men would
never have thought of it; I, for one, would have
sooner drawn my knife and fought. I asked why he
did not fight; he replied that he was afraid to move,
supposing that it would only infuriate the animal.
Such a caution, said I, would have been good in case
of a bear; but the panther is made of different stuff.
By nature a coward and a sneak, he has the cruelty
of cowardice, daring the combat only when he has a
sure advantage, and wreaking a bloodthirsty ferocity
most upon an unresisting victim. A determined
stroke with a knife, though it might not have killed,
would have terrified and put him to flight.

In the meanwhile, I stripped the coat from Solon's
back, and found his shoulders severely scratched by
the panther's claws. His neck, also, was badly bitten, but not dangerously; for the buckskin had fortunately saved him. Still the wounds were serious
enough to require the best of my surgical skill, and
I at once placed them under treatment. I led the
patient directly to a spring which was not far distant; and, making him bend over it, with a piece of
hollowed bark I poured water over his wounds, until

he complained bitterly of the cold. I then put on his shirt, saturated with water, and over that, his coat; and, drawing off my own coat, put that, also, upon him. This was an easy matter, as my shoulders were much broader than his, and, besides, my clothing was always worn very loose, so as to give me perfect freedom of action.

A further article of my prescription was, that he should drink as much water as possible; but he replied that he was not thirsty, and wished to know why he should do so. I explained the reason, by saying that he would soon become warm; the water would, more readily, induce perspiration, and that would ease his pains. He then followed the direction; and, as we returned to camp, though he started stiff, in a short time, by warming up and perspiring, he felt well, and travelled as comfortably as ever. My surgery, however, did not end here; for, upon reaching head-quarters, and examining the wounds closely, I found there were two, more serious than anticipated, in the back of Solon's head, where the marks of the panther's teeth were plainly visible. To reach them, it was necessary to shave the hair; and, as my bowie-knife was the nearest approach to a razor in the camp, it was not without wailing and gnashing of teeth that the tonsorial operation was accomplished. Indeed, before it was half done, the patient cried that I was worse than the panther. I excused myself by the wretchedness of my razor, and hacked away again; when he refused to submit any longer to what he called my horrible butchery. Like an expert

surgeon, however, I had Tuolumne holding his head;
and, though he gritted his teeth and shouted with
pain, I went on, with apparently the most unfeel-
ing coolness, with my work, until the hair was as
short as the nap of velvet; after which I bandaged
the wounds with wet rags, and put my patient to
bed.

Solon passed a good night, and the next morning,
seeing he could get along alone, I determined to hunt
up the panther; and, taking Tuolumne, proceeded at
once to the ravine where the accident had occurred.
We soon found the trail, here and there marked with
spots of blood, and followed it for more than a mile
over a hill into a deep cañon. We at last came to a
very rugged and brushy place, where it was necessary to creep; and, crawling along, we were suddenly
startled by a low growl, and, looking low under the
bushes, beheld the beast glaring upon us from a cleft
in the rocks. At her side lay five kittens; but there
was blood upon them and upon her, giving evidence
that my shot the day previous had not been harmless. Indeed, had it not been for that shot, I doubt
whether the panther would have allowed us to approach so near her den, without either attacking or
fleeing.

Our situation, under any circumstances, was not
without its danger; but so used to perils had I
become, that not for a moment did my judgment
desert me. It had always been my practice, when
out with Tuolumne, upon getting into danger like
this, to give him the first fire. He was a good

marksman; and, if he killed, it would be a great encouragement to him; if he did not, it would require a degree of coolness, which he did not possess, to fire an effective second shot. Accordingly, at my beck now, he discharged his rifle. He struck her, but not to kill, and the coward brute turned to fly; but, as she exposed her side, I bored her through the middle with my shot, and she dropped in her tracks. We immediately rushed up and secured the kittens, which were about a week old. We afterwards examined the dead body, and found, besides the wounds in the breast and groin which she had just received, that my ball, the previous day, had struck her shoulder, and buried itself in her neck. We then drew our knives and whipped off her skin, preserving the head and claws, and, taking it and the cubs, set out upon our return. On arriving at camp again, Solon complained of lonesomeness; but when I presented him with the skin of the panther, he grew cheerful, and enjoyed the story of our adventure with great relish; but he would have wished, he said, to have been in Tuolumne's place, and have had the first fire at the beast.

For three or four days after this, we continued our hunting, and, on several occasions, made efforts to kill more mountain sheep. These wary animals inhabit the rockiest and most inaccessible heights of the mountains. Wherever there is a high, rugged, jaggy, treeless waste, with only here and there a stunted bush, a clump of bushes or scanty bunches of grass, there may they be looked for, lurking in the clefts and nooks of the cliffs. It requires a good hunter to approach them; he must keep himself out of sight; he must allow no breath of wind to carry notice of his vicinity to their keen nostrils; he must be a sure marksman, for no second shot can be hoped for. In an instant's alarm, the shaggy flock, as if gifted with wings, fly up the precipices, and only the eagle can follow them.

Upon breaking up camp, to return to our general head-quarters on the Merced River, we had, besides numerous bales of dried meat and hides, quite a family of young animals, consisting of two bear cubs, two wolf pups, five panther kittens and two fawns, which we caught upon one of our excursions. These young animals we packed in boxes or baskets, and placed on top of the bags and bales carried by the horse and mules. Lady Washington also, on the journey homeward, was required to bear her proportion, which she obediently did, till the panthers, which constituted a portion of her burden, began to whine; and she then became so uneasy that I was compelled to lead her until they were quieted.

We travelled back over the mountains by slow and easy stages until we arrived at our old camp, and were welcomed by our faithful Stanislaus, who, during our absence, had protected our interests with remarkable ability. It was with satisfaction, therefore, that I presented him, as well as Tuolumne, with a new bowie-knife, a new suit of clothes, and new blankets, which Solon, in one of his trips to the mines, had purchased at my direction. Both lads, upon receiving their presents, repeated to me their assurances of devotion and willingness to continue in my service; to which I replied that the Rocky Mountains was the next mark of my ambition; and they answered that I should lead on, they were ready to follow.

CHAPTER IV.

PASSAGE OF THE SIERRA NEVADA.

Expedition to the Rocky Mountains. Preparations. My Compan-
ions. Gray. Contract with Gray. Digger Indians. The Phi-
losophy of Life. Indian Fellow-travellers. Their Improvi-
dence. Our Train. Respective Causes of Pleasure. The first
Day's Journey. The Road. Ascent. The Snow. Aid of the
Indians. The Heights of the Sierra. A steep Place. Our
Labor. Construction of a Road. Progress. A general Treat.
Camping in the Snow. Firewood. Tobacco. Night on the
Mountain-tops. A festive Camp. Notions about the Diggers.
Attack by Wolves. Adventure with a Panther. A narrow Cañon.
Lugging through a Pass. Pulling and Tugging. A Supper of
Panther's Meat. A quiet Camp. Blistered Hands. Packing
up the last Slope. The Summit.

IT was, if I mistake not, about the middle of April,
1854, after several busy weeks of preparation, that
we started upon our expedition eastward over the
Sierra Nevada, towards the Rocky Mountains. From
the commencement, I anticipated that this would be a
longer and more dangerous tour than the one of the
preceding summer; we would have to pass over deserts, traverse totally unknown mountains, and travel
through the countries of Indians who were often hostile to white blood. We were also going into the
haunts of animals celebrated for their ferocity; and
it was impossible to foresee the issue of the undertaking. Before starting, therefore, I sold off a number of my animals, and left my affairs in California in
such a condition that, should I never more be heard

of, my representatives would find little difficulty in settling up my worldly accounts and taking into possession all my effects. There was, it is true, quite a fortune of debts owing me; but I had long given up the hope of ever receiving a copper of them, and considered, in my inventory, only what was tangible, or what was due from honest men.

A few of my animals, or to give their names, Lady Washington, Ben Franklin and his foster-brother, the greyhound, which I called Rambler, I never for a moment thought of leaving behind; but all the rest were taken down to Howard's ranch, and left with the collection I already had there. My friend Solon, whom I endeavored in vain to prevail on to accompany me, had taken his cub, and also several other of the captives of the last expedition, and returned to his home; but, in his stead, I obtained the society of an old acquaintance, named Gray, a miner of Chinese Camp, who had frequently expressed a desire to accompany me upon a great hunt. This gentleman was a Mississippian, young, active, and hardy. Like most of the miners of the time, he wore a full beard, mustaches and long hair, which gave him a fine and manly appearance; and, as he was an excellent hunter and a trustworthy friend, I was fortunate in securing his companionship. In relation to terms, we soon came to an understanding very much the same as that between Solon and myself; I was to be the leader of the expedition, and direct all its movements; I to receive two thirds of the profits, and he one third. I was to provide a wagon, two oxen and two mules, which were to remain my property; and he to join in providing our outfit of ammunition and general furniture. He was to have the liberty of separating from me at the Rocky Mountains; and he candidly gave me notice that he should probably do so, as he desired to return to his native State. So determined was he upon this point, that he carried with him nearly a thousand dollars' worth of gold-dust, which otherwise, doubtless, would have swelled the liabilities of one of those magnificent banking concerns, whose failure, the next winter, consumed the laborious earnings of so many small proprietors, myself among the number.

While our preparations were progressing, the snow having now entirely disappeared from the lower portions of the mountains, the Indians, as was their annual custom, came up from the plains, and spread themselves along the mountain streams. These miserable people I had been accustomed to encourage in their search for a precarious existence, and frequently would give them a deer, or other large game, which, while it lasted, would afford them a great treat; and the poor creatures were truly grateful in return, and, whenever an opportunity afforded, would do me any favor in their power. When, in the beginning of my mountain career, driven by a sort of misanthropy, as related in the commencement of my book, I had foresworn my own color and exiled myself to the wilderness, the contemplation of these lowest specimens of the human family, and the pity which their extreme wretchedness drew from me, reawakened the feelings of humanity in my breast, and prepared my mind for a complete reconciliation with my fellows. Even these people, I convinced myself, Providence had created for a purpose which, I doubted not, they fulfilled; and I soon could not help reflecting that, whatever of evil or good there was in the world, and whether they did me harm or advantage, it was the part of philosophy and wisdom to take them as they were, and make the best of them. This, indeed, is the great, and, I may say, the fundamental, lesson of life; and it was thus and there, in the mountains, that I successfully worked out for myself the great problem which other men have to work out, each in his own way, before they can say that they live.

A number of these Indians, about twenty-five in all, men, women, and children, were at this time on their way across the Sierra to the lakes beyond, where they proposed spending the summer in fishing; and, learning that we were about setting out in the same direction, they begged to be taken in company. Anticipating a scarcity of provisions, I at first objected, but finally consented to take them; and, long before the passage of the mountains was completed, I had reason to be gratified with my second thought, for not only did my protection prevent great suffering among them, but they, in return, were of great assistance to me and mine, as will in a short time be seen. Before setting out, it was my care to see that they had provided themselves with blankets, and with such provisions in advance as, with their bows and arrows, they could collect from the country about camp.

Having thus made all our preparations, in the early dawn of the appointed morning I roused the camp; and, drawing out our old wagon, we placed in it our furniture, yoked in the oxen, and hitched the mules before them. Lady Washington I chained to the hinder axle-tree; Ben and Rambler, being still too young to travel, I placed beside the goods in the wagon; and the greyhound and Indian dog ran loose. The Indians took up their position at a respectful distance in the rear. We were all in the best of spirits, and each had his special cause of pleasure: I found myself once more at the head of an adventurous expedition; Gray felt that his long-cherished hope of a great hunt was on the eve of fulfilment; Tuolumne and Stanislaus paraded the new revolvers and crimson scarfs which I had just presented them; and the Indians rejoiced in the prospect of a safe escort and plenty of provisions.

As the sun rose, we got under way, and, travelling all day, encamped in the evening in a little valley covered thick with pine and fir-trees, near the head waters of the middle fork of the Tuolumne River. We had proceeded with comparative ease the greater part of the day, but in the afternoon reached the more rugged and difficult country, where, notwithstanding what was called the Emigration Road, there could hardly be said to be a track. Our ascent had been rapid; and, at this first camp, we were already in the midst of snow; so that it was easy to infer

that the labors of the passage were about to commence. Anticipating difficulties, I informed the Indians that I would the next day expect their assistance, and gave them a deer, which Gray had killed
on the road, as an earnest of my care for them, provided they would be faithful. They assured me of
their obedience; and we threw ourselves into our
blankets by the side of our fire.

The next morning, after starting ahead, the first
obstacle that opposed itself to our progress was a
mountain of about three miles steep ascent, which was
covered with snow four or five feet deep. The crust
of this snow thawed in the daytime but froze again at
night; and, on this account, it was fortunate that we
started early, while the crust was still hard; for as
the sun mounted in the heavens, it beat down pow-
erfully, and, had we been but a little later, our
wheels would have broken through, and the road
been entirely impassable. Even as it was, we did
not gain the top of the rise without great difficulty
and repeatedly calling into requisition the aid of the
Indians, who with ropes assisted in dragging the wagon up the slopes, and pulling it over the many obstructions which lay in various places before us.

The top of this rise was the highest point I had
ever visited upon this road; and from here, having
no guide, we had to choose out our way as we best
could. There was much more snow than was to
have been expected; and I knew that, if we should
be caught in a storm in the higher parts of the
mountains we might perish. In front of us rose

the broken summits of the Sierra, mountain over mountain, but we pushed on as vigorously as possible, taking the best road we could find, and overcoming difficulties as we were best able. In some places, we were compelled to take a circuitous course around the mountain-sides, which were frequently so steep that it was necessary to hold the wagon to prevent its toppling over; and at last we came to a place so very steep that I considered it impracticable to support the wagon in this way, and we would certainly have been stopped here, but, fortunately, we had several shovels and pickaxes in the wagon, which had been provided for digging out the holes of animals. The idea that they could ever be of use to make a road in a snow-bank never entered my head before, but they now stood me in good stead.

Turning to the Indians, I directed them to lay off their blankets and go to work digging a road in the side of the snow so that the upper wheels of the wagon might have a kind of track to run in. It was necessary to dig thus for the distance of nearly a mile, but I encouraged the workers by saying it would be soon finished and that they should have all the provisions they could eat in the evening. With this prospect ahead they all went vigorously to work, men and squaws, with three shovels, two pickaxes, two axes, and a number of pointed stakes which I prepared for the purpose. At the same time I directed two to cut with hatchets a number of small pieces of wood about two feet long, which, as the track was dug out, we placed crosswise over it to support the wheels and prevent them from sinking too deeply in the snow; and in this manner, after four or five hours' work, we constructed a passable road, and started ahead. Being myself something of a teamster, I yelled at my animals with great success upon this occasion, and helped them up the hill as effectually as ever the best driver in the world could have done. When we had thus made the pass, feeling very liberal, I went to the chest and drew forth my famous old leather bottle, which contained several quarts of the best brandy of Sonora. This I had taken along as medicine; but as the Indians had worked so faithfully, I determined to treat. I therefore had the company drawn up in a circle, and, pouring out drink after drink into a tin cup and directing Tuolumne to follow with water and Stanislaus with the sugar bag, I dealt out a fair drink to all,— braves, squaws, pappooses, and all; not enough to intoxicate, but sufficient to make all feel lively, — the brandy being high-proof, and a pint of it better than half a gallon of the ordinary liquor of the saloons. Having thus completed the circle, finding there was not more than a quart left, I looked up to heaven and made a vow that the remainder should be kept inviolate, except in case of sickness or urgent necessity.

We then proceeded on our way a mile further over very rough places, with plenty of snow to trouble us, and, as it grew dark, determined to camp under a huge pine-tree. It was so very cold and inhospitable that we resolved to allow the Indians to camp with us; and, accordingly, set them to digging out a large circle

of snow around the tree, and bringing in all the firewood they could gather in the neighborhood. These
improvident creatures usually build very small fires,
however inclement the weather may be; for the reason, perhaps, that they do not relish the work of collecting sufficient fuel; and I soon found that we could
not have a good fire without providing more than the
sticks and boughs which they brought in. Gray and
I, therefore, took our axes, cut several dry pine logs,
and thus soon had a large pile of excellent wood and
a rousing fire, at which we all sat down and roasted
an immense quantity of venison; none too much, however, for the ravenous crowd around it. After supper,
I went to the old chest again and took out half a
dozen plugs of tobacco, which I distributed among the
Indians; and they well knew the use of it, — all understanding how to smoke, and most of those who had
been contaminated by contact with the white man,
being acquainted with the mysteries of chewing.

The night was intensely cold, but the moon shone
and the stars twinkled with a remarkable brilliancy,
and for a long time none of the party felt disposed to
sleep. This being the case, we soon got the Indians
to singing, dancing, and whooping; and a jolly good
time we had of it till very late, when I ordered them
to their blankets, and they rolled themselves up in a
promiscuous huddle, men, women and children, — all
together. This sort of bundling would not be relished
by more advanced people; but among the Diggers
there appears to be no harm; and it is even said by
some that, except at certain periods of the year, just

as among animals, there is no disposition of the sexes towards each other; — but this wants confirmation. That they do approach the nature of mere animals in some respects cannot be disputed. After they were all fairly rolled together, I ordered them to lie still and not move about during the night; and then, leaving Gray on guard, I myself tried to sleep; but my repose was brief, for in a short time the whole mountain resounded with the cries and howls of panthers, wolves and coyotes, attracted by the scent of our cooking, and it required not only Gray, but myself and Tuolumne, to keep them out of our camp.

Towards morning, a gang of wolves, which seemed more determined than ordinary, approached and came up within a few yards of us. I raised my rifle to fire; but they fell back at the movement, and sitting down at a little distance howled in a most saucy and insulting manner. In a few minutes, emboldened by their own impudence, five or six of them again approached in a body, when, taking as good aim as we could Tuolumne and I fired upon them; and the cowardly thieves turned their tails and fled. Even the panthers and coyotes took the alarm, and in a short time all was quiet again. As daylight approached, we went out towards where they had been, and found one of the wolves with a broken spine. My bowie-knife soon put an end to his earthly career. We then rambled a little further, finding that the dogs were much excited, evidently on some fresh trail; and, in a few minutes, started up a panther. The dogs pursued; and, in a short distance, being hardly pressed and worse scared, he ran up a pine-tree, from which he grinned and growled at us in a very ferocious manner. With the remembrance of our disturbed sleep, we felt just as ferocious as he appeared; and, after breathing a moment, Gray and I fired, both at the same time and with double effect; Gray bored the heart and I the head. The panther fell dead, and, taking him, each by a leg, we dragged his body into camp; and, being in want of fresh provisions, threw him into the wagon for future use.

In the meanwhile, the boys had prepared breakfast; and, after partaking of it, and watering our animals by melting snow in all the available utensils, we started ahead again. Our road now lay up through a cañon which, in many places, was so narrow that it barely afforded room for the wagon to pass. With pulling and hauling, however, we managed to advance, until we came to a spot where the rocks jutted so far out from the opposite sides that there was absolutely no room to get past. The fact was, that we had missed the road and got out of the way; but the place was of such a kind that to turn back was impracticable, and nothing remained but to uncouple our wagon and lug the parts through. We accordingly put all the Indians at work, carrying portions of the luggage through the pass; and in the course of an hour or so the task was accomplished, and we were ready for a new start. All this time the snow had been melting, and our progress grew continually more slow and difficult. Coming to a steep place, we were again compelled to unload and carry the greater part of our luggage a quarter of a mile up the declivity; then, again, we progressed, and, by pulling and tugging, worked our way around towards the more northern side of the mountain, where the snow was firmer, and afforded a better road. Those who have never attempted the passage of a snowy mountain will hardly appreciate the difficulties we encountered this day. We felt them in all our bones, and, when we camped at night, were almost worn out with fatigue and exhaustion.

For supper, this evening, we served up the panther-meat, and found that it tasted well when roasted before the fire. We were now within a few miles of the summit of the Sierra, and, as no game was to be looked for in that freezing region at this time of year, the fear of running out of provisions for our large company gave the unusual meat a relish which, perhaps, it might not have had in the midst of plenty. This night we neither danced nor yelled, as we had done the previous one, but were very glad to sleep.

The next morning, before dawn, we took our posts again, so as to reach the summit as early as possible; but some of the Indians complained of blistered hands, and did not feel disposed to do much. Upon examination, I found the complaints to be true, much as it surprised me; but there was no help for it, and all that could be done was to press the sound ones into service; and with some encouragement, being told that this would be the last day of hard work, they took hold, and we advanced up the last rise. Before noon, all the Indians had their hands blistered;

and therefore, though the snow was hard, we were compelled, as a last resource, not being able to pull any more, to unhitch and pack the luggage on the backs of our mules to the summit, and then, returning with them, pull up the empty wagon afterwards. All this took till after dark, nor were we then through with the day's work; for, as the mountain-top was bare, we had to run down on the eastern slope a mile or two, to reach a spot which afforded firewood, and there we camped. As our labors were now nearly over, we were all this night in excellent spirits again, cheerful and vivacious; and we promised ourselves a day or two of sport on reaching the base of the mountains, to luxuriate among good game and recruit our strength.

CHAPTER V.

DOWN THE EASTERN SLOPE.

Pleasure of Difficulties surmounted. Deeds of great Captains. Magnificent Prospect from the Summit. A Trading-post. Wrecks of the Emigration. The downward Road. The eastern Foothills. Hunting in the eastern Foot-hills. Plans for an Antelope Slaughter. Our Success. Indian Arrows and Archery. Tuolumne's Adventure with a Bear. Profusion of Provisions. Arrival of Stanislaus. The Feast of Gladness. My last Shuffle.

THERE is a pleasure in great difficulties surmounted so exquisite that generous and ardent souls often undertake great works solely for the gratification of overcoming their obstacles and enjoying the inspiriting after-thought. Great captains have crossed great mountains, as the histories tell us, and gained great applause, and the meed of praise is doubtless due for their magnanimous plans, for the weighty responsibilities they bore, and the success which attended their efforts; but little, indeed, could have been their own toil in those great undertakings. It was the engineers, and the hard-fisted, brawny-backed soldiers, the unsung and unremembered many, not the deified one, who sustained the real labor. I claim no great credit for leading my army over the California Alps; but perhaps my difficulties were, in proportion, as great as ever were those of Hannibal or Napoleon. Had I commanded a larger party, and disdained to bend my own back to the task,— or better still, had I fallen upon the valleys at the eastern base of the Sierra with carnage and blood, I too might have gained a niche in the temple of fame, and my passage of the snowy mountains might have lived in story. But my mission was a peaceful and an humble one, and what I accomplished was the work of my own hands.

The next morning dawned upon a scene beautiful and grand beyond description. Having passed the summit in the night, we returned to the highest point, and arrived there in time to behold the sun rise. Not a cloud obscured the sky, and the ridges of the Sierra, far to the north and far to the south, glittered in their snowy mantles, which, as the sun rose, were flushed with crimson. To the west, faint in the distance, lay the plains of California; to the east, far away stretched hill and dale, lighted up with the russet tints of morning. So enchanting were the views that we remained full an hour enjoying the magnificent prospect, cold as it was; and then, hitching up our animals and placing lock-chains upon the hinder wheels of our wagon, we ran down the trail till towards evening, when we camped for the night.

There was, at this stopping-place, a log-house built by traders from Sonora, who, the previous summer, had crossed the mountains with goods to trade with the immigrants; but, at this time, as the regular trains could not be expected until fall, the place was vacant. On all sides lay old axle-trees and wheels, some broken, some perfect, melancholy evidences of the last season's disasters. There were also some complete wagons lying abandoned, and Gray proposed that we should pick out a lighter one than our own. At first I thought of following his advice; but, on second thought, I replied, no, — that the wagons were not mine, and somebody might yet claim them: ours was good enough, and we would certainly be much more at ease with it than with another, which might be claimed at any time by somebody else. Without disturbing the wrecks, therefore, we merely passed among them, wondering to whom they had belonged, and what difficulties had induced the owners, after crossing so great an extent of country and arriving at the very threshold of the promised land, to cast them aside, and leave them to rot and ruin. They induced much the same kind of reflections as are produced by the sight of a wrecked ship, which, upon entering port from a long voyage, drives against the rocks, and is broken to pieces by the merciless surges.

From this place we proceeded the next day, not without difficulty at many places, but with vigor and emergy, into cañons and out of cañons, over hills and down declivities, until afternoon, when we ran out of the snow entirely. The country was well timbered. We passed on till night, and camped in what may be called the eastern foot-hills, where we found dried grass of the previous year, and, here and there, new grass springing up; so that, turning our animals out to pasture, we determined to lay over and spend a day hunting. And it was, indeed, full time; for this evening our stock of provisions ran short, and over thirty of us were in an unknown country, with only about fifty pounds of dried meat, a bag of flour, half a bag of Indian meal, and a little sugar and coffee.

Our first day's hunt east of the Sierra gave us no reason to be dissatisfied. Gray prophesied failure; but I was confident, from the appearance of the country, that game must be abundant, and that we could not be far distant from plenty. At all events, necessity impelled us to do our utmost, — for without relief we would have been in a bad situation indeed. I accordingly mustered all our force, and found that, besides my own party of well-armed reliable hunters, there were twelve Indians provided with good bows and arrows. These I divided; and sending out six, with Tuolumne at their head and a mule to bear their game, towards the northeast; and Stanislaus, with four and a mule, towards the southeast; I took the other two, with Lady Washington, and proceeded eastward down the hills. Gray remained behind to take care of the camp, in which were left several old Indians, the squaws, children, oxen, and pets.

I proceeded with my party several miles, when suddenly, in a region of scrubby oaks, cedars and juniper bushes, we came upon a band of fifteen or twenty antelopes. Tying the Lady to a tree, I instructed the Indians how to creep around and decoy them,— and they started off to make a surround. Having waited long enough to enable them to accomplish the purpose, I advanced, and, mounting a knoll, beheld one of the Indians lying flat upon the ground and moving his cap gently on a stick, endeavoring to decoy the animals, which were not far distant; and so well did he work the plan that, although myself within rifle-shot, I remained quiet, with the determination of giving him the first shot.

The antelopes stood looking at his cap, and approached by degrees until they got within eight or ten yards, when, drawing his bow, the Indian sent an arrow into the side of one of them. As he remained concealed, the remainder of the band did not offer to fly, and he soon shot a second arrow and a third; but without looking to see any more, as a fine buck stood before me, I now levelled my rifle and fired. At the discharge, the band wheeled and looked towards me, and, as they did so, I raised a red Mexican sash which I wore about my waist. While they gazed curiously upon it, the Indian continued throwing his arrows thick and fast; but the band, not knowing whence they came, and attracted solely by the flaming sash, continued to advance,— except the wounded, which pranced around where they were, or tried to get away. As soon as reloaded, I fired a second time, and pierced a fine buck through the heart; but the fire and smoke alarmed the other animals, and they turned and ran. Only one lay dead; but there were three wounded, and, pursuing, we soon killed two of them. The third we followed a long distance, but after a long search were compelled to return without him. Upon getting back to the antelopes, we ripped them up, and, lifting the skin from the thigh of one, cut out some choice steaks; and the Indian having meanwhile built a fire, we soon satisfied our hunger.

Packing the rest upon Lady Washington, we then started back to camp, and on the way overtook the second Indian, who had killed several hares, an eagle, and several crows. These Indians used arrows tipped with flint or obsidian, and could easily kill the smaller kinds of game; but such weapons were not so effective with larger species, though one of the wounded antelopes had been pierced entirely through with a shaft.

When we got back to camp, Tuolumne and his party had already come in, and brought with them the body of a brown bear and a number of hares and birds, such as grouse, magpies, crows, and hawks. In giving his account of the bear, Tuolumne said that he had met it early in the day. He had fired and wounded it, when the beast showed fight, and four of the Indians ran. The other two, however, stood by him like men, and pestered the beast with their arrows till he was able to reload; and with a second shot he finished the business. As for Stanislaus and his party, they had not yet arrived; but, even without what they might be expected to bring, we now had plenty. Thus it was that, although in the morning we started out almost destitute, and with starvation staring us in the face, by good management and prompt action we had quite a market of game before the sun set; — indeed plenty smiled around us in those heaps of bear-meat, antelopes, hares, and birds. In thankfulness for our good fortune, and to show an appropriate gratefulness, I ordered a rousing fire to be built and a feast to be spread; and at the same

time directed the Indians to clear two rings, and prepare for the dance of gladness.

While all this was going on, I discharged my rifle
as a signal for Stanislaus, and in a few minutes the
report was answered from the hills to the southeast.
In a short time afterwards, Stanislaus and his party
made their appearance, with their mule loaded with
two deer and a third lot of hares and birds; so that,
if we had plenty of provisions before, we now had profusion. In jolly good mood did we then sit down to
our feast of roasted dainties. When we had despatched them, the Indians began their dancing; and
such a whooping and shouting and kicking up of heels
I rarely ever saw; and the sport was kept up with
various amusing episodes till a late hour. Even Gray
took part in the dance; and it furnished me with the
most lively amusement to watch him with his hoe-
down step in the character of an Indian brave. Once,
indeed, they induced me to get up for a few moments,
and I showed them how the Yankees used to dance
when I was a boy; but my gray head and long white
beard ill-comported with the lightness of my heels,
and the Indians, and particularly the squaws, almost
burst with laughter at the figure I made, so that I
soon resumed my seat and my old pipe, fully satisfied
that my dancing days were over.

CHAPTER VI.

WALKER'S RIVER COUNTRY.

Our Progress. Hunting on the Way. Camp on the Barrens. Provisions. Over the Barrens. Walker's River. Vultures. The
California Condor. Preparations for Camp. A strange Sight.
A Horse run wild. Night Alarm. A Bear in Camp. Attack
upon the Bear. The Bear among the Indians. Slaying of the
Bear. Plan to inveigle the Horse. His Capture. Building of
a Raft. Ferriage. Parting with the Indians.

THE next day we travelled on, following the emigration trail, and in the evening camped with good
grass and water; and the succeeding day we proceeded on, in hopes of reaching Walker's River, at
which the Indians were to leave us. On starting,
this day, I sent Gray, Tuolumne, and a number of
the Indians in different directions, with orders to kill
all the game they could; for I wished to leave the
Indians well provided, as they had been of valuable
service to us. The parties were to go a mile or two
on opposite sides of the road and advance parallel to
it, while I also undertook to hunt as we proceeded.
Having made this disposition of the forces, I drove
leisurely on, and, in the course of an hour or two,
perceived a band of antelopes crossing the road in
advance. Giving the charge of the wagon to Stanislaus, I went forward, but could kill only one. Throwing it in the wagon, I then took up the whip again;

and we travelled on till the middle of the afternoon, when, coming to a ravine with water and good grass, we determined to camp, though we had not yet reached the river.

The place of our camp this evening was a hard, dry country, without trees; and there was no wood, except drift which had been brought down by torrents from the mountains, and sage bushes which already began to form a feature in the landscape. As soon as we unhitched, I put the Indians to gathering what sticks were to be picked up for a fire; and, leaving Stanislaus in charge of camp, I sallied out with Lady Washington for an evening hunt. In a short distance I fell in with a band of antelopes, and killed two; and soon afterwards met Gray and his party, who had also two antelopes, besides two wolves and a number of hares and squirrels. Upon getting back to camp, Tuolumne and his party had arrived, bringing one antelope, a lot of hares and squirrels, and a number of sage-hens, making in all a fair supply of provisions.

We were on the way again early the next morning, when, seeing that everything was in proper order, I left Gray to drive, and, taking Tuolumne and the Lady, started on in advance, so as to hunt as far as Walker's River, and wait there for the team. The country, as we proceeded, became more and more sandy and level, and we could see a long distance. There were no bushes, save a little sage and weeds, and no game, save squirrels and prairie-dogs. After travelling seven or eight miles, we came at last in sight of the timber of Walker's River, which was

eight or ten miles ahead.   We travelled on, and, upon
approaching it, again met antelopes and killed two.

Walker's River, where we struck it, is usually nearly
a hundred yards wide, and deep, though fordable in the
summer time.   The surface of the water is considerably lower than the surrounding plain.   Timber is disposed in belts about half a mile wide along its banks,
and consists generally of cotton-wood, button-wood,
ash, birch, and black alder.   In this timber, at the
time of our visit, there were great numbers of vultures and buzzards, which made the trees look almost
black, until we killed the antelopes above referred to,
when the birds took wing, sailed around us in circles,
now and then darted down, and indeed seemed determined to take the meat by storm.   Some were very
large, — one in particular, which was of the species
sometimes called the California condor.   As he
was sailing in grand style, with a majestic swoop,
like a king of the vultures, I determined to kill him;
and, seizing the opportunity as he swept towards me,
fired and broke his wing, so that he wheeled to the
ground.   We then approached, but he was so savage
that he darted at us with the most ferocious energy;
and, not liking to test the strength of his powerful
beak, I directed Tuolumne to put a pistol-ball into
his head, which he did.   After this, we made preparations for a camp; but as yet, there was no appearance of our company although we could see four or
five miles over the plain.   We waited some time;
but as they still did not come, we took our rifles and
went out to meet them.

It was now approaching evening and becoming dusky. As we passed along a few miles from the river, our attention was attracted to a large object nearly a mile to our right, which we could not make out. It looked as if it might be a buffalo, but still the shape was singular, and for a long time we were not able to conjecture what it could be. The most familiar things, sometimes, under certain circumstances, assume strange shapes, and when we have found them out, we are astonished that they could ever thus have excited our wonder; and so it was in this instance; for upon approaching the animal, which I had almost thought an elephant, it proved to be only a horse, which, doubtless, had been left by some hapless emigrant, or had broken from some passing drove the previous season. We tried to approach him, but he was too wild; and we therefore left him for the time, and proceeded on to our company, which we soon met; and, returning with them to the river, made our camp on its bank, and, being all fatigued with the day's labor, turned into our blankets at an early hour.

We were troubled this night again by the howling of wolves and coyotes; and about midnight, Gray, who was on watch, woke me up to say that he heard footsteps, and feared an attack of Indians; and wished to know whether he should not put out the fire, so as to blind the enemy. I answered, by all means not to do so; for the Indians, if such there were, could certainly see much better than we in the dark. I then arose, and went with him to his post and heard the footsteps; but soon perceived that they were made, not by Indians, but by beasts. "Now," said I, "if I am right, a whistle will tell the tale." Preparing my arms, I then gave a sharp, startling whistle; and it was immediately answered by a snort of a bear, which was but a short distance off, though we could not see him. He had evidently come to procure a supper from our supplies; and, after a little reflection, I determined to allow him a good square meal, and then give him the dessert.

Our game lay by a stump near where we stood, but, to give the bear an opportunity to approach, if he dared, we removed, and took up our positions behind trees a little further off. The way being thus left clear, the bear soon approached the meat, and, sitting leisurely down, began enjoying himself, and smacking his chaps over the luscious morsels. He sat with his back towards us, so that we could not procure aim; nor indeed was there light enough to enable us to do so at any rate. To do the best under the circumstances, however, I again uttered the bear-yell; and, as he rose and looked towards us, we simultaneously fired, and bored him through the middle.

During all this time, the Indians, who were camped close by, sat in great trepidation, and it was as much as Tuolumne could do to keep them quiet. But, as soon as the shots were fired, they commenced jabbering like a flock of blackbirds, and got up to come towards us; when the bear, not yet dead, rushed into their midst, and began pawing right and left. For a moment or two the scene, or as much as could be seen of it, was altogether indescribable. The bear managed to get an Indian down, and bite him terribly in the thigh, and the poor fellow roared and yelled for pain; but as Gray and I rushed up on both sides and plied our knives, we soon made the enemy loosen his hold and roll over dead, — though, in the encounter, I received a severe wound in the left arm, and the Indian was grievously hurt.

The next day, we laid a plan to capture the horse which we had seen on the plain the previous evening; and, for this purpose, put a number of the Indians to work making a small corral, or brush inclosure, near where, as we could see by the tracks, he was accustomed to come for water. Putting the oxen and a mule in it as a decoy, I sent Tuolumne with the other mule to endeavor to drive the horse in; but all his efforts were vain, for the animal, whenever disturbed, would run off towards the mountains. As thus this manœuvre did not succeed, we waited until evening, when, taking a small party, I went out myself; and by forming a semicircle and moving gently forwards, we drove the horse before us, and finally he walked into the corral, as we wished. He had barely entered it, when we threw several lariats over his head and secured him. He proved to be a good American horse, six or seven years old, wearing the galls of harness, but high-spirited enough to protect himself from the assaults of wild beasts; from all which I inferred that he had been abandoned by some emigrant as worn out, but had recuperated and managed to live through the winter.

In the meanwhile, having inspected the river and found it too deep to ford, on account of the floods from the melting snows of the mountains, we made a raft of cotton-wood and prepared to cross the next morning. When morning came, we gave all our game, with the exception of a couple of days' sufficiency for ourselves, to the Indians, with whom we were here to part; it being their purpose to go down the river to the lake, and spend the season in fishing there, while our course was to cross the stream and strike over to Carson's River. Two of the Indians desired to go with us, and, as they were active young fellows, I consented; but the rest we left upon the bank, watching our movements as we ferried our wagon and baggage over the stream, and evidently wishing that we had remained, to provide them with venison and bear-meat.

THE PANTHER.

CHAPTER VII.

THE HUMBOLDT MOUNTAINS.

FROM Walker's to Carson's River, a distance of
forty miles, we travelled over an uninviting region
without trees, grass or water, nothing but sage
bushes and weeds. We had taken the precaution to
carry some bags of water with us from Walker's,
but before the two days during which we were upon
this desert were over, all suffered much from thirst.
Towards the end of the second evening, as our sufferings were becoming aggravated, I mounted my
horse for the first time, to ride in advance and
reconnoitre. I found that long freedom had rendered
him impatient of restraint, but in a short time he
recollected the bit, and I rode off like a nabob at a
rapid gait for more than an hour, in search of the
river, and at last reached it. Carson's is a larger

stream than Walker's River, and there is good grass along its banks, but no trees in this place; so that, being unable to find firewood, we were compelled to take our food uncooked; and to add to our discomfort, the night was damp and foggy.

In the morning we hurried off very early, desirous of leaving the place as soon as possible, and proceeded down the river towards the great bend, where it was our intention to cross, and from there, strike for the Humboldt Mountains. Of these mountains I had heard much from emigrants of 1849; it was said that there were strange animals there, among them the purple panther and black and white wolves. We travelled about twenty miles this day, and came opposite a little island in the river, covered with cottonwood timber, where we camped. In the evening we caught a fine lot of salmon-trout, using grasshoppers for bait, and in the night killed half a dozen beavers, which were very tame. The next day we continued our journey, and the day after we reached the bend.

At this place the river divides and forms an island, which was the place I chose to cross. We accordingly went to work making a raft of cottonwood; and, upon getting it ready, loaded everything upon it, and crossed the first branch of the river. which was comparatively easy, as we could reach bottom with our poles and thus push ourselves over; but, upon rounding the point of the island and committing ourselves to the second branch, the water became so deep that our poles were of no use, and our raft was carried down the stream. The current was rapid, and I became, for a while, much alarmed, lest we would be swamped in the eddies of the bend; but it was fortunately not long before we reached shallower water; and, again finding use for our poles, we finally reached shore, and disembarked. Having no further use for the raft, we left it tied to the bank, for, although there was no probability of our ever seeing it more, others might come along and find use for it; and this was my invariable rule, not to destroy an article when the destruction could serve no good end.

Upon leaving Carson's River we entered a country almost entirely unknown; but, after travelling some distance, a faint line appeared in the eastern horizon, which we knew could be no other than the Humboldt Chain. It was sixty or eighty miles off, a mere line of blue in the distance; but the sight invigorated us, and we pushed on with energy. We travelled three days, seeing the mountains plainly in the clear mornings, but losing them in the smokier after-parts of the day; and, on the third evening, we camped on a small stream, which showed, by its sparkling waters, that it was born in the hills, though it wasted itself in the sands of the plains, — the same as thousands of other streams in the great basin. Along this stream we travelled the next day, gradually making our way through the hills, until we came to the mountains proper, which presented an almost unbroken barrier to our progress. We skirted this barrier for fifteen miles, when we found a rugged cañon with precipitous sides, which served for a pass, though it was barely wide enough to admit the passage of a wagon. A little brook rushed along the bottom of this cañon, and, in the course of four or five miles, we were compelled to cross it at least a dozen times, but we finally came into a beautiful little valley, a few miles long and half a mile wide, inclosed with high hills, which were covered with oaks, pines and cedars. The valley was level and grassy, with here and there a few treès, and, on one side under the hills, with a placid sweep, wound the stream. Here we pitched our general camp and determined to hunt for a week or two.

Throughout the whole distance from the Sierra we had seen no human beings save those of our own party; it was too early for emigrants, nor did we see Indians. After leaving the emigration road at Carson's River, we passed through an entire wilderness; not a track or anything to denote that man had ever trod the waste could be found. Until we reached the neighborhood of the mountains, there was also no edible game to be met with; and when we finally camped, our stock of provisions was very low. But all the way our animals thrived well, and travel seemed to affect them but little. As to the pets, Lady Washington had steadily followed the wagon, tied to the hinder axletree; but Ben Franklin and his foster-brother, Rambler, I kept in the wagon, where they spent most of their time in tussling with each other or sleeping. Sometimes I would take them out, and, when the road was pleasant, let them chase each other over the grass, or while away the time in the chase of hares, squirrels, and prairie-dogs, in which they found much to amuse and occupy them.

Upon reconnoitring in the Humboldt Mountains the first day, they did not promise us much. We went in an easterly direction with our mules, passing over a country rough with hills, rocks, gullies, and ravines, here barren, and there scantily covered with scrubby timber. We killed several deer, a few grouse, hares and squirrels; but could find no traces of more ferocious beasts. The next day we took a southerly direction, and coming to a very rough and rugged mountain, left our mules, and climbed over into a deep gorge full of ledges of rocks, holes, clefts, chaparral and brush;—a place which, if there were savage animals in the region, appeared exactly suited for their dens. Nor were we mistaken; for we soon found fresh tracks of a panther, which discovery enlivened us much; and visions of the purple panther, an animal with which we were totally unacquainted, danced before our eyes.

The two Indians who had come with us gave me to understand that they were expert in following a track, and they soon demonstrated their ability; for they pursued the panther trail through many winds and turns for several miles down the cañon, till they came to the great ledges and shelving cliffs, curious to see, — such as vultures build their nests in. The rocks were large, and left many holes and clefts; and in various places among them there were white bones of different kinds of animals, which seemed to have been thrown there by the savage tenants of the caves.

Upon reaching this place, we built fires, and endeavored to drive the smoke into the caves; but the wind being unfavorable, the plan did not succeed, and watery eyes were our only recompense. We then lighted pine torches, and entered a number of the caves, but could find nothing. At last we came to the determination of watching the place all night, and in that manner learning where the game lay; and accordingly, as it grew dark, we selected a ledge of rock where we could defend ourselves, and, wrapping our blankets snugly about us, began our observations. I can never look back to our position there without thinking of the famous valley of diamonds in the story of Sinbad the Sailor, with its high, steep, and inaccessible sides.

As soon as it grew quite dark, our ears were regaled with a concert of panther shrieks, quite astounding. We were so situated that every shriek was repeated by a dozen echoes, and the cañon fairly rung with terrific noises. We could also hear the beasts rushing along in the brush, but could not see them. At midnight it became more silent, but towards morning the concert was repeated; from which it appeared that the beasts had left their dens in the evening, hunted for prey during the night, and returned towards morning. Our watch, therefore, convinced us of the presence of many beasts; but it was impossible to see where they retired, and we knew not how to proceed to hunt them. As we were thinking this matter over, however, one of the Indians announced that he had discovered a panther's den, where there

were young ones, and described it as being about a
mile further down the cañon, in a spot very difficult
of access.   Upon questioning him, I perceived that
he understood the signs and proofs of the brute nearly
as well as myself; and we resolved to proceed at once
to the place.

The road was one of the utmost difficulty, on account of the thick brush, precipices, ledges and rocks,
which were piled together in great confusion the
whole way.   In some places we had to let ourselves
down, at the risk of breaking our necks, from one
shelf of rock to another; and the place itself, as we
found upon reaching it, was of most gloomy description, but exactly calculated for the dens of ferocious
beasts.   It seemed a perfect Golgotha of the animal
creation; for the bones of deer, antelopes, wolves,
coyotes and birds, together with feathers and hair,
lay scattered about in every direction.   Some of the
bones were yellow with freshness, others perfectly
bleached, and many crumbling with age.   The place
indeed bore the appearance of having been the den of
beasts since the days of Methuselah.   After viewing
the premises attentively, we came to the conclusion
that a particular horizontal opening in a ledge of
rocks led to an immense den; and we determined to
await the pleasure of the inmates to come forth.   We
accordingly posted ourselves, Gray and an Indian at
one place and I and an Indian at another, within fifty
yards of the den, and in such positions as to have fair
aim and be able to assist each other if necessary.

It was about sundown when we took our positions,

and we had not waited long before I had the pleasure
of seeing two panthers come out of the cleft of the
rocks. They played with each other, wrestled and
caressed, and I soon saw that one was a male and the
other a female. Never in my life before had I seen
two large beasts play so prettily, and I therefore
watched them without disturbing their gambols. In
a few minutes afterwards three small kittens came out
of the cleft and commenced playing also, springing
upon their parents' backs, and off again, and growling
with pleasure. I could have watched a long time,
but the opportunity being too favorable to be neglected, I drew my rifle, and, giving a whistle as the
signal agreed upon with Gray, fired at the female and
pierced her through the heart. Gray also fired, but
unfortunately at the same animal, so that the male
remained unscathed. He could not see us, however,
and, being confounded by the unaccustomed sound, did
not fly, but pranced about, jumping over the dead
body of his consort, looking in every direction, and
screeching every few minutes. I reloaded as quickly
as possible and fired a second shot, but without the
fatal effect of the former one. The beast was however struck; and making a tremendous spring, he
bounded in the direction of Gray. I thought he was
springing for my comrades; and in an instant, drawing
my knife and uttering the loudest yell that ever
passed my lips, I rushed forward; but the panther
was only scared, for, passing by them, he bounded
over a cliff into the bushes out of sight; and this was
the last we ever saw of him.

After waiting until his screeches had died away in the distance, we approached the den for the purpose of securing the little ones; but they evaded all our efforts. We used our buckskin coats to throw over them, but they dodged and jumped with such rapidity that our endeavors were useless; when we thought we had them surely, they were not there; and finally they ran into the den, and buried themselves in its recesses. There remained but one resource, that of following; and, making a large fire at the mouth of the place and procuring a number of pine torches, I prepared to enter. Gray was much opposed to this step at first; but I represented that the old ones were certainly disposed of, and there could be nothing else to fear. He replied like a man, that if I was determined to go in, he would share the danger; and accordingly he prepared himself to follow. I then took my buckskin coat and wrapped it about my neck, making thus a kind of battery for my face and breast, and placed a little Cayenne pepper in my pocket, which would serve to blind an opponent, if necessary. It was rare indeed that I was not provided either with pepper or dry snuff, though seldom that I ever had occasion to use them. In my left hand I carried my torch and drawn knife, in my right my revolver; and Gray was provided in much the same style.

It had now become dark, and the region dreadfully gloomy; nor was the appearance of the place benefited by the fire, the light of which, flickering upon the angular projections of rock, increased the blackness of the recesses. Any but a tried man would have drawn back from the adventure; but we were both firm of nerve, and, after deciding, would not be stayed. We accordingly entered the cleft, and crept forward eight or ten feet, over skeletons and bones, which rattled as we passed. Coming to a narrow hole, we passed through it into a second cave, five or six feet in extent, and then into a third, larger than either of the others. The most absolute silence reigned, and nothing was to be seen, until, as we approached a few broken rocks in a corner, the little panthers bristled up, and, with flaming eyes, began to spit at us. Seeing that we had no other beasts to encounter, we laid aside our arms, and I untied the coat from my neck; but, in consideration of the trouble already experienced from the active little brutes, I took a small quantity of pepper in my hand, and, watching an opportunity, dashed it into their faces. We then, in an instant, rushed upon them with our buckskins, and in a few moments had them in our arms; after which we made our way out of the close and now smoky cave as soon as possible.

The Indians, in the meanwhile, had remained at the fire at the mouth of the cave; but they were terribly frightened when they heard us coming out with the young animals screeching in our arms, for the acoustic peculiarities of the place were astonishing, and, hearing so great a noise, they knew not what was coming. When, however, they saw us emerging safely with our trophies, they looked upon our success as heroic, and, with a sort of reverence, cried "Bravo! bravo!" I myself exulted, believing that I had procured the famous "purple panther ;" but, on skinning the dead dam before the fire, I was undeceived. She was as tawny as the sands, and in all respects the same panther, called by naturalists the cougar or concolor, which is common to the whole country.

CHAPTER VIII.

AMONG THE DENS.

Discovery of a Wolf's Den. Wolves' Dens in General. A Night-
watch. Digging out the Den. Construction of the Den. Lost.
Adventure with a Bear. Our Position. Second Visit to the
Panther's Den. Explorations. A Panther. Adventure with the
Panther in her Den. Its Incompleteness. Conversation with
Gray. Reëntry of the Den. Seizure of the Kittens. Gray hor-
rified. Gray's manful Aid. The Purple Panther ?

THE recesses of the Humboldt Mountains afforded
us many adventures. The day after we stormed and
took the panther's den, one of the Indians reported
the discovery of a wolf's den, and said that he had
seen whelps playing at its mouth. We determined at
once to proceed to the place, and he led us a long
distance through a rocky and mountainous couutry,
with much chaparral among the gullies, but otherwise
barren and desolate. We arrived at last at a hill-side
in which there was a kind of tunnel-like cave; and
this was the den. Wolves sometimes have such dens,
but probably dispossess other animals to obtain them.
I have known them in different parts of the country
to dispossess coyotes, which had previously dispos-
sessed badgers, woodchucks or prairie-dogs. They
sometimes, however, dig holes for themselves; but
do not, generally, go very far into the ground, and
especially where the earth is in any respect hard. In

the present case, it seemed, from the general appearance of the place, that the hole had once been a bear's den, and that the wolves had taken possession after the original occupants had vacated it.

Upon examining the spot, we saw that it would require much labor to dig the whelps out,—a mode of procuring young wolves frequently practised, — and particularly as we had no spades or crow-bars with us. But as the Indian insisted that there were wolves there, we determined to watch the den during the night, and, if necessary, dig into it the next day. For this purpose we accordingly stationed ourselves, and kept a sharp look-out until morning; but no wolves appeared, and nothing was heard but the shrieks of panthers and the howls of coyotes in the distance. I concluded that the den had been deserted; but Gray, pointing to the fresh tracks, which were to be seen in abundance, was anxious to dig; and finally I acquiesced. The word was given; and, all going diligently to work with pointed sticks, we dug, and pried, and removed stones, until, after three hours' hard labor, we penetrated the hill five or six feet, and arrived at the inner chamber of the den. This was an apartment three or four feet in diameter and several feet high, nicely lined with leaves and also with some hair. It seems that wolves, when about to whelp, will frequently chop off a portion of their own hair, besides picking up all they can find, to make a soft nest for their offspring. This is a lesson that Nature, mother of us all, teaches them. We examined the den carefully, but there were no wolves of any kind about it, though appearances indicated that they had deserted the place but a short time before our visit. The old wolf had doubtless discovered the Indian scout; and, as it is the nature of the beast to remove her young when disturbed, she had probably taken the first opportunity to do so. Thus we lost four and twenty hours of hard watching and hard labor, and got nothing for our pains.

The provisions we had brought with us were now nearly exhausted, and we determined to scour the region for game. We started out, and travelled till nearly night, but, to our astonishment, found nothing but a barren, rugged country. As it grew towards evening, we did not know where we were, and began to suffer from thirst and hunger, when suddenly one of the Indians whispered to me. "There's a bear!" I looked in the direction in which he pointed, and saw a bear crawling slowly up the side of a ravine opposite us. It appeared to be lounging along, searching for roots and squirrels, in a manner customary to the animal after drinking; and I at once concluded that there must be water in the ravine; so that here, at once, food and drink were presented to us. We immediately separated, and, while Gray took one direction, I took another. He was most lucky in his path, and reached a suitable point of attack before I could; for when I had stationed myself in a clump of bushes near the top of the ridge I saw him below, preparing to fire on the beast. He did not know I was near, nor did I give him notice, but waited until he fired, and then ad-

vanced. His ball, although it struck, did not kill;
but this was of little advantage to the bear, for I soon
placed mine in his heart, and it fell dead. We drew
our knives, and, ripping out a ham, rushed down the
declivity to a spring at the bottom, where, building a
fire and partially roasting the food, we devoured it
like savages, — for we were nearly starved. After
satisfying our thirst as well as our hunger, we returned to the body of the bear, and, building a fire
near it, spread our blankets and fell into a sound and
comfortable sleep.

The next morning we ascended a hill to ascertain
our position, and found that we were but a short distance from the cañon of the panther's den. As we
wished to examine that den more at our leisure than
we had been able to do on the first visit, I despatched
the Indians to camp for Tuolumne and the mules, to
remove the bear; and, after they started off, Gray
and I went down to the den. We provided ourselves
with torches, as before; and, having lighted them,
crept into the apartment where we had found the
kittens. Upon removing a few loose stones, we unexpectedly discovered another crevice, which led in
among the rocks, and, passing through it, we entered
another apartment, and then another, until it seemed
as if we would never be able to find our way out
again. Presently, however, Gray remarked that he
thought he could see light ahead; I told him to place
his torch behind, and, doing the same with my own,
we both saw plainly that there must be a second entrance eight or ten yards in advance. We groped

along very cautiously now, being satisfied that we
were in another den, and having nothing but our
bowie-knives and pistols to defend ourselves, our
rifles being still at the mouth where we entered; but
we still continued to crawl forward in spite of danger.
It inspires me with more dread to recall the low,
narrow, tomb-like place now than when, under the
excitement of the hunt, I crept into it. All of a sudden, Gray cried, "A panther!" which startled me
terribly. I had neither seen nor heard anything;
but, upon halting a moment, plainly heard a low
growl, and, rising a few inches, I saw cowering in
front of me a huge living form, with a pair of flaming
eyes.

My first thought, at this startling discovery, was to
turn back, — but this would have been madness; our
only chance was to proceed, and beard the brute.
Should we turn, the beast would surely attack us;
but, with a bold front, armed as we were and with
fire, that terror of beasts, we were more than a
match for the brute, even under the disadvantages
of our position. Accordingly, drawing our weapons,
we advanced; I first, and Gray at my heels, — for
there was not room to proceed side by side. The
panther, meanwhile, continued growling more and
more angrily, and did not seem disposed to retreat.
For a few minutes we eyed each other, and I began
to fear a sudden spring; when, pointing my pistol as
directly at her eyes as possible, I fired. The animal
gave a tremendous screech, and we heard a terrible
growling and scratching, but, paying little attention

to these, and wishing to take advantage of our attack, we crept on as quickly as possible, continuing to fire and yell as we advanced. All this terrified the beast, which wheeled, rushed for the opening, cleared it at a bound, and escaped; but she was no sooner gone than I was sorry I had not seized her by the tail and plied my knife. Frequently have I thought of the matter since, and regretted my want of readiness; for the adventure lacked this of being complete. I indeed rushed after her, and paid no attention, for the time, to her kittens, which sprawled in her lair; but when we got out of the place, and looked about us in every direction, no panther was to be seen; she had vanished.

Our search for the dam being vain, I turned towards Gray and asked him to go in and catch the kittens. He replied that we should both go. I answered that such a plan would never do; for one must watch outside and keep off the dam, which was much more dangerous than to catch the little ones. I knew very well that there was no probability of the dam returning after the fright we had given her, but I spoke so to try my comrade's courage. All I could say, however, was of no avail; for, as I soon found, Gray was afraid of other old beasts in the den, and this was the reason of his refusal. This circumstance afforded me an opportunity, not only of ridiculing his fears, but of testing his faithfulness in the hour of need.

With torch in one hand and knife in the other, I again crept through the narrow opening, and soon

reached the panther's bed. Finding five little panther kittens, I placed them on my coat, which I had
drawn off for the purpose, and, doubling up the
bundle, began crawling out. But upon reaching the
narrow entrance, where Gray could see me, I began
twisting my face into a look of horror, and cried that
he should help me for mercy's sake. In an instant
Gray darted towards me, and asked frantically what
was the matter. I replied, "The panther! the panther! pull me out! pull me out!" and at the same
time worked my body from side to side, threw my
face into the most frightful expression, and kicked as
if a panther had me by the legs. Gray manfully
seized my arms and pulled me out, when, jumping
upon my feet, I slapped him on the back, and remarked that, though he had acted the coward before,
he had fully redeemed himself by his prompt action
now.

I was in hopes that these at least were the purple
panthers, — the animals we were so anxious to procure, — and resolved to lay in wait for the return of
the dam, in order to ascertain. We accordingly took
up positions near the den, and occasionally pinched
the tails of our little captives to attract her; but in
vain, — nothing more could we see or hear. As it
began to grow dark, we took up our prizes and arms,
and proceeded to camp, from which we had been
absent several days.

CHAPTER IX.

A HUMBOLDT TEMPEST.

THE next morning was one of the most beautiful that could well be imagined. The sky was clear, not a cloud to be seen; and a fine haze, like the commencement of Indian summer, gave it a peculiar charm. There was something so soft, and at the same time so fragrant, about the air, that it seemed to ravish the senses. It was not the invigorating atmosphere which incites to labor, but a luxurious one, as if of a perfumed bazaar under a Persian sky. I therefore felt little disposition to go upon the hunt, and chose to marshal and review my animals in camp. The pets were thereupon all brought out together upon the green sward, and, for an hour or more I had them gambolling and playing together, bears, dogs, wolves and panthers. From an early period in the life of my bear, Ben Franklin, it had been my intention to teach him to be a hunter, and I

had therefore taken every means to cement the
friendship which existed between him and the greyhound, Rambler; and so intimate had their relations
become that they passed their time together by choice,
always keeping in company in their plays. Ben was
now growing finely, and had far outstripped his foster-
brother in size; but they were still brothers. As for
the little panthers, they were all doing well, and gam-
bolled with the bear and dog, as if all had been reared
in the same family. Taking all in all, the sight was
one of great interest, and much did I enjoy it that
beautiful morning.

Such was the forenoon of this remarkable day in
the Humboldt Mountains, but in the afternoon clouds
rose. At first they seemed like huge banks of snow
rising over the mountains; but the higher they rose
the darker they grew. I was not acquainted with
the climate of the region, but it soon became evident
to me that a storm was brewing; and I therefore ordered the animals to be placed away, and everything
to be prepared for a rough time. Little idea did I
have, however, of the tempest which was about to
burst upon us. We had, indeed, barely rolled away
our rifles in blankets, and piled large chunks of wood
upon the fire, when the heavens became black, the
wind blew with terrific force, and large hailstones began pouring down. I soon discovered that a tremendous whirlwind was roaring near us, and that our
danger was imminent. Some of the party ran towards the wagon, with the intention of finding shelter
under it; but I forbade them, and directed all to

throw themselves flat upon the ground, and draw their blankets over them; and well it was that they did so, for in a few minutes the whirlwind suddenly took up the wagon, whirled it over, and scattered the luggage in every direction. The stronger it blew, the harder it hailed, and the firmer we had to hold ourselves to the ground to keep from being carried away; for the violence of the storm was so great that trees but a short distance from us were twisted off or torn up by the roots, and thrown about like straws. The devastation was frightful; but, as is the case with all violent things, the storm soon spent its fury, and passed over us. We were all bruised by the hail, and drenched by the rain, and rendered a truly sad looking set; but in the course of an hour or two the extinguished fire was relighted, we gathered up our scattered goods, and soon afterwards the sky cleared, and the sun shone pleasantly forth again.

I was in hopes, after such an afternoon, that we should have a calm night; but no, this tornado was but a prelude to a still more dreadful one, which might have been disastrous had we not had warning in time, and prepared for it. Seeing in the evening that it would come, we unpacked the wagon, took off the wheels and turned the bed bottom-upward, placed everything we could under it, and loaded it down with large stones on top. The animals we placed in bushes, and did the same with ourselves; and in a short time afterwards the storm came, bringing torrents of rain, which drenched us to the skin, and formed a sea of rushing water on every side.

There was thunder and lightning too, frightful, terrific; never in my life, before or after, have I seen
anything so appalling. But fortunately the wind did
not lift our wagon-bed; and when the tornado was
over, although it took a long time to dry our clothes,
and much of our property was ruined, we at last
made ourselves comparatively comfortable, and the
next morning rose upon us bright and clear.

We had now made as long a stay in these mountains as our time would allow, and began to prepare
for our journey over the Great Basin to the Rocky
Mountains. In view of the desert road before us, we
determined to devote ourselves, during the remainder
of our stay here, to collecting a store of dried provisions; and accordingly, on the day after the storm,
we started out with the horse and mules, and soon
killed four or five deer, which we hung up as usual.
Towards evening we came upon a bear, and crept
upon him, when Tuolumne, according to arrangement,
fired the first shot. No sooner had he done so, however, than the beast made a rush for him. There was
a small cedar-tree at a short distance, and Tuolumne
was soon in its branches; but the animal was close at
his heels, and would perhaps have caught him, had
not Gray and I, after vainly firing our rifles, seized
our knives and run to the rescue. Although Tuolumne discharged his pistol in front, our attack in the
rear diverted the animal's attention; and, after a
fight in which both Gray and I used our knives too
freely, he expired at our feet. He had a beautiful
skin, and when I saw how much it was injured by our

slashes, it grieved me that I had not been alone in the fight. But so it generally happens where several persons hunt in company, animals are spoiled by too much killing. I have, therefore, when collecting peltries, always preferred to hunt alone, which is also safer; for then a hunter has to look out only for himself and the game; but in a company, the attention is distracted by considerations for the safety of one's companions in addition.

The next day we again took the field, and, after a short hunt, perceived a large band of antelopes. We crept up on different sides with flags, until an old buck happened to see the decoys at nearly the same time. He looked first on one side and then on the other, and for a while it was uncertain which way he would go; but, by a waving of my flag, which was of an attractive red color, I drew him towards me, and the band followed. As they came down the knoll, Gray ascended on the opposite side, and, upon reaching the top, fired; whereupon Tuolumne and I discharged our pieces also. The shots had the effect of killing three, and so amazed the band that they began tramping around in a panic, while we rapidly reloaded and fired four additional times; and at last the band broke away and escaped, but left nine dead and four wounded ones behind.

A number of other antelopes and bears, deer, wolves and foxes, we likewise killed, and our camp for several days presented a busy scene of meat-drying and buckskin-making. After procuring as much provision as our journey would require, we packed it in such a manner as to economize room, having a journey of several hundred miles over a comparative desert before us, and knowing that we would have to carry water as well as provisions. We also greased the wheels of our wagon; and having thus prepared everything, and made all necessary arrangements for a start early the next morning, we gathered around our last camp fire in the Humboldt Mountains, and speculated upon the character of the desert over which we were to go, and the kinds and numbers of the animals of the Rocky Mountains, towards which we were now to travel.

There is something attractive in the very name of the desert. It is invested in our minds with the stories learned in childhood, of its wonderful wide stretches of sandy wastes, its mirages, and its caravans, all of which have been so generously adorned with the splendors of diction, and dressed out in the gorgeous robes of imagination. The poets have peopled its fearful solitudes with the creations of fancy, until the desert of the books is far from being the desert of reality. One who sits in the midst of plenty, to indite his experience of a travel over the plains, is apt to forget the desolation he has passed, and to describe inadequately the fearful loneliness he has traversed.

On the appointed morning, having yoked up at an early hour, we drove down a valley in the mountains, and the same day ran out into the hills which border the plains of the Great Basin. I had come to the conclusion that Ben Franklin was now old and strong enough to travel on foot, and allowed him to run the whole day in company with the greyhound, — a privilege which he seemed to enjoy as an acknowledgment of his majority; though a grizzly bear can hardly be said to have come of age until several years old. Lady Washington was chained to the axle-tree, as usual; but Ben seemed rather to harmonize with the greyhound than with his relative, and I had no disposition to interfere with his inclinations.

The next day we ran out of the hills, and camped upon what we supposed would be our last watering-place for several days; so that we considered it prudent to fill all our vessels and bags with water for use upon the wastes. The lower hills had a little timber and a little grass, but as they stretched out before us into the plains, the land became parched and sandy, with only a few weeds and sage bushes, and dreary indeed. As we pushed forward the next day, the country became more and more dreary, assuming a volcanic aspect as if burnt, having small stones scattered about, and in many places coated with a soda-like substance, very disagreeable to the sight.

We were in hopes this day of reaching a spring of which we had been told, but after a drive of forty miles, were compelled to camp without any signs of it, and during the night we used up all the water we had brought. Besides, there was neither grass nor firewood anywhere to be procured, and our stoppage, therefore, did little towards affording us the necessary refreshment. We passed a night of torment indeed, and, in the morning, were so thirsty that I became fearful of the consequences. All that could be done, however, was to ride ahead and search for relief; and, accordingly, while Gray was to follow leisurely with the team, I mounted the horse, and rode on a long distance; but nothing was to be seen, save a blank waste, without signs of water or vegetation. I hardly knew in which direction to turn, when at last, far in advance, I perceived several mounds, which we had been told indicated the situation of the springs. They were, however, not less than twenty miles distant from where the poor animals were panting with exhaustion; and when I bore the good tidings to Gray, he declared that they came too late.

It was, fortunately, now nearly evening, and the poor cattle seemed to revive as it became cooler, but, had it not been for the hardy mules, it is doubtful whether we could have reached the springs that night, and perhaps not at all. I sent all the party ahead to refresh themselves, and took charge of the team alone; but it was only with much coaxing and painful slowness that I succeeded in making progress, and managed to reach the springs, such as they were, in the morning. The water was brackish and unpalatable, but still acceptable under the circumstances; for, after the dreadful drive of the last two days, we considered ourselves very fortunate to procure any drink at all, however bad it might be.

CHAPTER X.

THE GREAT BASIN.

Recruiting. Our Route. Exhaustion. Ben Franklin's sore Feet. His Moccasins. Over the Great Basin. Travellers. Utah Lake. Mired. Around the Head of Utah Lake. Game. A Buffalo Hunt. Blackfoot Visitors. Another Buffalo Hunt. Among the Mountains. Discovery of a Rocky Mountain Grizzly. My Feelings. Slaying of the Bear. Characteristics of the Rocky Mountain Bear. Progress. Game. Camp on Muddy Fork.

AFTER a stay of two days at the mounds, recruiting our animals upon the scanty herbage which skirted the springs, and refilling our water-bags, we started again over a country similar to that which we had just passed, and camped at night on the desert. The whole of the next day we travelled on, and that night our supply of water failed again, with no prospects of relief. The next day we travelled forward, in the expectation of reaching springs; but the hope was vain, and the sufferings of the cattle became even greater than before. The route we had taken no emigrant had ever travelled, and all our information in regard to it had been derived solely from an old hunter named Walker, whose account, though perfectly truthful, was difficult to understand. We had endeavored to follow his directions implicitly, but it soon became evident that we were out of the way; and therefore, when we stopped at night, I rode out

to reconnoitre and explore, and, in the course of the
night, I found springs very similar to those we had
last been at, about ten miles distant. The next day
we proceeded towards them; but so dreadfully exhausted were the animals that they merely staggered
along, and it was night again before they could wet
their parched lips. To be broken down in the desert
is like being dismantled at sea, except that, in many
respects, the former is the more dreadful of the two;
but a happy escape in either case seems to be almost
a special providence.

Besides the want of water, which gave me so much
uneasiness, my bear Ben Franklin's feet became very
sore, by passing over so many sharp stones and so
much hot sand. I feared that he would be perma-
nently injured, and for some time could think of no
remedy. At first, I put him in the wagon, but he
had become so delighted with the privilege of following in freedom that he would not remain there; and,
rather than have him fret and worry himself sick, I
determined to allow him his liberty. Before doing
so, however, I placed moccasins upon his feet, — consisting of soles of elk-hide and uppers of buckskin,
sewed together with thongs. These were bound
tightly to the feet, and were intended to remain until
entirely worn out. As was to be anticipated, the
bear at first endeavored to tear them off; but they
were so tightly bound that he found himself unable
to either bite or tear them, and at last made no further attempts. They remained on for a couple of
weeks, and served the intended purpose admirably;

for in that time the feet were perfectly healed. The plan thus adopted I made use of on several occasions afterwards, not only with Ben, but also with Lady Washington.

After several days of recruiting we again advanced, expecting that the next water we would strike would be Utah Lake; for, since leaving the Humboldt Mountains, we had travelled about two hundred miles or more. During this day, we met six horsemen driving a few packed mules, — the first white men we had seen since leaving California. They had wintered at Salt Lake, they said, and were on their way to the Pacific. After a few moments' conversation, neither of us having time to delay in the desert, we proceeded on, and at night camped as usual. The next evening we came in sight of Utah Lake, a large body of water with tules growing profusely around its edges, and multitudes of birds, such as geese, ducks, tule-hens, and others, flocking about it. The following day we struck to the southeastward, and in the afternoon came to a stream, where we got mired in attempting to cross. The mud was very black and foul, and so thick that we were compelled to uncouple our wagon and pull it out by piecemeal. But however disagreeable in one respect, the mud was not without its benefit; for it showed us elk-tracks, and gave us to understand that we were again in the country of game.

The next day, passing towards the east around the head of Utah Lake, we crossed a number of sloughs, and, towards evening, arrived on the bank of a deep and muddy stream, which had a few cotton-wood trees growing on its borders. It was necessary to build a raft to ford it, and this detained us for an entire day. During the next several days we travelled on, crossing various streams, some of good size, others small, the country every day becoming more hilly and better stocked with game, until at last we camped in a valley, which I think was as beautiful a one as I ever saw. The undulating hills were covered with scattered trees of large size, such as oak, pine, cedar and fir, and the bottoms thickly swarded with grass; and on every side there were indications of deer, antelopes, elks, buffaloes and bears.

We determined, on the morning after camping in the valley, to replenish our diminished stores before proceeding further; and therefore, taking the horse and mules, we proceeded eastward in search of buffaloes. After going five or six miles, we came upon a small herd, and by surrounding and rushing upon them, managed to kill two. We might, perhaps, have slain more, but our animals were so jaded and worn out with their exertions on the desert that the buffaloes easily outran them. While cutting up the game, a small party of strange Indians approached us. They seemed to be hunters, and were well armed; but I gathered from their broken English words that they had been unsuccessful, and wanted something to eat. I of course gave them what they wanted, and they soon after went off, saying that the Indians were brothers of the white men, and apparently very well pleased with the acquaintance. Upon returning to camp that evening, we had a grand buffalo roast, and enjoyed ourselves with our first good meal since leaving the Humboldt Mountains.

The next day we killed several deer, an elk and six antelopes; the next, four deer and seven or eight foxes; and the next, had another buffalo hunt. On this occasion we discovered a large herd in a steep, rocky ravine. As we approached, they raised their heads, snuffed and blew the air, and then, turning their tails, ran up the ravine. We followed, and, upon firing, wounded two, one of which Gray pursued, and Tuolumne the other, while I followed the main herd. The course they had taken rose very rapidly, and this worried them so much that I soon overtook and wounded a third, which Gray and Tuolumne, who had despatched theirs, assisted me in killing, — by which time the main herd had reached another valley and disappeared. Having as many as we wanted, we pursued no further, but set ourselves to work dressing the game thus procured and packing it to camp. On the road back, we killed an elk and a number of foxes, the skins of which, as well as those of the buffaloes, we were careful to preserve.

After spending a day in preparing our provisions, we proceeded again in a northerly direction, through a rough country. In the course of a few hours, we fell in with several white hunters, who told us that we would have to travel about seventy miles before we could meet the emigration trail running through Salt Lake City. We travelled along in a mountain-

ous country that day, and the next morning started
forward before sunrise, being anxious to reach the
trail. Gray rode ahead to look out the route, but he
soon came hastily back to say that, if I wanted to
fight a Rocky Mountain grizzly bear, he could take
me to one in a few minutes; but he added that it
would be foolish to go after him, as our team was
already loaded down. It would be foolish, I replied,
to allow the first Rocky Mountain grizzly we had met
to escape; and I at once determined to give him
battle.

Directing Tuolumne to follow, I started off in the
direction pointed out, and, upon reaching a bushy
ravine, saw the bear busy eating berries in the bushes.
We looked with curious eyes on the beast, of whose
kind we had heard so much and knew so little. He
appeared small in comparison with the grizzly bear of
California, but so many stories had been told of his
ferocity that it was not without misgivings that we
commenced the attack. As there were trees in the
neighborhood, I felt pretty safe in any event, and accordingly, creeping up, gave a sharp whistle, such as
invariably starts the California bear; but it appeared
to have no more effect upon the Rocky Mountain grizzly than the singing of the birds. I then uttered a
yell, to see if that would rouse him; and he looked up
and snuffed, but did not seem to be very much disturbed. I at once saw that I had a different animal
to deal with from the California grizzly, and for a
while his imperturbability appeared terrible, — like
the consciousness and carelessness of immense power.

The reputation of the beast made me feel nervous, and it was some time before I could steady my aim; indeed before firing I was extraordinarily careful to see that my pistol and knife were ready for a close encounter, and that a tree was near by for refuge. Having thus provided for the worst, I drew up my rifle, and bored the bear through the heart. He bounded up a few times, and fell. I hastily reloaded, and, though I knew from the struggles and character of the groans of the beast that he was dying, planted a second bullet under the butt of the ear, and stilled him forever. Thus was I victorious over the first Rocky Mountain grizzly I ever saw.

Proceeding, according to my practice, to cut the bear's throat, I noticed that he had light-colored eyes, and coarse, long, shaggy hair, almost white. He would weigh about five hundred pounds, and was as large as any bear I saw in the Rocky Mountains; for it is seldom that they ever exceed this size. Taking the hide and a portion of his meat, Tuolumne and I proceeded on and soon overtook the team, managing, on the road, to kill a beautiful silver-gray fox, the skin of which we also preserved. We travelled thence till late at night over a rugged but well-timbered country, and camped on a small stream. Throughout the day the signs of game were plenty on every side, but we did not delay; and for several days longer we continued our route, until finally, in the neighborhood of where the emigration trail crosses Muddy Fork, we made a general camp.

CHAPTER XI.

THE ROCKY MOUNTAINS.

IT had been my intention, in travelling to the
Rocky Mountains, not only to hunt and collect animals, but also to trade with that great stream of
migrating humanity, which, in search of the gold-
bearing hills or the stock-raising valleys of California, poured over the Rocky Mountains by thousands
during the whole summer. Before commencing at
this business, however, I determined to visit Salt
Lake City, which was only fifty or sixty miles distant, and see that noted head-quarters of polygamy
and the Mormons. It was now the first day of July;
and, as it is the custom of all true Americans, in
whatever place they may be, to make the Fourth of
July a holiday, I planned the trip in such a manner

as to give us the Fourth in the city. We accordingly packed up our mules and horse with meat and hides, and taking also two young panthers, two young wolves, and two fawns, set out towards the Mormon head-quarters. On the road we overtook many wagons and families, and disposed of our meats to them, long before our arrival in the city. The greater portion brought a fair price, but much we gave away to wayworn and weary sufferers, of whom there were very many in whose behalf our sympathies were called into exercise.

After travelling two days and a half, we reached the city on the afternoon of July 3rd, and soon sold our hides and young animals, at excellent prices. We then took a view of the city, and spent the rest of the day in passing around and looking at the wide, square lots into which it is divided. On the Fourth, there was a celebration and a speech in the temple, but I paid little attention to the Mormon talk. I thought then, as I think now, that it does no good to listen to what the Mormons have to say, but it may do much to look at what they have done, and what they are doing.

It has been usual to call these singular people fanatics, and I can see no harm in giving them their proper names; but when it is considered that all the world is more or less fanatical, and that it is the privilege of only a few to deserve the name of true liberality, I can hardly look upon the Mormons with what is generally considered orthodox contempt. There must be something good, among the much evil, to keep them together, and their wonderful labors in their Rocky Mountain city attest the fact that there is at least earnestness and vigor in their counsels. They are equal to the Jews of old in their hatred of the Gentiles; but it seems to me that their entire organization and polity is much more of a political than of a religious character.

Upon our return, we spent a day in putting things about camp to rights, and the next day set out upon a buffalo hunt, and managed to drive a large herd up a rocky ravine in the side of a mountain. Gray wounded one, which turned to fight; but Tuolumne laid him low with another ball. At the same time I wounded a second, which we also killed. Pursuing up the ravine, we killed a third, when the drove passed over into another ravine and escaped. After dressing our meat, we watched it through the night, and the next morning Gray and one of the Indians took a portion of it on the mules and horse to the emigration trail, to trade it off, while Tuolumne and I used Lady Washington to pack the remainder to camp. The Lady was almost as tractable with Tuolumne as with myself, and would obey him with nearly as much submission. She was thus, under all circumstances, a very valuable assistant; and it may truly be said, that on many occasions she was of as much use to us as a mule or a horse would have been.

For a week or two we continued in this neighborhood hunting buffaloes and other game, and trading; but the market by degrees became dull, and we moved up past Fort Bridger to a spot on Ham's Fork,

between the trails to Salt Lake City and the bend
of Bear River. Here we made a general camp again,
and commenced a system of hunting and trading,
which we carried on with more or less success for a
week and more, during which time we also had several notable adventures with grizzly bears.

On the day after arriving there, as Tuolumne and I
were hunting, we discovered a grizzly in a ravine.
He had been wallowing in a pool, and was covered
with mud, which dripped from his long and shaggy
hair. As he came leisurely towards us, he would
now and then lie down upon the grass and endeavor
to rub the mud from his coat; as he drew near, snuffing the air as if he suspected an ambush, I fired and
struck him in the nostrils. Tuolumne immediately
stepped from his concealment to shoot; but the bear
seeing his movement made a rush towards him, and
with such ferocity that the boy dropped his rifle and
sprang up a pine-tree, which happened to stand convenient.

The bear stopped when he came to the rifle, which
he poked and smelled and snuffed for a considerable
time, notwithstanding Tuolumne used his pistol and
fired six shots into him. The balls, however, appeared not to penetrate through the fat, and the brute
paid little attention to them, merely grunting. After
turning the rifle over several times, the beast placed
one paw upon the stock and the other under the barrel, as if about to break it, and, in doing so, rose on his
haunches. This afforded me a fair aim at his breast;
and being by this time reloaded, I planted a ball in

his heart, where the first ought to have struck. And yet even this did not kill him, so tenacious of life was he; on the contrary, he ran at least three hundred yards to the pool in which he had been wallowing. I pursued, but, finding him in his death-struggles, did not fire again. Upon examination we found that my rifle-ball had passed through the apex of the heart, but the pistol-balls were only imbedded in the fat of the sides.

After cutting up the bear and washing the hide, we made a dinner of bear-meat, and then threw ourselves in the shade of a tree to pass the heat of the day. In the evening, soon after we started on our return to camp, we discovered another grizzly bear upon a knoll. He saw us as soon as we saw him, and I supposed he would attack us; but, instead of doing so, he merely rose on his hind legs and looked curiously at us. I directed Tuolumne to fire, which he accordingly did, but at the discharge the beast gave a tremendous growl, and bounded off over the hill out of sight. Had he been a California grizzly, he would doubtless have attacked us, at least after the fire; but the Rocky Mountain beast is not always so ready to fight. He is more dangerous than the California grizzly in his disposition to follow up a trail, but in a fight, though terrible enough, he is not to be feared like his cousin of the Sierra.

The next day, Gray having succeeded well in disposing of meat to the emigrants, we made another buffalo hunt. After going a few miles we came upon a herd of about one hundred, which we surrounded.

At a concerted signal the whole party advanced, and the buffaloes were so bewildered that for a short time they knew not which way to turn; so that we were able to rush into their midst and fire at close quarters. The leg of one was broken, but the others fled. Leaving the Indians to finish the wounded one, we pursued the drove, and managed to overtake and kill another. Upon our return to camp, we unexpectedly met a little brown bear cub, about four months old, which seemed to be lost. I endeavored to catch it, but not being able, fired; and that evening we had supper of its flesh.

During all the time that we were in this country, we continued night after night to keep a guard over our camp; for though there was not much to lose in the way of property, it was still all that we possessed. The guard usually consisted of two persons, relieved at midnight by two others. The last guard, on one particular night, were Tuolumne and one of the Indians, who reported to me in the morning that a strange bear had entered camp, made the acquaintance of Lady Washington, and, after a *tête-à-tête* of an hour or so, had retired again, in a very peaceable and orderly manner, to the mountain from which he came. They had not called me because of my fatigue during the day, they said, and because the visitor had been so civil that they did not think it necessary to disturb me. I however directed that if such a case should occur again, they should not fail to let me know.

The next night the visitor returned, and, being in-

formed of it, I got up. It was about midnight, but
the moon was shining, so that we could easily see him
approaching the Lady, who was chained to a tree as
usual at night. I took my rifle with the intention of
killing the beast, but, on second thought, concluded
that it would be more to our advantage to give him
the freedom of the camp, and, accordingly, did not
disturb him. He remained until dawn, and then
retired. On the occasion of his return the next
night, — for, like a loyal lover, he was very atten-
tive, — Gray advised that he should be killed; but I
opposed the proposition, and, for what I know, he still
roams in his native haunts.

By this time we had amassed quite a sum of cash
by selling buffalo-meat to the emigrants, and had
purchased for ourselves a second horse among other
things; but these adventures filled my head with ideas
of bear hunting, and I determined to give the buffaloes
respite, and turn my attention to the grizzlies exclusively. We accordingly moved on to a deep ravine,
covered with chaparral and trees. Soon after reaching it, we found a fresh bear-track, and, hitching
our horses, followed it up by crawling among the
bushes, and presently came upon an old bear playing with two cubs in a pool. She would poke one in
the water with her paw, and then the other, and,
as they jumped back towards her, she would poke
them off again, — presenting thus an interesting and
beautiful sight; for what can be more interesting or
beautiful, among animals as well as among human beings, than to see a mother playing with her offspring?

I looked a considerable time upon the scene, and did not fire till she appeared about ready to withdraw, when, as it happened, I merely broke her shoulder. She rushed for me at once, but I seized my rifle by the barrel and struck her over the head, and then jumped to the bed of the creek and drew my knife, with which I dealt her a stab in the flank. As I struck, she reared upon me and bore me to the ground; and, while she placed her paw upon my head, bit me severelv in the shoulder, the marks of which I still bear. I lay perfectly still, however, and in a few minutes the cubs began bawling, when the old bear, seeing no resistance in me, turned to them. Seizing this opportunity, I sprang to my feet again and drew my pistol; but, observing at a glance that the stab in the flank was fatal, I did not fire. The poor brute was evidently dying, though she tried to pacify her cubs. Although I stood but a few yards distant, she had not the strength to come at me; for she had bled, and was still bleeding, profusely. As I watched her licking her young and giving them her last attentions, as if conscious of the approach of death, I thought there was something of the human in the bear, and was sorry I had shot so affectionate a mother.

As she expired, I looked around for my companions, but they were nowhere to be seen. I looked up to heaven, and exclaimed to myself, "The cowards leave me;" then I called as loud as I could, "Gray, Gray!" He answered, "Halloo!" "Where are you?" cried I. He replied at a distance of about

a hundred yards, "I am here." I asked if he expected to help me there? and called that he should
come and catch these cubs, for I had despatched
the bear; but he asked, "Is she dead?" This
made me angry, and I replied, "She is dead, but
it was no coward that killed her." Gray grumbled
something in return, and came poking and cracking
through the brush, and exclaimed, "Adams, I thought
you were gone this time." "It is only cowards,"
said I, "who are *gone* in the hour of danger. You
have acted in this affair like a miserable coyote."
This language, at another time, would certainly have
been resented; but when a man accomplishes any
difficult deed, and particularly under such circumstances as these, he enjoys a certain degree of immunity, and can growl as he pleases.

I now directed Gray and Stanislaus to catch the
cubs; but, seeing that they were not quick enough,
I cried out impatiently, "You are more clumsy than
cowardly; see the Old Hunter catch them." I then
took off my cap, and, leaping with it upon the head
of one of the cubs, seized him with a powerful grip,
and, holding him up, cried, "See there!" Sanis-
laus answered he could catch the other, and, in a few
moments, did so; and thus we had two additions to
our stock of live bears, besides the body of the dam,
which we cut up as usual. The cubs were not more
than a month or two old, and had no teeth worth
mentioning; and, in this connection, it may be stated
that the grizzly bear generally cuts its teeth at about
two months. It does not have full teeth till its matu-

rity, at about two years of age, though it has a dangerous mouth at six months. Every year a ring is added to its tusks, — the first ring being for the second year; and as the animal sometimes reaches the age of fifteen or sixteen years, a corresponding number of rings are found.

We camped this night near the scene of the capture, partly on account of the lateness of the hour, and partly on account of my wound, — which, however, gave my companions more alarm than it did me, or than it merited. During the night our cubs yelped dreadfully; and, as we had nothing to feed them with it was impossible to quiet them until we reached the general camp the next day, when we gave them water, flour, and sugar, mixed together, and they thrived well. One of them, which I subsequently named Funny Joe, became a companion for me, next in my esteem to Ben Franklin and Lady Washington.

In a few days after this adventure, finding the buffaloes growing scarce in the region, we moved on over a rugged, mountainous country to Smith's Fork of Bear River, where we hunted for several days, and had good success. One evening, while here, we came across a grizzly feeding on the carcass of a buffalo. As he was very busily engaged at his meal, I had no difficulty in approaching, and fired at his heart. The ball appeared to strike correctly, but had a singular effect; for the bear, instead of rushing at me or running off, wheeled around like a dog trying to catch his tail, — different from any bear I ever saw before or since. He seemed, indeed, to be crazy; probably some nerve intimately connected with the brain had been injured. He continued thus to turn around until Gray and Tuolumne rushed up and planted their balls in his body, when he jumped up and rushed towards us; but, as he did so, I planted a fourth ball in his breast, and he fell dead. I had some curiosity in examining him afterwards, and found that my first ball had struck the spine; and this, I presume, was the cause of his singular action. It is, doubtless, no impossible thing for a bear to be affected with insanity, even without mechanical injury to the brain; but this disease is one of the greatest of rarities, except among domesticated animals, — and even among them only in cases where the laws of nature are outrageously violated. Disease of any kind among wild animals is rare; and I am well satisfied, reasoning by analogy, that the long list of ailments which plague the human family are nearly all of its own making; in other words, they are adjuncts of the abuses of civilization.

CHAPTER XII.

THE SIERRA NEVADA AGAIN.

ABOUT the first of August, Gray came in one evening and stated that he wished to close our engagement. He said that he had met friends, who were on their way to the Atlantic States, and that he desired to accompany them. I did all in my power to dissuade him, but found it of no avail; and we moved up to the trading-post, where his friends were recruiting, and proceeded to settle our accounts. We sold out everything we could, and divided the proceeds and the remainder of the property in accordance with the provisions of our agreement, — he receiving one third and I two thirds. When all was done, I had left, as my portion of the wild stock, besides the Lady and Ben, two bears, two panthers — which soon afterwards died, — two deer, two wolves, various foxes and skins, and about one thousand dollars in coin. After the division, Gray withdrew and took up his camp with his friends; and this was the last I ever saw of him. He was a good hunter, but, like most hunters, not over fond of grizzly bears.

The day after Gray left us, I concluded to make a safe deposit of my money, and sent Tuolumne, Stanislaus, and the Indians on a hunt, for I did not wish to let them know anything about it. When they were well out of sight, I pried up the bed of my wagon, and, going to work with auger and chisel, cut a hole several inches in extent in the heavy white-oak axletree. In this I deposited my purse, containing the money, and after plugging it up covered it over with tin, and then replaced the bed. While working, I was asked several times, by persons who happened to pass, what I was cutting the hole for; and they remarked that it would certainly weaken and injure the axletree. I replied that I wanted to have a mortise in which to hoist a pole, and stretch a canvas; but in every case the questioners seemed to cast a look of compassion on me, possibly thinking I was not very sound in the head, and passed on.

The next day we set out on our return to California, intending to take the emigration road, and hunt only sufficiently to provide for our own wants. Accordingly we proceeded by the way of Fort Hall and Lewis's Fork, along the regular road, until we again approached the boundaries of California. In the course of the travel, we picked up three horses, six cows, and two oxen, which had been abandoned by the emigrants; and travelling along slowly, as was neces-

sary with these worn-out animals, we reached the foot
of the Sierra Nevada, (near where I had crossed in
the spring,) towards the end of September. There
was already considerable snow on the peaks, and before attempting to cross I directed a camp to be
made, and determined to spend several days to recruit.

Since leaving the Rocky Mountains we had not
seen a single bear except our pets, but as soon as we
camped under the Sierra, the beast was not long in
paying his attentions to us. The very first night of
our encampment I was waked up with information of
beasts among the cattle, and going out to ascertain
the difficulty, discovered the long, whitish hairs of a
huge grizzly waving in the breeze. He had killed
one of my cows, and was lapping the blood as it ran
from her neck, into which he had eaten. There was
only starlight, but I knew my game intimately, and
did not for a moment think of letting him off without
full payment for the care and trouble I had had in
nursing the cow. Accordingly, posting Tuolumne and
Stanislaus in positions behind trees, as a reserve in
case of necessity, I crept up to a small clump of
bushes near the bear, and, preparing my arms, raised
my rifle. The bear was busy tearing the flesh of the
dead cow, and did not perceive me; but as I whistled
he jumped upon his hind legs and fronted towards
me, and I planted the ball in the right place. He
fell over, and, at the same moment, drawing my knife,
I leaped upon him and plunged it to his heart; for I
knew that should he have time to get up, my life

might pay the forteit of my slowness. Happily the
ball and knife together gave him his quietus, and,
with the exception of being knocked over by his
death-struggle, I escaped unharmed. As I fell, the
boys rushed up to assist, but the bear expired in a
few moments; and we cut him up, and fried out of
him about fifteen gallons of oil at our leisure.

On the fifth day after reaching this place we again
yoked up, and commenced the passage of the mountains, which we accomplished in a few days. The
soft snow which we encountered gave us much difficulty, and kept us diligently at work brushing it from
the wheels of our wagon, but by persistently pushing
along we succeeded in reaching the summit, and then
ran down as fast as possible on the California side,
through familiar scenes. All this then wild region
has since been taken up by private owners, and an
immense reservoir of water, for mining purposes, has
been made of the flat which I used to cross daily with
my team. And thus, I have no doubt, it would be
found that in many of the spots where I fought bears,
and saw nothing but a wilderness, there is now im-
provement and civilization. The varied drama of
social life, not the adventures of a lonely hunter, is
now being enacted there.

In the course of a few days I reached my old camping-ground near the head waters of the Tuolumne
River; but, alas for the stability of earthly things!
there had been a fire in the region, and my old habitation and all my traps had been burned to ashes.
With the exception of the tools, which had been con-

cealed in the old cave, not a vestige of my camping fixtures and apparatus remained. However, we had stout hearts and willing hands, and going to work, put up, in the course of a week, a new cabin and stable, both snug and tight, and laid in a stock of hay for winter consumption, and also built three traps. In a few days after all this work was done, the Indians who had been with me during the summer took their departure; and, as they went, I gave them enough of an outfit and money to make them nabobs among their people; but Tuolumne and Stanislaus remained and assisted in the duties of camp.

In a few weeks after my return, I received letters from my brother William, who was then at San Francisco, informing me of a contract he had made to send two large and one small grizzly bear to Lima, in South America, and requesting to know whether they could be provided at short notice. I replied, by letter, that I had a large and a small bear, — referring to two at Howard's, — and thought that in a few weeks I could provide another; — and, as fortune willed it, in a few nights afterwards we caught a large bear in one of the traps. I now immediately wrote my brother that I would deliver the three bears at Stockton at a certain time, when he should be present, or have an agent present, to receive them. I then set to work to build a cage for the last bear, and in the meanwhile despatched Tuolumne to Howard's for a team, which he brought up; and in a few days afterwards, everything being prepared, I set out with the bear in its cage upon the wagon for Howard's. There, I engaged a teamster to haul the bears which were at Howard's, and we two set out in company for Stockton. Nothing worthy of special note occurred until we approached the city of Stockton, when a blacksmith of the place accosted us, and wanted to know what we had in our wagons. I answered that we had grizzly bears. He replied that we had no business taking bears into the city, and went on to say that a man named Dunbar had been killed by one a few days before; "and," continued he, "we are not going to have any more fights in this city." Now, as this blacksmith was a citizen, and talked like a citizen, he put me in mind of a certain public-spirited smith, named Demetrius, who once stirred up a sedition in the city of Ephesus, as is related in the Acts of the Apostles. I called the modern smith's attention to the ancient smith's story, cautioned him against the dangers of uproar, and drove on.

I suppose I must have presented quite a figure with my buckskin costume and unshaven face at Stockton, for I found myself followed by a large crowd; and when the cages were placed upon the wharf for shipment by steamer to San Francisco, there was a great multitude of people collected. Some of them, more curious than wise, poked sticks at, and otherwise annoyed, the bears, until one individual happening to get too close to one of the cages, suddenly lost a pawful of meat, the want of which probably interferes with his comfort, while sitting, to this day. The consequence at the time, as was to have been anticipated, was an excitement; and the gentleman, so unceremoniously treated, drew his pistol and swore revenge. Now, I have always been an admirer of that passage in Hamlet which runs, "Nay, an thou'lt mouth, I'll rant as well as thou," and snatching out my own pistol, I informed the gentleman that the bear had committed nothing more than a justifiable assault and battery, and I would, therefore, stand by it to the last wag of my eyelids. The gentleman swore not a little at this, and I ranted in return, while the crowd shouted, "Hurrah for the Wild Yankee." This interference of the crowd cooled the gentleman's ardor, and he soon afterwards withdrew; but the crowd remained, and, as soon as the animals were shipped, I could do no more than ask them to drink at my expense; and they were not backward, as my purse soon experienced.

A Californian crowd is very different from a crowd in any other part of the world of which I have had any experience. It is usually composed of men who have seen much of life, and learned much of human nature. Though given to excitement, and disposed often to disregard the formulas of society, they almost invariably arrive at the moral right of a subject, and do justice with more unerring certainty than the most nicely-adjusted legal tribunals, which are too much bound up and hampered by antiquated dicta and decisions. A spectator is surprised at the order and temperance of counsel, which actuates the motions of a California meeting. Although a thousand technically unlawful assemblies have taken place in the State, there has seldom been such a thing as a tumult.

CHAPTER XIII.

SAMSON.

The Tracks of a huge Grizzly. On the Watch. Appearance of the
Bear. Building of a Trap. The Snowy Season. The Tracks at the
Trap. Watching the Trap. The Roaring of the Bear. The Grizzly
in the Trap. The Violence of the Bear. Subjugation. Samson's
Size and Disposition. Removal of Camp. Trapping at the Mouth
of the Merced River. Willow Timber. Final Departure of Tuo-
lumne and Stanislaus. Their Character. Engagement of Combe.
Condition of Samson. Caging of Samson. Loading the Cage.
Howard's Journey to Corral Hollow. Corral Hollow. Contract
with Wright. Our Hunting. The Kern River Emigration. Combe.
Wright's Fear of Grizzly Bears.

I HAVE come now, in the course of my story, to the
capture of Samson, the largest specimen of the grizzly species, perhaps, that ever was taken alive. I discovered his huge tracks in a ravine which was full of
rocks, trees, and bushes, a few days after my return
from Stockton to my mountain camp. No sooner had
I seen the prints of this magnificent animal's paws than
I determined to capture him at all hazards; and the
next morning, before day, I placed myself upon the
watch, for the purpose of finding out the locality of
his den, and choosing the proper spot for a trap.

After lying behind a rock for about an hour and a
half, happening to cast my eyes down the trail, I beheld the monster advancing, with his head raised and
snuffing the air. I had never seen so large a bear

SAMSON

before; he looked like a moving mountain, and my heart fluttered for fear of being discovered; but he passed on up the ravine, and disappeared in the chaparral. I had seen enough for my purpose, but, as a matter of precaution, remained still for some time after he had disappeared; and then, getting up, I chose a spot, which he would certainly pass in his nightly excursions, and to which there was a fair road for a wagon. The next day I took the boys and the oxen, and we went to work felling and hauling logs, and in the course of a week finished the largest, strongest, and best trap we had ever built.

It was now about the middle of November, and the rainy season, or what in the mountains is more appropriately called the snowy season, had set in. The game had commenced moving down the Sierra, and we killed various bears, deer, and other game; but for a week or more we neither heard nor saw anything of the big bear, and feared that he had left the region. One morning, however, when we had nearly despaired of ever seeing him again, it was evident that he had not only visited but actually been in the trap. His tracks were plainly to be seen, but for some unaccountable reason or other the trap had not sprung. The fact of his presence renewed my almost extinguished hopes, and I immediately adjusted the trap with the greatest nicety; and to make still more sure, I determined to pass the next night within hearing distance; so that, in case of catching, I might be certain of securing him. At the same time, as it was necessary to be particular not to disturb the trail, —

as when disturbed bears will often leave a region, — I erected a small tent about half a mile down the ravine, and about five hundred feet lower in level than the trap, where Tuolumne and I slept for two nights without either provisions or fire; and, as will be readily imagined, we had rather a comfortless time of it, and particularly so as we waited in vain to hear of our expected visitor.

In the middle of the third night, however, I was waked out of sleep by a terrific roaring. It was the awfullest roaring and echoing in the mountains I ever heard, with the single exception of an appalling thunderstorm in the Humboldt Mountains, which occurred the summer before. I jumped up at once and ran out of the tent to listen what could be the cause of the noise, and soon concluded that it could be nothing else but the bear in my trap. The night was cold, with a light snow on the ground, but I called Tuolumne, and we at once lighted our torches and proceeded to the trap. As we approached, the bear made a tremendous lunge towards us, and I thought for a moment that he would burst out; but the trap was made of the strongest timbers, and withstood his assaults. We directly built a rousing fire, and then went to work securing the trap with additional timbers; for, by peeping in at the cracks, we soon satisfied ourselves that our prize was one of the largest in the land.

I was compelled to watch this trap night and day for more than a week, during which time Tuolumne brought provisions and water, and some nights would remain with me. During this time, the bear continued violent; he would bite and tear the logs with his teeth and claws, and frequently made the structure fairly tremble with his prodigious strength. We had sometimes to beat him with an iron rod, and at others to throw in firebrands — which he fought with the same effect that the viper bit the file — to prevent him tearing his prison to pieces. On the eighth or ninth day, however, his spirit weakened, and he appeared to grow reconciled to his fate. When this species of subjugation takes place, there is no further trouble with a bear until he is removed to a new cage; and then the same process, though usually not so severe, has to be gone through with.

Such was the manner in which I caught the huge Samson, whose weight is over fifteen hundred pounds, and whose massive proportions have for years been the admiration of all who have seen him. He was then in his prime, and has grown none since; the only effect of confinement and good living has been to make him lazy and imperious, like a pampered monarch, and to change his shaggy, coarse hair from gray to brown. His strength was so immense that for a long time I was compelled to keep him in the trap in which he was caught, it being dangerous to remove him; and when, in the course of a few weeks, my business called me away to another part of the country, I engaged four wood-choppers, who were at work cutting timber for a mining flume in the neighborhood, to feed him; and it was not until more than a month afterwards that I felt safe in caging and hauling him away.

Meanwhile the season advanced towards the middle
of the winter; and, finding game becoming scarce in
the higher regions of the mountains, we moved our
camp to the Merced River below Yosemite, taking
with us all our camp-fixtures, stock, and animals, with
the exception of Samson, who, as above stated, was
too large and savage to be removed. We also built
traps there, and managed, in the course of a few weeks,
to capture several grizzly bears, which we disposed of
at good rates. One, a female weighing about six hundred pounds, gave us trouble of a peculiar kind; her
capture forming a unique example in the many curious
adventures of my career. She had entered a trap
at night, but, by the time we reached it, she had
gnawed off one of the timbers, and had her head
through the hole, and, indeed, was about escaping.
Seeing the position of affairs, I leaped from my horse
and hastily cut a stout switch, with which I gave her
a smart rapping over the nose and face before she
would draw back. The timber thus gnawed was willow, which we had foolishly put into the trap; but
now we replaced it with oak, though it took us a long
time, with much prying, lifting, and tugging, to get
the oak in the right place. While we worked, we
also had to fight the bear continually, as she seemed
determined to come out; but at last she was secured.

Towards spring, I had occasion to go to Hornitos,
and desired Tuolumne to accompany me; but he
replied that there were bad people at Hornitos, and
he would rather not go. Whom he spoke of he did
not specify, nor could I get from him his reasons;

but finally he said that he had not seen his own people for a year, and wished to make them a visit, — to which, of course, I readily consented. I then gave him and Stanislaus a horse, complete suits of buckskin clothes, and about one hundred dollars in gold coin, with which they set out, highly delighted, promising to return in a month; but this was the last I ever saw of these two excellent boys, for in a few weeks after this time I removed from the region, and never returned, except for a few days at a time. In recalling their many good qualities to mind, I cannot but remark that, in comparing ourselves with the Indians, we are all too apt to disregard the centuries of slow advancement which have removed us from the savage state. We are apt to look upon the roaming tribes as an inferior race, but the inference is unauthorized and unjust.

Upon my return from Hornitos, I met a young man named Combe, and, he being a robust fellow in want of employment, I hired him to take care of my camp, while I made arrangements to bring down my big bear Samson. I then proceeded to Sonora, where I purchased a large cage, and engaged a teamster and a yoke of oxen, with which, in addition to my own, we drove up the mountains to where Samson was confined. It was now nearly two months since his capture, but we found that, although he had fallen away somewhat in flesh or fat, he was nearly as savage as at first; and it required several days of great trouble to get him into the cage.

The manner in which we finally succeeded in

removing him from the trap to the cage, was notable. Finding it impossible to drive him from one to
the other, as they were placed side by side with the
doors open between them, I determined to pull him
with oxen; and, taking a log chain, managed, after
great difficulty, to get a loop of it around his neck.
I then passed the chain through the door of the trap
and through the cage, and hitched a yoke of oxen to
the far end. While the oxen pulled in front, I poked
with an iron rod behind, and thus he advanced inch
by inch, until he got to the doors leading from one to
the other, when he suddenly bounded into the cage,
and commenced tearing around, as if he were going
to demolish it. The teamster, during this time, was
on the top of the cage, and I called to him to drop
the door. He did so, and thus we had the bear
caged; but he continued to act so violently that I
had to remain at the cage the whole night, and use
the iron rod and firebrands to quell his turbulent
rage, pretty much in the same way as when he was
first captured.

The next morning we took off the wheels on one
side of the wagon, and, proceeding much the same as
persons who load saw-logs, we managed to boost the
cage up, and, replacing the wheels and yoking up,
started on our road. The load was so heavy and the
way so bad, however, that our progress was very
slow; and it took three days to reach Howard's,
where I determined to leave Samson, as also most
of my pets, during the coming summer. I had as
yet chalked out no campaign for the season, but,

having heard that there were many California lions in
Corral Hollow, near Livermore's Pass, in the Coast
Range, I determined to go there, and, accordingly,
soon broke up camp on the Merced, and sending all
my animals, save Lady Washington, Ben Franklin
and Rambler, to Howard's, we drove over to that
place, reaching it in two or three days' travel.

Corral Hollow is a narrow valley, nine or ten miles
long, with steep mountains on both sides. A stream
of water runs through it during the winter and
spring, discharging into the San Joaquin plains; but
in the summer this is mostly dry. A wagon road
from San Francisco to the San Joaquin passed
through the valley; and, at the time of which I
speak, there was a small public-house there, kept by
two men, named Wright and Carroll. With the former of these men, I soon made a bargain to hunt in
the neighborhood; and we immediately set ourselves
to work and built three traps, choosing out the wildest, roughest, and rockiest cañons of that very rough
region for their positions. When the traps were
completed, we hunted deer with success, and sold
their meat with profit to persons who passed along
the road.

It so happened that this was the period of the Kern
River excitement, and hundreds of people were pouring
into the San Joaquin Valley from all quarters, on their
way to the famous Kern River mines. Those who
came from San Francisco and the regions thereabouts,
travelled generally by the way of Livermore's Pass
and the Hollow, and we thus had the opportunities of

a fair market, — an advantage which we were not
slow to improve. During the hunts here, Combe,
who evinced little hunting spirit, remained in camp;
but, as I had engaged him principally to take care of
and feed my animals in my absence, I did not find
fault with his want of enterprise or lack of courage.
My hunts were made entirely alone, or with Wright,
who was a good enough hunter of deer, but, like all
other men who have had little experience, he was
dreadfully afraid of a grizzly bear.

CHAPTER XIV.

CORRAL HOLLOW.

The Devil's Den. A Grizzly Dam and Cubs. Wright's Flight. Attack upon the Bears. Wright on Top of a Rock. My second Shot. Combat with the second Cub. Passage of Words with Wright. Kern River Adventurers. Their Admiration. Red Woods Hunters Their Marksmanship. My Decision. Return to the Sierra Nevada. Perilous Adventure with a Bear. Assistance of Ben and Rambler. Our Wounds. Care of Ben. My Gratitude to him. Return to Corral Hollow. A scoundrel Visitor. His scurvy Trick. Pursuit of him. The Oil of Panthers. Visit of Scarf. Our Meal on Panthermeat. My sudden Sickness. My Medicine. A Night of Agony. Scarf's Sickness. Poison. The Wretch's Boasts. Speculations about the Poisoning. Cautions.

ONE day Wright and I were hunting in what is called the Devil's Den, a dreadfully rough and deep cañon, full of brush and rocks so heaped and piled together that a person has almost to crawl wherever he passes through it. I had discovered a bed of coal there, and also sulphur springs, and I was pointing them out to Wright, when suddenly we were startled by the snort of a grizzly dam which had two yearling cubs. When we first became aware of her presence, she was standing just before us on her hind legs, and evidently offering battle. I saw at a glance that Wright was not the man for such a situation, for he trembled like a leaf, and then, turning his back, cried out to run; and suiting the action to the word, on his own behalf, he soon left me alone. I knew very well there was no use of running, under the circumstances; nor indeed did I feel any disposition to do so, for it was seldom that I ever let a bear escape me; and it was pretty evident, on this occasion in particular, that if I did not kill her, she would kill me. As there was nothing to be hoped for from Wright, I paid no attention to where he went; but, giving my whole attention to the bear, I watched my opportunity as she came snorting towards me, and planted a ball fairly in her heart. As she received it, she fell over backwards, and never rose afterwards.

No sooner had I thus fired than I began reloading, and, without looking up, cried out to Wright why he did not fire at the cubs. His voice quivered as he answered, that they kept bobbing around so that he could not procure aim. I turned to see where the man was, and there he sat on top of a high rock, vainly trying to hold his rifle steady, while the cubs were bawling and yelping about their dying mother. "When you do get aim, shoot," said I; and at the same time, running up to a clump of bushes within a few yards of the cubs, I stretched out one by a ball at the butt of the ear; when directly, crack! went Wright's rifle; but his ball could hardly have come within twenty yards of the cub. Wright always pretended that he did really shoot at it, but I questioned it then, and I doubt it now; he was too much scared to shoot at anything.

I immediately proceeded to reload a second time, but the remaining cub discovered and charged at me too soon. Seeing that I could not get my rifle loaded in time, I dropped it and drew my knife. There was no great danger, except of being scratched, so I met the cub half way; and as he reared to strike, I caught him with my left hand by the long hair on the under-jaw, and plunged my knife into his abdomen, burying it to the hilt; then ripping it out, I thrust it in behind the fore shoulder, and reached his heart. He had given me a severe blow upon the thigh, but only one; and as the life poured from his side, I let him drop and die at my feet.

Having thus killed the three bears, I turned to see what Wright was doing by this time; and there he still sat on the rock, just as he had been sitting before. He had not even reloaded, nor made any attempt to do so. As I turned towards him, he cried, "Are they dead, Adams?" "No," said I; "you had better stay there till they stop kicking." "Well," continued he, "I thought they would kill you, surely; and I saved my life while I could." "That's a comfortable doctrine," said I; "but your bones too would have whitened this valley, if they had killed me. You are a good climber, I see, but when you talk of running up rocks, look at these claws." Thus I talked while cutting the throats of the bears.

We let the bodies lie where we had killed them, and returned to camp, where we found a party of Kern River adventurers. When we told them the story of the three bears, a half dozen volunteered to go along and help pack the bodies in. They would hardly believe our report, and wanted to see with their own eyes; but when shown the truth of the story, by the wounds on the bodies, such as we had described, their incredulity gave place to wonder, and, if I mistake not, to some admiration of my powers.

In the course of a few days after this adventure, three hunters from the Red Woods came to my camp, and, stating that they had heard of my hunting, asked the privilege of accompanying me for a few days. I acquiesced, and we took a hunt, in the course of which we came on a she bear with a yearling cub. I soon stretched the dam upon the ground, and directed the Red Woods men to kill the cub. At the word, all three discharged their rifles, and the cub fell; but, when I came to examine him, I found but one wound. Upon calling attention to this curious circumstance, a contention sprang up as to who it was that fired that ball. Each one gave so many reasons why he could not have missed, that I amused myself for a long time laughing at them. They at last appealed to me to settle the controversy; and I decided that they had all shot into the same hole, — which was very satisfactory to all parties.

About this same time, Lady Washington presented me with a valuable addition to my collection of animals, which gave unmistakable evidences, in the form of the body and in the color of the hair, of having the blood of the Rocky Mountain bear in its composition; and I rejoiced that I had exercised so much forbearance towards the Lady's lover, the previous summer east of Salt Lake. The little fellow thrived well, and grew up to be the one known as Fremont, — a bear of considerable intelligence and sagacity, though not equal, in these respects, either to his dam or to Ben Franklin.

I had occasion, during my stay at Corral Hollow, to return for a few days to my old camp in the Sierra; and hitching up my wagon, and taking my bear Ben Franklin and my dog Rambler along, in a few days reached that favorite old spot. I anticipated that it would be my last visit to the place, and determined to have one more hunt before leaving it, perhaps, forever. Accordingly, calling my bear and dog, I started out, and made the old mountains ring again with the sound of my rifle, until, fatigued with roving, I turned back towards camp

As I was leisurely passing through a thicket of chaparral, I heard a stick crack at my side, and, upon turning, beheld a huge grizzly, which had three young cubs, in the act of springing at me. I tried to raise my rifle, but in an instant it was struck from my hand by the bear, and, with the same blow, I was thrown to the ground. Ben and Rambler were but a few paces behind at this time, and rushed forward, Rambler seizing the enemy's thigh, and Ben attacking her at the throat. This distracted her attention for a moment, at which I seized the opportunity to snatch my rifle and spring to one side, while the savage bit terribly into the head and neck of poor Ben. I uttered a terrific shout, and the old bear rose for an instant, when I fired a ball into her heart, and she fell over backwards. I then jumped upon her, and bathed my knife several times in her heart's blood.

All this was the work of a moment; but when I looked for Ben, he was bounding off for camp, with the blood streaming from his head, and yelling at every leap. I endeavored to call him back; but the little fellow was scared nearly to death, and soon disappeared. As for myself, I did not know at first that I was hurt; but, in a little while, the blood commenced dripping over my clothes, and I found that my scalp had been dreadfully torn by the brute; and she had bitten through my buckskin coat and flannel, making wounds, the scars of which still remain, in my neck.

With considerable difficulty, I managed to reach camp, where I found Ben lying under the wagon, licking his bleeding sides. The poor fellow had certainly saved my life, and I felt so grateful that at once I took him into the cabin and dressed his wounds before I dressed my own; and I continued paying unremitting care to him for nearly a week, when, finding him well enough to travel, I settled up my business in the region and departed. That was one of the narrowest escapes I ever had in all my hunting; and, as my preservation was due to Ben, the circumstance explains, to some extent, the partiality I have felt towards that noble animal. He has borne the scars of the combat upon his front ever since; and I take pride in pointing them out to persons who, I think, can appreciate my feelings towards him.

Upon my return to Corral Hollow, I learned that a large panther or cougar, such as is usually known as the California lion, had been prowling about one of the traps, and, on the next day, I went to the place, and set the snare with particular nicety, confidently expecting a prize in the morning. That same evening, as I was sitting at my camp fire, a shaggy-looking scoundrel, who carried a shot-gun, pistol, and bowie-knife, came up and asked the privilege of stopping overnight. He had a bad countenance; but never in my life did I turn a weary or a hungry traveller away from my fire, or refuse the offices of hospitality; nor did I now. On the contrary, I freely offered him a portion of my supper, a place to sleep at my fire, and a hearty, wholesome breakfast in the morning. I not only fed him, but I talked with him, and in answer to his questions spoke without reserve of my business in the Hollow, and the hopes I entertained of entrapping the lion. After breakfast, the scamp went away without thanking me; and in an hour or two afterwards, when I went up to my trap, I found that he had been there before me, and had shot, dragged out, and cut off and carried away the tail of, the panther, which, as I expected, had been trapped overnight. I knew that it could have been no other person than this fellow, who had played such a scurvy trick, and, being mounted and very angry, I took the road to Livermore's Pass, in the hopes of overtaking and punishing him. I rode nearly all day, but, not being able to find where he had gone, came back, packed the dead lion on my mule, and returned to camp.

The oil of panthers is good for sprains and bruises;

and with the intention of frying out some for future
use, I sat down at the root of a tree, and began cutting the body up. While so engaged, a man named
Scarf, the keeper of a sheep ranch five or six miles
below, happened to pass, and remarking that the
meat looked very nice, proposed making a meal of
it. I asked whether he had ever eaten any of the
kind. He replied that he had not, but, from the appearance, he knew it must be good. I remarked,
that I had frequently eaten panther's meat, and knew
that, though not the best of meat, it was certainly
not the worst; and forthwith we proceeded to roast
portions of the tender-loin and liver, of which we ate
heartily and with very good relish. After the meal,
Scarf smacked his lips, and proceeded on his way.
It was now nearly evening, and having one of my
traps to look after, about a mile distant, I ran up
towards it, but, getting into a perspiration, began to
feel disagreeable and very queer; — and God knows
I had cause. So ill did I soon become that I had
difficulty in getting back; my head was dizzy, my
eyes nearly blind, and all my members staggering, so
that I supposed death was approaching.

It happened that Combe was absent at this time,
but I managed, without assistance, to get at my stores,
and, taking out a bunch of wild tobacco, made and
drank a decoction, which caused me to vomit violently; and afterwards, I rolled myself in my blankets and tried to sleep; but my head felt like bursting
with pain, and during the entire night I lay in agony.
I thought that morning would never come, so pain-

fully did the time pass, — but it came at last; yet I
was unable to rise, and continued lying, more dead
than alive, until the sun rose, when I was suddenly
aroused by the voice of one of Scarf's men, who had
hurriedly come up to ask whether I was sick too. I
replied that death had a firm grasp upon me. "You
are poisoned," said he. "Poisoned?" said I; "that
cannot be; for there is no poison about camp." "It
was the wretch," said the man, "who killed the panther. He passed our ranch day before yesterday,
and had a bottle of poison, which he showed me.
Scarf is poisoned too, and is suffering in the same
manner as yourself." The man and I then compared
notes, and we soon concluded that his master and I
had been poisoned with some deadly drug contained
in the panther's meat, which we had so unsuspect-
ingly eaten. A few days afterwards, I learned from
one of the Livermore family that a fellow, answering
the description of the wretch who had fed at my
board, had visited the Pass, and exhibited a tail in
corroboration of a wonderful story which he told of
a fight with a panther in the mountains.

It has always been a source of speculation with me
in what manner the poison was introduced into the
panther, — whether before or after its death; but the
most plausible theory I can form is, that the wretch
tried the effect of the deadly drug upon the encaged
beast first, and shot it afterwards, — though he may
have poured a few crystals into the bullet-hole, after
shooting it. However this may have been, one lesson
I learned from the great jeopardy in which this ex-

periment placed me; and this was, to beware of game
not killed by myself or my friends in a country where
phosphorus, arsenic and strychnine are used for so
many purposes as they are in California. Indeed,
where such deadly poisons are daily employed for the
destruction of squirrels, panthers, bears and other
animals, too much care cannot be exercised in avoid-
ing flesh affected with them either directly or sec-
ondarily.

CHAPTER XV.

ALONG THE COAST RANGE.

THE Kern River excitement was one of those periodical visitations of a mild species of insanity, with which the people of California seem to have been afflicted from time to time, ever since the early days. It originated out of vague reports of gold in the gulches of the Kern River country, and in the course of a few months all the avenues leading to the region were crowded with adventurers. Miners passed daily on their way thither, during the period I was in Corral Hollow; but it was not long before they began returning, disappointed in their anticipations of sudden wealth, and deeply cursing the infatuation, which had induced them to go so far with so little profit.

It had been my object before this period to hunt in

the southern country, and as the Kern River emigration afforded an excellent chance of trading, I seized
the opportunity for a summer's hunt in that direction,
intending not only to visit the mines and sell game
to the miners, but to collect animals and see the
country. I accordingly provided myself with two
good horses in addition to my mules, and loaded my
wagon with stores of flour, coffee, sugar, tea, tobacco;
and among other things a keg of whiskey, which proved
a curse. I took also a quantity of mining tools, picks,
shovels, crow-bars, boards for rockers, buckets, pans,
and other mining implements. It had been my intention also to take my young man Combe along, but,
finding him not much disposed towards the romantic
trip, I engaged another young fellow named Drury,
a smart enough boy, but very lazy, and shamefully
fond of strong drink, as I soon learned to my cost.
My bear Lady Washington I chained as usual to the
axle-tree, but the bear Ben Franklin and his foster-
brother the dog Rambler followed loose.

We left Corral Hollow early in the morning, and
travelled southward along the eastern base of the
Coast Range of mountains till evening, when we
camped on a small stream, called Roro Mocho. Upon
unhitching, I directed Drury to prepare supper, and
busied myself with picketing the horses and feeding
the animals, which engaged my attention for an hour
or more; but what was my disgust upon returning to
the fire to find that Drury had broached the keg of
liquor, and was so much intoxicated as to be insensible. The beastly condition of the fellow gave me

unpleasant feelings, and boded bad for the future. I was perfectly willing that he should drink in moderation, but this was such an open and outrageous abuse at the outset of our journey that I determined to check his propensities in the bud; and, accordingly, lifting the keg from the wagon and seizing an axe, I knocked in the head, and poured the liquor out upon the ground. Without saying a word to Drury, I then prepared and ate my supper, and, wrapping myself in my blankets, went to sleep, leaving him to recover as he best could from the situation to which he had reduced himself.

About midnight I was aroused by the fellow's calling upon me to give him water; but I refused to get up and wait on him, and said that if he would make a beast of himself, he must take the consequences; if he wanted water, he had better crawl down to the creek, and throw himself into it until he soaked the liquor out, and then I would help him. He grumbled at this, and rolled about complaining of my hard treatment for about an hour, when, finally, I got up, gave him his blankets and fetched him water, of which he drank a large quantity, and soon fell into a sleep. In the morning I rose early, fed the animals, got my breakfast, and, being ready to start, called the fellow; but he still complained of being very sick. I retorted that he had made a hog of himself, and, therefore, I could feel no sympathy; and if he was too sick to come along, he might remain behind. At the same time I cautioned him that, if he repeated this conduct, I would be under the necessity of discharging

him at once from my service; and it would make no
difference where we might be; no confidence could
be reposed in a man who would get drunk.

In a few minutes afterwards I started on, as I had
said I would, and Drury followed with the dog and
bears. We continued thus a mile or two, when noticing that he had difficulty in keeping up, and that he
grew very pale, I took him in the wagon, and driving to the next ravine, stopped and put him to bed.
Leaving him sleeping, I went out with the Lady, Ben
and Rambler, on a short hunt, and killed three antelopes, which afforded provisions for several days. I
afterwards made supper and gave Drury a cup of
strong coffee, which had a good effect; and the next
morning he felt comparatively well, and we started
on our road very early.

As we were travelling along about mid-day, Rambler
started up an antelope, which seemed to be alone.
There were no trees near us, nothing but the grassy
plain stretching from the mountains to the San Joaquin, a distance of fifteen or twenty miles. The antelope, on being started, ran towards the faint line of
cotton-woods, which skirted the river; and Rambler
and Ben pursued as fast as their legs would carry
them. It was the most interesting race I ever saw,
for while the antelope ran for life, the hound kept
close at its heels. As for poor Ben, he tried with all
his might to keep up, but the further he went the
more he fell behind; and, in the course of a few minutes, he was loping over the ground perfectly alone.
He kept at it vigorously, however, until in about a

mile, finding that his wind was giving out, he stopped, and came back with a look in his countenance, which showed that he did not wish to be considered as having been in the race. In the meanwhile the antelope and greyhound kept on, as I could see with a spyglass which I had with me. For about eight miles the hound kept within a few leaps of the antelope, when they reached the brush near the river. The hound then turned to see whether I was following; but, finding I was not, he gave up the chase and turned to rejoin me. I drove on, and in about an hour afterwards he came up, seeming to be very tired. He, however, ran directly to Ben, and whined and jumped about him; and it really appeared to me that he was trying to tell the bear what a fine race he had had, and reproaching him for his want of bottom to run. Ben used often to run in this manner, but of course could not keep up with the greyhound. As for the antelope, I believe that on a stretch like that, he is the fleetest animal in the world.

That evening we camped in a ravine at the foot of the mountains, in the neighborhood of large herds of cattle, which were grazing in the plains. The herdsmen, or vaqueros, when they saw us, came up and talked awhile, and then proceeded further up the ravine to their ranch, leaving the cattle to themselves. About sundown I heard a tremendous commotion among the cattle, and, going out to see what caused it, beheld a huge grizzly bear rolling and tumbling in the grass, while the cattle were gathering around him, and bawling as if crazy. I immediately took my rifle

and went around in such a manner as not to disturb
either cattle or bear, — my object being to get up near
and witness the motions of the bear, which, I correctly
supposed, was playing one of the most wonderful tricks
known to his species. I had frequently heard of the
sagacity of the grizzly in decoying cattle within his
reach, and had a great curiosity to see it for myself.

I accordingly ascended a small hill near the spot,
and reached a place from which I could easily witness
the whole affair. The bear was in the long grass,
rolling on his back, throwing his legs into the air,
jumping up, turning half somersets, chasing his tail
and cutting up all kinds of antics, evidently with no
other purpose than to attract the attention of the cattle. These foolish animals crowded around him; some
bulls running up as if to make a lunge, and then turning aside, and all bawling violently. At last a young
heifer, more bold than the rest, lowered her head and
ran up, to thrust her horns into him. In an instant
the bear rose upon his hind legs, and, making a leap,
caught the heifer around the neck, and fixed his jaws
in her nose. She made a jump to get away; but the
bear, with a peculiar jerk of his head, threw her upon
her side, and, without loosening his hold, turned his
entire body upon her. He then let go his hold upon
the nose and seizing her by the neck, tore it open;
the blood gushed in torrents from the severed arte-
ries; and in a few moments she was dead. No sooner had she stopped struggling than he got off, and
leisurely began sucking up the blood, and enjoying
the supper which his trick had procured for him.

The other cattle drew back at first, but in a short time they seemed to gather courage, and again approached. As they came close, the bear left his victim and rushed at them with a terrific growl. This frightened them off for a while; and then the bear would resume his meal. He drove them off thus a dozen times; and I relished the scene so well that, without interfering, I lay looking at it until it became quite dark, — thus neglecting the opportunity to have a fair shot at him. As he was about turning to leave, however, I crawled down and fired at him; but it was then so dark, and the distance so great, that I missed. At the crack of the rifle he rose upon his legs, uttered two or three savage growls, and then put off for the mountains.

In the morning I sent Drury to the ranch to give information of what I had seen; and in a short time he came back with the vaqueros and two of the ranch owners. I told them the story, and they seemed much interested. They said they were much troubled with bears, and offered to give me one hundred dollars a month and all the beef I wanted, if I would remain and hunt there a few months. I laughed at the proposition, and replied that a gold-hunter on his way to Kern River could not be purchased on terms like those. They laughed in turn about Kern River; and, after talking in good-humor some time, I took a portion of the dead heifer with their consent, and, bidding them good-bye, proceeded on my journey.

We proceeded this day to the neighborhood of Pacheco's Pass, which opens a passage in the Coast

Mountains from the San Joaquin to the ocean near Monterey, and camped. The next morning I drove up to a ranch at Pacheco's Pass, where there were about a hundred persons, some of them rancheros and some returning Kern River miners. They all wondered, seeing me drive up with the bears, and wanted to know where I hailed from, and where I was going. I answered their questions frankly, when they replied that I was out of the road which led to Kern River. I rejoined that I knew it well, but that there were certain valleys in the mountains which I wished to visit, and that was the reason I came that way. They kept eyeing me, and looking suspiciously at the beef, horses, and mules, as much as to say they suspected me to be a rascal and thief, though they threw out no insinuations in words. I stood their treatment as long as I thought proper, and then spoke as follows: "Gentlemen, you look at my beef as if you were hungry. If you desire, you can share with me, and you will find that it is neither stolen nor poisoned." At the same time, I looked full in the faces of the rancheros, who, when they see a stranger have beef, suspect at once that he has been killing their cattle, and generally with very good reason; and as I saw they understood my meaning, I narrated the story of the grizzly bear, and how I came by the beef. This seemed to please them all, and they invited me into the house to take breakfast; but I thanked them, and replied that I never breakfasted so late in the day. I however went into the house with them, and, getting into conversation, gathered all the information

I could about the country in the mountains, and a certain valley of which I had heard, abounding in game.
They told me that the valley was distant about three
days' journey over a rugged road, and that it was
very uncertain whether a wagon could get along, as
none was ever known to have passed through.

Notwithstanding this unfavorable intelligence, we
started into the mountains, and travelled during the
day a considerable distance, passing three or four
ranches, and seeing a few wild mustang horses, — for
we were getting into a region where there were many
of these animals. The subsequent day we travelled
till noon, when we came to a great hill, of which I had
heard much at Pacheco's, and, ascending it with difficulty, found that there was a sort of jumping-off place
on the other side, as had been told us. Taking out
my glass here, I examined the road further on, and
saw, nearly a thousand feet below me, a large, grassy,
and comparatively level plain, covered here and there
with antelopes and mustangs, and in the distance a
line of cotton-wood trees, indicating a stream. The
difficulty was to descend the side of the hill, which
was almost a precipice, with scrubby oak-trees about
the top, and rocks towards the bottom. It seemed to
be almost a hopeless job to get down; but we commenced the labor by taking down the horses by themselves first. I intended to lead the Lady down also,
but, finding it so tiresome to ascend, lengthened her
chain, and left her tied, and then, fastening several
strong lariats to the axle, had Drury take hitches with
them around trees, and aid in that way in letting the

wagon down as lightly as possible. Besides this, we locked two wheels, and then attempted to go down with the mules, wagon, and all together. We descended thus about half-way, when, having to turn to one side, the wagon was brought into a sideling position, and Drury had to stand on one of the upper wheels to keep it from toppling over. We went thus a few hundred feet further, when, smash! over went the whole concern, tumbling and scattering the goods into the brush, overthrowing and crippling the mules, tearing the harness, twisting off the tire of one of the wheels, and breaking the tongue square off near the whipple-trees. To add to the misfortune, the sun was beating down fiercely upon us; and there was no water near, and no help.

To be thus circumstanced is one of the discomforts which hunters have to expect in new and untried countries. It is almost enough to make a man sink into desperation, and forswear an adventurous life forever. But the difficulty is soon forgotten when a man goes energetically to work to repair damages; and, when all is over, he looks back upon the occasion as one of the bright spots in his career, and dwells upon it as a pleasure and an honor. There was here nothing to be done but to do the best we could. First, I gave my attention to Lady Washington, who, in the general disaster, had been pitched over with so much violence that her nose ploughed up a furrow in the ground. As she recovered herself, she seemed frightened, and snuffed and snorted, and her hair stood on end in great agitation; but I went up and patted her head, and in a few moments she appeared to be pacified, and licked my hand, as if she understood the affair was only an accident and entirely unintentional. I then took the packsaddles, and, placing them on the mules, loaded upon them portions of the luggage, and sent Drury to the foot of the hill with them; and, by repeating these trips several times, we finally got all the luggage down. In the meanwhile, I managed to replace the tire on the wheel, and, cutting two oaken timbers, lashed them with lariats and thongs of green hide on both sides of the broken tongue, in such a manner as to make it temporarily sufficient. Next, I mended the torn harness with buckskin and raw hide; and, by night, we succeeded in getting the wagon down, repacked, and were on our way again.

All this time, however, we were suffering dreadfully from the want of water; but, fortunately, there was a clear, starry sky, and I determined to travel on till we reached the stream indicated by the cotton-wood trees which we had seen from the hill-top. We accordingly proceeded slowly and painfully all night, refreshed a little, it is true, by the cool night-air, but still suffering the torture of thirst; and as morning approached, we found ourselves near the cotton-woods. There we expected water; but, upon reaching the banks of the stream, we found it entirely dry, and no water or sign of water was to be seen. I had been told by the rancheros at Pacheco's Pass that we would probably find water in pools along the creek; but now everything seemed to be entirely dried up.

The creek had a sandy bottom, and bore the appearance of rising and sinking again every few miles, like many other streams in the southern portion of California; and I directed Drury to dismount and follow the bed, searching for pools, while I would drive along the bank. He dismounted, very unwillingly however, and wanted to know why he could not ride, instead of walking. I told him there were two reasons: first, it would not be easy to get the horse down the bank into the bed of the creek, and, secondly, he could travel over the loose sand in the creek on foot better than the horse, and would be more likely to find water. He rejoined in a tone of discontentment, but finally threw himself down the bank, and commenced making the search. I drove along on the bank for nearly an hour, but heard nothing of Drury, and began to think he had deserted me. A thousand suspicions, indeed, passed through my mind, as is usual when we have no confidence in persons whom we are compelled to trust; but, finally, he made his appearance from a clump of bushes, and reported water.

The pool which he had discovered was situated under a cleft of rocks in a deep place, about fifty feet below the bank, which was there very steep, and covered with trees and bushes. On the opposite side of the pool, the bank sloped more gradually; but as we could not reach that side without a wide circuit, we were under the necessity of carrying the water up the bank to our animals. Ben and Rambler, however, no sooner saw the water than they plunged down the bank, and, running up to their middles, satisfied their thirst, and then wallowed and rolled with the most luxurious satisfaction. So great had been our trials for the previous twenty-four hours, and so fatiguing and harassing our long and weary march, that it was absolutely necessary to recruit; and we accordingly unhitched at this place, and, after a hasty breakfast, having first attended to our animals, we threw ourselves in our blankets under the shade of the cotton-woods, and enjoyed a sound and refreshing sleep.

CHAPTER XVI.

JOAQUIN'S VALLEY.

WHEN I awoke from my sleep, it was the middle
of the afternoon; but I determined to push ahead as
far as we could before evening, and then take a good
night's rest. As we were hitching up, however, I
noticed the bear and dog pricking up their ears and
exhibiting signs of uneasiness, as if there was something in the wind. Leaving Drury to finish hitching,
I took my rifle and stepped back towards the pool.
The bear and dog seemed anxious to pass ahead, but
I made motions and signs for them to keep back, and
they dared not do otherwise. On reaching the bank
and looking over, I beheld a band of antelopes standing at the water, and drinking as if very thirsty. I
immediately drew my rifle and fired, and one dropped,
when the others turned and ran up the slope of the
bank out into the plain. I cried to the dog and bear,

WILD CATTLE.

and they set out in pursuit, the former, of course, taking the lead.

The grizzly Ben started with the greatest courage and the most resolute determination; but, after loping four or five hundred yards over the sand, he wheeled around to see whether I was doing my part. Seeing I was not following, he at once decided that such treatment was not justice; and, returning, sat himself down on his haunches in front of me, as I began to skin the antelope. The noble fellow was already so well trained, that he never presumed to touch anything till I gave it to him; but he had a way of grumbling for food, when hungry, that was irresistible. I shall never forget how he sat there, wistfully eyeing my carving, looking into my face, and remonstrating about my strictness with him. His perquisites were generally the entrails of game, of which he was remarkably fond; but as he now had to wait until they were removed, his impatience at last assumed such a pitch, that he got excited, and grumbled more than ordinarily. I resolved to try him a little, and placed food in such a way as to tempt him; but the faithful fellow continued true to his training, and the meat remained inviolate. Seeing this, I threw his portion to him, and he ate until I almost thought he would burst, — devouring the entrails, and lapping up the liquid of the antelope's stomach, which to his palate seemed as sweet as honey.

As soon as Ben was done, I carried up the meat to the wagon, and, finding all ready, we started off; and, travelling till sundown, we arrived at the mouth of a cañon, which led up into the valley of which I was in search. It was a very rugged opening, the rocks rising nearly perpendicularly on each side, leaving but a narrow place for the passage of a small stream of water which came from the valley. There was no wagon road, and as difficulties were to be anticipated in winding up into the valley, I determined to take the next morning for it, and camped for the night.

The valley, which I had thus reached, was noted at one time as the head-quarters of Joaquin, the famous robber, who, during his brief career, spread terror over the southern country. I had been advised, at Pacheco's, not to go there, as the danger of being robbed, and perhaps killed, by straggling remnants of this lawless desperado's band would be imminent; but as it was not at all certain that any were there, and as our danger in any one part of the country was nearly as great as in another, so far as these active and ubiquitous thieves were concerned, I paid no attention to the caution, and, as the event proved, never was molested.

Upon advancing up the cañon the next day, — and to do so we had to cross the creek at least a dozen times, and once to unload, — we found one of the most beautiful valleys in all California. It was about six miles long by one wide, covered with grass and grove-like clumps of trees, and surrounded by mountains which, in some places, were so precipitous that it was impossible for a man to climb them. In the centre of the valley was a ridge of slightly elevated land, dividing into two branches the stream which sprang from fountains at its head. A stock-raiser could not desire a finer location; and had I not been a hunter of wild animals, I should certainly have wished to settle down here, and devote my attention to the rearing of domestic ones.

After pitching camp under some fine trees in this beautiful valley, and eating dinner, I took my rifle, and, accompanied as usual by Ben and Rambler, took a stroll towards the nearest tongue of mountain, which came down on one side. As we approached it, Ben snuffed the air, and Rambler grew uneasy, which was sufficient notification that there was game near by; and looking carefully around, I discovered a female grizzly with two cubs, feeding in the bushes about a hundred yards distant. I restrained my animal companions immediately, and made them lie down. Then creeping around, unobserved by the bears, which were very busy, I raised my rifle, and, upon firing, pierced the dam at the first shot. Ben and Rambler, at the discharge, were on their feet, and would have rushed forward, but I still kept them back, and, reloading, killed one of the cubs. There being but one cub left, I allowed the bear and dog to advance, and in a moment they were upon it. Rambler seized a leg, but Ben took it fairly by the neck and shook it terribly, and so determined and persistent was he that I had difficulty in making him release his hold. Indeed it was necessary to give him several good bouts over the head, before he could be induced to forego the pleasure of shaking the saucy little cub into pieces. I took the poor thing to camp afterwards, and gave it a cage for preservation, but it was fatally injured, and soon died.

The next day, after hunting in the valley and killing an antelope or two, we left camp unprotected, and paid a visit to a high peak at the head of the cañon. It was a queer-looking mountain, with shelving rocks hanging on its sides, and pine-trees about its summit, which led off by ridges to mountains beyond. I had been told that wild cattle frequented the highest parts of these mountains; and it was in the hopes of seeing them, that, with great fatigue, we ascended the peak. When we reached the top, we obtained a grand view over all the country round about. Towards the ocean, which, however, could not be seen, the land was rugged and broken. On the opposite side, a range of hills shut out the San Joaquin Valley, but far beyond we could see the Sierra Nevada, a line along the horizon. Below us was the delightful little valley where our camp was pitched; and beyond, the larger valley through which we had travelled at night, when suffering from the want of water.

Having satisfied ourselves with the prospect, we advanced a short distance into the mountains, and soon discovered a herd of half a dozen wild cattle, which, of all the animals I had ever seen, were the most savage looking. I thought I had seen large horns when passing through Mexico, but they were not to be compared with these California specimens. The cattle themselves were extraordinarily large; and having these immense horns, with shaggy hair about the shoulders and head, they presented an appearance almost terrific. Notwithstanding their fierce looks, however, they fled upon seeing us; and, it being nearly night, we turned towards camp without attempting to pursue them.

Upon clambering back to the brink of the mountain, and looking down into the valley, I was astonished to see that my camp was in the possession of strangers. At first, it seemed as if my eyes must be deceived; but, upon drawing forth my glass, I could distinctly make out four or five men and a number of horses; yet who they were it was impossible to tell in the dark. They had made a fire and usurped my camp; so that the suspicion at once flashed across my mind that the reports about Joaquin's band were true, and that here I had fallen into their hands. Under the circumstances, I knew not for a while what to do. I had read, during my younger days, the stories of famous brigands and robber captains, and retained, doubtless, too exalted an idea of their magnanimity; but my maturer judgment counselled me that not a spark of generosity can animate the soul of a cut-throat or a thief. I resolved, however, to run the risks of facing the strangers, whoever they might be; and, preparing my arms for use in case of necessity, we descended the mountain, and approached the fire around which the strangers sat. Instead of finding robbers, I had the pleasure of meeting two American gentlemen and five Spaniards; the former from San Francisco, on a visit to certain quicksilver mines in that vicinity, and the latter be-

longing to the neighborhood of Tulare Lake, where
they had corrals for the capture of mustangs. They
appeared to have heard of me at Pacheco's, and had
purposely stopped at my camp to procure meat.
When I told them of the thoughts which had been
suggested to me by their appearance from the mountain, they were highly amused, and assured me that
none of Joaquin's followers were in that part of the
country.

The next morning, after the Spaniards left, the
American gentlemen induced me to accompany them
to the mines of quicksilver, which were eight or ten
miles distant. We proceeded thither, and spent the
day in the neighborhood of the mines, examining them
and picking up specimens of the cinnabar. We then
returned, taking with us an old Spaniard, whom we
found living at the place, having been left there by his
companions, who had gone to San Luis Obispo for
provisions. I had no knowledge of quicksilver mining; but was told that the ore there was good, and that
the mines would one day be valuable. At that time,
they had not been worked much; and, at the then
high rates of labor, it would not justify to build works
and employ the necessary hands to carry them on. I
spoke of the beauty of the valley, and the gentlemen
agreed with me about its value when the mines should
come to be extensively used. Recalling my impression of the place, I often think that, had I
only sat down and taken up the valley, I might
now have been a kind of a monarch, the possessor
of a beautiful little kingdom, with uncounted herds

and flocks on every side. But such was not my destiny.

The next morning, after the Americans left, we determined to have an elk hunt; and the old Spaniard took us to a ravine among the mountains, where he informed us there were elks; or if not, he said it would be of no use to look further, and we might conclude that they had all gone over into the tulés of the Tulare Lake country, as they generally did in the warm season or fly-time. When we reached the place, we soon discovered a band of a dozen or fifteen elks, with half a dozen young. The little ones were what we especially sought; and I at once laid my plans for killing an old one or two, and capturing the young. To the Spaniard, accordingly, I gave a horse with several lassos; and Drury I stationed at the mouth of the ravine with a rifle; while I myself crept up among the bushes to the neighborhood of the elks, to try the flag operation, which sometimes works well with elks as well as with antelopes. Arriving at the desired situation, I raised a red silk handkerchief on a stick, and imitated the elk whistle, all of which had the wished-for effect. The animals stopped eating and gazed at the flag. I remained concealed; but as they came up close, I fired through the bushes and killed the nearest one. This appeared to bewilder the others; and, as they continued to approach, I quickly reloaded, fired a second time and disabled a second elk. A third time I reloaded and fired, when the wounded elk bleated; and the Spaniard, supposing that to be the signal agreed upon, advanced with his

lassos. Before I could reload a fourth time, he
plunged among the elks, and soon threw a lasso over
the neck of one of the little ones; while the others
turned and ran down the ravine. I sprang forward
and took the lasso, while the Spaniard pursued the re-
treating band, and managed to overtake and lasso a
second little one; so that the result of this hunt was
three old ones killed, and two young ones captured,
both of which I subsequently managed to raise.

The next day, having jerked the elk-meat and left
it to dry, the Spaniard and I ascended the mountains
for the purpose of seeing the wild cattle again; and
we soon came upon a herd of fifteen or twenty. I
tried to induce the old man to lasso one of them; but
he replied that it would be impossible, as the ground
was too rough and the cattle too strong and desperate
to attack in that way. Giving up this idea, therefore, I
crept around among the rocks within range, and fired
at a bull, which I wounded so badly that he was not
able to keep up with the flying herd; and with
another ball I managed to kill him. He was a great
curiosity to me, and differed so much from ordinary
cattle that I felt almost disposed to believe him of a
new species. It is generally considered that these
cattle are the offspring of cows which escaped many
years ago from the rancheros in the valleys, and that
they have become perfectly wild. Be this as it may,
their hides are thicker, their hair longer and shaggier,
and their eyes more like those of the buffalo than those
of any domestic cattle. The horns are very large,
and I have frequently regretted that I left those of

this bull lying, when I might so easily have packed them with the meat to camp, and hauled them along with my other curiosities.

Upon reaching camp again, I concluded that it was time to resume the journey towards Kern River; and accordingly, the next day, after making the old Spaniard some acceptable presents, we hitched up, and passed out of the valley by the same road by which we had entered it, and then travelled towards the San Joaquin River over a hot, sandy, waterless plain. We must have gone, I think, about thirty miles, when Ben Franklin exhibited so much fatigue that we were compelled to stop. There were no signs of water, except a line of cotton-wood trees away off to the east, showing the line of the river; and, for fear we could not reach it, I sent Drury ahead on horseback with a leather bag, directing him to fill it and return as quickly as possible. As soon as he was gone, I started slowly ahead, encouraging my jaded animals as much as possible; but in a few miles was again compelled to stop, finding that Ben had entirely given out. The poor fellow's feet were dreadfully blistered by the hot sand, and do what I might he refused to budge. I wound pieces of cloth about his paws, but they did no good; he stretched himself out, and could not, or would not, march any further.

CHAPTER XVII.

TULARE LAKE AND KERN RIVER.

THE condition of my poor Ben, as he lay panting on the sand of the San Joaquin plains, unable to follow me any further, and looking up affectionately, but despairingly, from the midst of his pain, in my face, grieved me to the heart, and gave me great uneasiness. He was my favorite; I could well have spared any other animal rather than Ben; and I feared he would die. I reproached myself for having brought no water along, but as the fault could not be helped by reproaches, I hastily split some pieces of board from my wagon, and erecting a frame and throwing a large blanket over it, so as to make shade, left Ben and Rambler there, and then I drove on with the intention of procuring water and returning more speedily than Drury, who had no interests at stake, would be dis-

posed to do. In the course of four or five miles I
met Drury with his bag of water; and, hastily handing
him the reins, with directions to drive on, I mounted
the horse and galloped back to where Ben lay suffering. It was dark when I reached him, and to all appearance he had not moved from the position in which
I left him. He had life enough, however, to express
his gratitude, and drank several quarts of water with
avidity. I then endeavored to coax him along, and
he took a few steps; but neither flattery nor blows
could induce him to move far.

Seeing that it was impossible to get him along, I
again let him lie, and rode ahead for the wagon, which
I found at the side of a spring. The mules and
horses were turned out to graze, and Drury was lying
asleep at the fire, which he had hastily kindled. I
roused him, and ordered him to assist in hitching up
the wagon again, to go back for Ben. He obeyed,
and we soon unloaded the heaviest of our articles,
and, leaving them at the spring, drove back. As the
country, however, was new to us, and the night dark,
we by some means or other missed the way, and could
see no signs of what we sought. We looked about
all night till daylight, but there was no Ben in sight.
I at last sent Drury in one direction and myself took
another, by which means we succeeded in a few hours
in finding the trail, and finally discovered the bear
lying under his blanket. We gave him water again,
but still he could not walk, and we had to place him
in the wagon, — which could not be done without some
difficulty, as by that time he would weigh in the

neighborhood of four hundred pounds. When at last we did get him in, partly by our own strength and partly by his assistance, we drove on to the spring, and camped.

On account of the bear's condition, we were compelled to remain two days at this spring, during which time I doctored him. My treatment met with success, and we soon got him on his legs again. In the meanwhile, as his feet continued sore, I made moccasins, as I had done on the Humboldt plains, and poured bear's oil in them, — which was an excellent salve for the blisters. The moccasins were bound tightly to the feet, and a muzzle was put over the nose, to prevent him from tearing them off. They worked well, and on the third day after reaching the spring we hitched up again, and drove on to the edge of Tulare Lake.

The head of the San Joaquin Valley consists of a vast area of nearly level country, inclosing several lakes, the largest of which bears the name of Tulare, — an extensive body of water, surrounded by a selvage, many miles in extent, of tules, or bulrushes. There appears to be a drainage from the lake into the San Joaquin River, but no large stream; and at the time I passed, though there were some sloughs with water in them, I may almost say that we crossed the valley dry shod. We could see nothing of the lake itself, but miles after miles of tule country spread out before us; and far to the east we saw a line of trees, which denoted the position of King's River. As we passed along, we heard the whistling of elks in the tules, but did not stop. We proceeded on around the end of the lake, until we arrived in the timber on King's River, where we camped. The rivers in this part of the country are very peculiar. After leaving the Sierra Nevada, they divide into a number of branches, in some instances reuniting, and in others running separate to the lake. King's River reunites; but the next stream, called Four Creeks, after leaving the mountains as one stream, divides into four, which spread out from one another like the ribs of an open fan. Their banks are timbered, and particularly those of the Four Creeks, which presents a most beautiful and rich valley, full of fertile land and fine timber. The King's River country is rolling and rather barren, but in the neighborhood of the lake there is timber and tule, and game is plenty. We stopped there several days, and killed a number of elks, besides capturing one young one, which we placed by the side of the others that we had brought with us in our wagon from the Coast Range.

On the borders of the lake, near the mouth of King's River, there was an Indian village, which we visited on the day after our arrival in the neighborhood. There were about a hundred Indians in it at that time, and I engaged two boys of them to take me to an island in the lake, where there was said to be elks in abundance, and birds of various kinds in astonishing plenty. We set out on foot from the village, where I left my animals, and, after wading through the tules nearly a mile, reached a canoe, which was made of several logs fastened together side by side, and calked with tules and mud. In this, we crossed an arm of the lake, and landed on a small wooded island, which was a place of birds indeed. There were birds in almost incredible numbers, — ducks, geese, swans, cranes, curlews, snipes, and various other kinds, in all stages of growth, and eggs by thousands among the grass and tules. There were also beavers' works in every direction; and we saw also elks in numbers, which fled into the tules at our approach.

Upon reaching the island, the Indian boys at once began gathering up young birds and eggs; but Drury and I pursued the elks, one of which I killed outright. Drury managed to wound a second, and, after reloading, followed it into the reeds for another shot; but the animal turned upon him, and struck him down into the mud. He roared for help, and I rushed to his assistance, in time to kill the elk and save his life. As I pulled him out of the mire, notwithstanding the serious nature of the accident, I could not help laughing at the pitiful face he made; but he took my laughing as an offence, and became so very sulky that for the remainder of the hunt I had to do all the work alone. While, therefore, Drury sat on the grass doing nothing, I took my rifle and rambled out among the small mounds which rose here and there among the tules, after more elks. While creeping along, I happened to see a fawn a few days old, which was so well hidden away that had it not been by mere chance I would not have seen him. His body lay flat, almost entirely covered with young tules, and only his eyes peeped out. I feared frightening him, but slyly laying aside my rifle, and creeping up, I made a sudden leap, and seized him. He however bleated so loudly that, fearing his cries would attract his dam to dispute my prize, and make a combat necessary, I held his jaws, and muzzled him. Soon afterwards we embarked again in the canoe, with the fawn, the slaughtered elks, and an immense quantity of young birds and eggs, and returned to the village, where the Indians gathered around, and discussed our successful hunting with great interest. Altogether, this island hunt was as pleasant and interesting to me as any I had enjoyed during the season.

The next day we proceeded on our journey. We travelled over a rather barren country, with the tule marshes to our right, and the white line of the Sierra Nevada far to our left. We passed a band of splendid mustang horses, to which we gave chase for a short distance without being able to overtake them, and then proceeded on our way southward. The next day we reached the Four Creeks, where there was scenery of a very beautiful description, and a country rich, well timbered, and well stocked with game; but as we were now well provided, and there was no advantage to be gained by delaying, we pushed on from this point for a number of days, until we arrived in the neighborhood of the Kern River mines, where we camped.

The whole of the next day after reaching the mines, I spent among the miners, looking at their work, hearing them talk about their claims, and examining their returns. From this one day's investigation, I became satisfied that there was nothing to be done at mining. There were, however, a large number of persons in the region who had to be fed; and I at once determined to turn my attention to hunting and supplying game, which brought a good price. The very next day, accordingly, I forded Kern River, and proceeded about ten miles into the mountainous country beyond; where, finding the signs of bears and deer in abundance, I made a general camp, and prepared for general hunting.

The next morning early, I started out, accompanied by Drury, my bear Ben, and my dog Rambler, on a hunt. In a short time, we saw three large grizzlies feeding among the chaparral on the side of a rocky ravine. They were far off, and it was difficult to approach on account of the brush; but, creeping around, followed by my companions, I got within sixty or seventy yards. The bears, in the mean time, evidently suspected danger, and began snuffing the air, rising upon their hind legs, and looking about as if to see where it was. I gave them, however, little time to consider their situation; for, drawing my rifle and firing, I bored the nearest through the heart. As he fell, I seized Drury's rifle and fired at the second, when the third turned and fled. The second bear was evidently wounded, and I urged on Ben and Rambler, who were uneasily waiting my permission to rush forward. It required but a word, when the faithful creatures bounded forth; and a terrific combat took place between Ben and the wounded bear. Meanwhile, I had drawn my knife, and was rushing forward through the brush to assist Ben, when the enemy suddenly turned tail and plunged down the ravine, with Ben and Rambler at his heels. I followed, and, upon reaching them, found the bear at bay, with his back in a dark hole which was choked up with rocks and brush, while Ben and Rambler were attacking him in front. I reloaded as quickly as possible, while they were snapping at each other, and fired again, but under so great a state of excitement as to miss my mark; and the bear again put off, followed by Ben and Rambler as before. We pursued at least half a mile, when the country became so rough as to be perfectly impracticable; and, resolving to give up the chase, I called off Ben and the dog, and returned to where the first bear had fallen.

Upon our reaching the spot, the bear was nowhere to be seen; but a line of blood indicated the direction in which he had crawled off. Ben and Rambler took up the trail, and I followed them three hundred yards through the brush, into the bottom of the ravine, near a pool of water, where we found the old fellow stretched out and dead. The ball with which I struck him had passed through his heart; and yet he lived long enough, and had strength enough, to drag himself thus far. He proved to be one of the largest bears I ever shot, and I congratulated myself that the others had not remained to make a more determined fight. Often since then have I thought of the rashness of my rushing into the brush after them, and can only explain it by the fact that it was my first bear fight for several weeks.

After cutting the meat up, I proceeded to the mines and disposed of it, together with a quantity of venison which I had killed. In a day or two afterwards, we had another bear adventure. On this occasion, we came upon a female grizzly and two young cubs, playing on a hill-side. I fired, and wounded the dam, and then set Ben and Rambler on her; but the cowardly thing ran, and deserted her cubs, — an action which a bear of more northern latitudes would not be guilty of. It is only in the south, where heat enervates the species, that such despicable natures exist. As the dam ran, Ben followed her; but Rambler seized one cub by the ear, and held it till I came up. We then rushed at the other, and, with some chasing, succeeded in securing it also. We then called Ben back and returned to camp.

A few evenings after this, having shot a deer near camp, I went out upon a mule by moonlight to pack it in. Upon approaching it, I heard a noise, and, after listening a few moments, satisfied myself that a bear was making his supper of the game. I dismounted, and, motioning Ben and Rambler to keep behind, I crept up within fair distance, and fired as well as I could in such a poor light. Fortunately, the ball struck the bear a serious blow, and I allowed Ben and Rambler to rush forward. Ben seized hold immediately, and a pretty even fight took place; Ben sometimes on top, and the other sometimes. I ran up within three or four yards, so that it was easy to distinguish between them, Ben being considerably the darker in color. As the struggle went on, Ben suddenly threw his adversary on the ground, when, seizing the opportunity, I fired a pistol ball into the latter, and soon afterwards managed to thrust my knife also into him. He fought well, but I think Ben could have vanquished him in a fair fight.

CHAPTER XVIII.

THE TEJON.

A FEW days after the last adventure, business becoming dull about Kern River, I struck my camp; and, taking all my animals and goods, such as were not consumed or disposed of at the mines, I proceeded towards the Tejon Pass. It is in the neighborhood of this place that the Sierra Nevada and Coast Range mountains interlock their rugged chains. My object here was to hunt cinnamon or red bears, which were reported to be found in abundance in the region. After travelling a few days, and approaching within about thirty miles of the Pass, we camped.

Upon making an early morning excursion into the hills, we soon came across an old bear and three cubs of the desired species. Their fur was long and waving, and looked beautiful and glossy in the rays of the morning sun. I crept up without being ob-

served and shot the dam; when Ben and Rambler
rushed forward, first at the old bear, but finding her
dead, then into the bush after the cubs, which had
endeavored to hide themselves. In a few minutes
Ben seized one of the cubs and shook it dreadfully.
I ran up to save it, when a second cub jumped up before me, which I seized in one hand, and rushing up
to Ben made him drop the first; but it was too late,
his teeth had crushed its ribs, and the poor thing after
a few gasps expired.

In the mean time Rambler had ferreted out the
third cub, and now had his paw upon it, and appeared
to be biting it in the neck. As I approached and
seized his prize, the sagacious dog looked up with a
most expressive face and wagged his tail, as much as
to assure me he had done his duty faithfully, which
indeed he had; for I received the cub uninjured.
We soon had the two secured; and packing the dead
ones upon mules, carrying the others, we returned to
camp.

The same day, after a hearty dinner of bear's meat,
I started out for an evening hunt; but soon began to
feel queer, though I did not know what was the matter. The farther I went the worse I felt, and at last,
becoming very weak, I sat down to rest; but, continuing to grow worse, I got up again and attempted
to return. By this time, however, my head ached
dreadfully; and, after a few steps, I was compelled
to sit down again, and all at once was taken with a
violent shivering and shaking. Being unable to proceed I lay down until the chill was over, when a burn-

ing fever came on; but nevertheless I managed by degrees to crawl back to camp, where I immediately turned into my blankets. During the entire night a fearful fever raged in my veins, and a dreadful headache drove me almost to distraction. Indeed, I found that I had a severe attack of chills and fever.

The next morning the first thing I did was to dispatch Drury on a mule to the Government post at the Tejon Pass, to purchase quinine, and he started off. I hardly knew what to do during his absence; but, as it happened, the chills did not return that day The next, however, they came back with increased violence. Upon feeling their approach, I placed myself in the sun, and piled all the clothing and skins I could rake and scrape together on top of me; still I shook as if I were going to shake to pieces. In the course of a few hours my head ached as if it would split open, and then a distracting fever came on, when I became delirious, and dreamed the most dreadful dreams, — in the midst of which I appeared to wake by fits and starts and see strange sights. At one time I thought I was burning up with thirst in the Colorado desert; at another time I was fighting the judges and lawyers of Sonora; and at another I thought I was having a desperate encounter with a grizzly in the mountains, and that he was literally tearing the flesh from my bones. Again I imagined that I was condemned, although not conscious of having ever wronged my fellow-man, and was suffering the most excruciating pains in the place of torture. How long these dreams lasted I do not know, but it seems that

I must have passed by degrees into a kind of stupor; for about dark I was roused from a deep sleep by a violent shake and some one calling, "Americano! Americano." I raised myself, and found before me an old Spaniard, who by chance had stopped at my camp on his way from the Tejon to the Tulare country.

The old stranger asked permission to pass the night with me, which I gladly accorded. I was now perfectly conscious again, and described to him my condition. He said that he thought he could cure me, and immediately went to work preparing a mess, containing liberal quantities of willow bark and red pepper, which he told me to swallow. I tasted the mixture, and remarked that it was too hot. He replied that it was just right; and I at length worried the horrible stuff down. The old man then, at my direction, made himself a cup of coffee, and we both turned into our blankets. I slept quietly till midnight, when two more Spaniards, attracted by our fire, rode up, and asked to stay the night, — a request which I never refused. I told them to help themselves to supper; and when they had done so, they also turned into their blankets on the other side of the fire, by the side of the old man, and we were soon all soundly asleep.

How long after this it was I know not, but I was in a profound repose, when a piercing shriek from the old Spaniard suddenly aroused me. Supposing that some diabolical murder was going on. I sprang to my feet in an instant, entirely forgetful of my sickness, and seizing my rifle in one hand, and drawing my bowie-knife with the other, I stood on the defensive. It was starlight, and I could see a movement among the Spaniards, but it was too dark to ascertain exactly what the trouble was. I, however, called out in a loud tone to know the difficulty, when one of the Spaniards replied, that the old man was bitten by a tarantula. The very name of this poisonous spider, shocked my whole system, and caused the blood to run cold to the extremities of my body; the idea of the miserable death he would have to die, almost overpowered me; and for a few minutes I had not the power to move to his relief. But as the shock passed off, I seized a torch and passed over to the old man, who was sitting up, gasping and looking ghastly pale. I supposed he was dying, but mechanically turned to the blankets, and remarking that I had seen no tarantulas in this part of the country as yet, turned them open, when out fell — a wounded scorpion.

The old man supposed, as we all did, that death was upon him; but the moment he heard the word scorpion, he brightened up in an instant, and when I held the reptile up before him, it acted as well as the best medicine in the world could have done; for he well knew that a scorpion's sting is not necessarily fatal. We then examined the wound, which was in the thigh, but fortunately not near any large or important blood-vessel, though it was already dreadfully inflamed and swollen. The Spaniards remarked that tobacco was good for such a wound, to which I replied yes, but I had something better, — referring to a

weed which is used by the Indians in cases of rattle-
snake bites, a supply of which I carried in my wagon,
and proceeded at once to get it, together with a plug
of tobacco. These we picked to pieces, and made a
poultice of them, with which we bound the wound,
and then gave the patient tea made of the snake-weed
to drink. Whether the medicine cured the wound or
not, it might perhaps be difficult to tell with certainty;
but the next day, after a good long sleep, the old man
eat a remarkably hearty dinner of roast bear meat,
and pronounced it *mucho bueno.* — He was cured.

For a day or two after this, I continued doctoring
myself according to the old man's prescriptions, and
with an eventual very good result. I took the
pounded bark of common willow, and made a strong
infusion, which I drank upon feeling the premonitory
chill on the next regular day of attack. It seemed
to break the disease; and, subsequently, when a
slight fever came on, I crept down to the creek, upon
which I lay camped, and took not only a hearty drink,
but at the same time washed my head and shoulders
repeatedly. This treatment, although contrary perhaps to all the rules of therapeutics, worked admirably; as the fever went down, I returned to my blankets, and was soon in a sound and healthy slumber; and
I was never afterwards troubled with chills and fever.

This attack of ague, the origin of which was,
doubtless, my constant exposure, for some weeks
previously, to the malarious atmosphere of the Tulare
marshes, broke up my hunting on the San Joaquin
side of the mountains; and I determined at once to

cross over to the Colorado side. I was the more induced to do this, by news which reached me of the conduct of Drury, whom I had sent to the Tejon for quinine, as before stated. The idle fellow, upon reaching the settlement, had fallen in with certain Spanish women and Indian squaws, and, without a thought of his duty, spent the money I had committed to him, for liquor, and gave himself up to all kinds of vice and immorality. This news gave me great uneasiness, showing how utterly worthless he was, and how impossible it was to place any confidence in him; though I had cause to expect nothing better from his conduct, upon setting out, in the spring, from Corral Hollow.

On the evening of the day previous to my intended departure, as I sat crouching over my camp fire, reading those strange fancies which appear to spring out of the changing hues of burning coals, I was unexpectedly aroused by the appearance of the fellow coming back. He saluted me as if nothing had happened, and I returned his greetings; but my manner was certainly not very gracious. He noticed this, and, seeing me not so communicative as usual, volunteered a pitiful story about having lost his mule at the settlement, and the great trouble he had been at to regain it. This falsehood was merely adding insult to injury; and, turning towards him, I recalled his beastly conduct in the commencement of the campaign, and accused him of a repetition of it. I made use of the information I had gained from others, of his conduct at the Tejon, to confound him; and he soon stood abashed and ashamed. Had it not been inhuman to dismiss him in so wild a place, I should at once have sent him off; but, as it was, he was allowed to remain.

The next day, we packed up and started off into the mountains; and, after several days of travelling over a rough country of cliffs, ledges, and rocky places, arrived at the mouth of a gorge on the southern slope of the mountains. In the upper part of this gorge there was a spring, but the place was too rough to reach it with our wagon; and we were therefore constrained to leave it below, and pack our goods up to the spring, where we pitched our general camp. From this point the Great Basin, like a sandy sea, was seen lying at our feet; and, from our height, we could look out over the dreary, desert expanse, with the feelings of men who view the ocean, — knowing that but a fraction was seen, and that uncounted miles lay beyond, with their curious and strange wonders.

We were weary with the labors of the day, and turning into our blankets early, fell into a deep sleep. I was suddenly aroused at midnight by a fearful snuffing and snorting among my animals; but what to make of the noise I knew not, except that there was danger at hand. It was starlight, but too dark to see; and raising myself in my blankets and seizing my rifle, I listened with all attention. In a short time, I distinctly heard the lapping of water at the spring, which was about fifty yards distant; and, looking in that direction, beheld two spots, like balls of fire, glaring at me. I expected an encounter, and prepared myself for it; but the stranger beast unexpectedly, after uttering a low growl, turned and leisurely retreated, as if he did not deign to attack, much less to fear me. I could see that he was of large size, — a majestic animal of the lion genus; but this was all I could see.

THE JAGUAR.

CHAPTER XIX.

JAGUARS.

MY curiosity, as well as my love of adventure, was so much excited by the sight of the magnificent but unknown beast, that during the remainder of the night I could think of nothing else. My imagination presented me with the picture of an animal whose capture would exceed in interest all the adventures of my previous days; and no sooner was it light in the morning than I started out with Ben and Rambler to follow the track and reconnoitre the country. The trail led us four or five miles over a rough country, and at last into a gorge, — one of the roughest and craggiest places man's eyes ever beheld. The only way I could work through it, was by crawling, clambering, climbing, and pulling myself from cliff to cliff, and thus getting along by slow degrees. In among the huge rocks, which were scattered all over the country, there was here and there a space of soft earth, where the prints of the animal's feet were plainly to be seen; and it was by these marks that I pursued the trail into the gorge. Here the marks were better defined; and after following them across the gorge up to the face of a ledge of rocks, I came to a cave, which there was no difficulty in recognizing as the den of the animal.

The cave was elevated on one side of the cliff, so that a man could with difficulty reach it. In its mouth, and scattered below it, were multitudes of bones and skeletons of various kinds of animals, and among others, of mountain sheep, making the place look like the yard of a slaughter-house. I endeavored to reach the cave for the purpose of looking into it, but was unable to do so, and therefore withdrew to consider plans for operations, determined as I was to leave no stone unturned in my efforts to secure the unknown but evidently ferocious animal which made it his haunt. Considering the matter in every point of view, I resolved at last to build a trap on the trail, near the den; but, there being no trees in the neighborhood, before proceeding farther I had to go out and search where I could find timber.

The country in the vicinity was the roughest that can well be conceived; and it was only with great labor that I was enabled to climb the side of the gorge, and pass along the ridge which separated it from another of much the same character. After travelling a few miles, however, I saw, at the distance of four or five miles farther on, a valley containing trees; but as the sun was now declining, I did not visit it this evening. Turning back towards camp, on the contrary, with the intention of taking the next day for visiting the wood, I proceeded over the ledges for some distance, and suddenly came in sight of a flock of forty or fifty mountain sheep, which were grazing on the scanty herbage of the cliffs. They were very wary, constantly keeping their eyes about them. While feeding, they would slap their heads down, pick up a bunch of grass, and then look around as they were chewing; and thus they seemed to be continually on the look-out. As there was a number of them, some heads would be up at every minute, so that it required the greatest care not to alarm them. With extreme caution I managed to creep upon them, and taking two in range, fired. My rifle had been loaded heavily, in expectation of larger game, and the ball passed through the heart of one sheep into the neck of the other; so that I got two with one bullet. The remainder of the flock of course scampered off at the fire; and as it was impossible to pursue and keep up over the rocks, I did not attempt it.

After dressing the meat of those I had, I took one hind-quarter on my shoulder, and proceeded towards camp. It was now dark, and in the course of a few miles I was startled by the howl of coyotes, which were attracted by the smell of the meat, and pursued me. Ben and Rambler, who during the whole time had faithfully followed my footsteps, wished to turn back and fight when the coyotes opened on the trail, but for some distance I would not allow it. The coyotes, however, became very saucy and impudent, and at last approached very near, when I gave the word to the bear and dog, and they turned in a moment upon the pursuers. They both seized upon the most forward coyote, and in a few minutes tore him to pieces, while the remainder of the cowardly pack ran off, and we went the rest of the way undisturbed.

The next day I explored the country farther, and visited the timber which I had seen the day previous, where I found good grass and water. I at once determined to remove my camp to that place, and accordingly did so, although it was eight or ten miles from the den of the beast, with which my imagination was now filled. As, however, it was the nearest timber to the cave, there was no other way than to cut the logs for our trap there, and transport them the best way we could; and, accordingly, going to work, we cut a number of cotton wood logs, which were light, but at the same time sufficiently strong for our purpose. When we had enough to pack the two horses, two mules, and Lady Washington, — the sticks being about ten feet long, and six or eight inches thick, — I fastened two on each side of each horse and mule, and one on each side of the bear, — the logs being tied to the saddles at one end, and the farther ends dragging on the ground. With this singular looking caravan, followed by Ben and Rambler, we proceeded up the heights towards the den.

Most of the way was very rough and uphill, and it took quite half a day to reach the spot pitched upon for the trap, which was a small rocky rise in the midst of the gorge, about a quarter of a mile from the cave. At the same time I took up my tools, as it was my intention to commence the work immediately; and as soon as the animals were unloaded, I sent Drury back with them to cut more timber, and bring it up next day in the same manner. The bears and dog I kept with me, and they were good company as I worked upon the timbers in that wild and lonely region.

Upon the approach of night, I picked out a spot to sleep, but did not allow myself a fire, for fear of disturbing the game. I went to sleep, but in the course of the night was aroused by a roar, which I supposed to be that of the beast which I was hunting; it was loud but clear, short but piercing, different from any roar I had ever heard; and, as a new fact in regard to the beast, it added to my wonder, for I had already come to the conclusion that the animal was of a different species from any I had ever known. The track was peculiarly large and firm, indicating an animal of great strength and noble bearing.

It is unnecessary to detail day after day the progress of my trap building here, and the slow and tedious manner in which we had to transport our timber from a distance of eight miles. Suffice it to say that the arduous undertaking was at length accomplished, and the trap completed. No sooner was it finished and baited, than I picked out a hiding-place, about three hundred yards from the cave, and in such a position

that I could see the length of the trail, the trap, and
the den; such a place, indeed, as would give me a
full and fair view of all that took place in the gorge.
Taking Lady Washington, Ben, and Rambler to this
place, I tied them together, and seating myself at the
side of them with my blanket about me, I determined
to watch the first night and see how the trap would
work.

There was at this time a new moon, and the gorge,
a doleful place even in daylight, was darker than I
liked; nevertheless, I could see if any animal passed
the trail, and this would be some satisfaction. I therefore watched the twilight passing over the mountains,
and saw it grow dusky, and at length dark, when,
overpowered by the fatigues of the day, I curled
down by the side of Ben, and fell into a slumber.
Barely were my eyes closed, however, when a roar
roused me, and I started up and strained my eyes
along the trail from the den to the trap, but could see
nothing. In a few minutes the roar was repeated,
but in an apparently subdued tone; and directing my
eyes in the direction from which it proceeded, I saw
a spotted animal, resembling a tiger in size and form,
with two young ones. The view was very indistinct,
but I could see that the animal was crawling out of
the rocks. She went ahead for a little distance, then
turned around, and appeared to call the little ones,
which followed, playing like kittens. My first thought
was to kill her and catch the young; — and I have
often regretted since that I did not take the risks and
fire; but I considered that the trap which we had

built, would be both a safer and a more certain method to secure them.

Remaining silent, therefore, I watched the beasts disappear in the darkness, and neither saw nor heard anything more of them till near morning, when I was aroused by the same masculine roar, which I had heard two or three nights before. I recognized it immediately, and strained my eyes to see the possessor of that lordly voice. It was, however, so dark that I could not see, though I distinctly heard the tramp of the beast; and it seemed that he was accompanied by his consort and the young ones, which I had seen in the evening. It was evident to me that they had passed near the trap, but they had not entered it; and on examining the tracks in the daytime, I found that they had passed around it.

Seeing thus that the trap had been passed by, I determined to dig a pit with a falling door; and, accordingly, going to work, in the course of a few days we completed such a trap, eight feet long, six feet broad, and ten feet deep; and fixed a door over it, swung upon an axle in such a manner as to turn and drop any animal, that trod upon it, into the pit. The door was covered over with dirt, grass, and leaves in such a manner as to resemble the ground about it; so that I supposed it would be impossible for an animal to detect the deception. I then hung a piece of raw mutton over the door, and retired to my place of concealment, to watch during the night, as usual.

Soon after dark the male animal again made his appearance. As he came to the mouth of the den, he looked around and snuffed the air, and then leaped down, and going a few yards placed his paws upon a rock, and stretched himself, yawning at the same time as if he were waking up out of a sleep. In a few minutes afterwards the female appeared, and approaching, lapped his brawny neck. Pleased with this conjugal attention, the male threw himself upon the ground, and after rolling for a few minutes, stood up, shook himself, and then, with a proud step, trod away towards the traps; and his consort followed him. Their manner towards each other induced the reflection in my mind, that nature works much the same in all species of animals; for even among human beings, I had rarely seen a more expressive indication of conjugal love than was exhibited here.

The male beast, as nearly as I could see, was twice as large as the ordinary cougar, and appeared to be covered with dark round spots of great richness and beauty. His mien was erect and stately, and so majestic and proud in bearing, that it was with pleasure I contemplated him. As he approached the pit, my heart fluttered; now, thought I, is the time of my success; but, alas, for my hopes! the animals, when they reached the place, evidently suspected something wrong; and, after smelling about suspiciously, made a circuit and passed on. They next stopped at the trap, which they appeared to examine attentively; they even entered it, and I strained my eyes to see the doors fall; but no, alas, for my hopes again! the animals came out and went off, without disturbing the bait, and soon disappeared over the ridge. I watched the remainder of the night, but neither saw nor heard anything more of the beasts.

For several weeks after this time, I continued making all endeavors to trap these animals. I caught live bait, and tried to inveigle them with the choicest morsels, but all in vain. On several occasions, subsequent to those mentioned, I obtained a sight of the animals, but only a passing one; and at last, confident that it would be impossible to trap them, I determined on the first opportunity to shoot. The male I never afterwards saw; but the female and her cubs I unexpectedly came across one day, in a gorge far removed from the one containing the den. Ben and Rambler were with me at the time; and, as I fired upon her, they bounded forward and engaged with her in a terrific combat, but she tore them dreadfully, and managed to escape. Poor Ben was so badly injured in the encounter, as to require my surgical care and assistance for a week or more afterwards; but, though I hunted and hunted, I could find no more trace of the beasts, or of any animals like them. I was, therefore, not able then, nor am I able now, to pronounce with certainty upon their character. If they were not jaguars, which had strayed up beyond the usual range, I know not what to call them.

CHAPTER XX

THE COAST RANGE AGAIN — CONCLUSION.

THE fall now approached, and the rains might soon be expected, so that we prepared to return to winter-quarters, either in Corral Hollow, or in my favorite ground in the Sierra Nevada. Accordingly, gathering up and packing our animals, we hitched up our wagon, and took the road over the mountains back to the Tejon, and thence to the west of Kern Lake, intending to take the west side of the Coast Range of mountains on our way back.

In a day or two after leaving the Tejon, we came to a camp of persons engaged in catching mustang horses, — multitudes of which covered the country in all directions. Here, unfortunately, during my absence hunting in the neighborhood, Drury allowed my two horses to break away and get among the mustangs. I knew it was doubtful whether I would ever recover them again; and the most desponding thoughts took possession of me for a while. I could expect nothing better of the fellow; but to think that I had passed through so much, and to lose them at last under such circumstances, appeared to me a peculiar hardship; and for several days I was morose to the last degree. However, I searched the country far and near, and used every possible exertion to recover them, but all to no purpose; I could neither see nor find a trace of them, and at length gave them up and turned my hope and trust to the mules, — those patient animals which had stood by me so long.

While in this country, I made several excursions after mustangs, and succeeded in shooting a number. They were small, but in good condition, and their flesh made very good eating; indeed, many an excellent steak of horseflesh have I enjoyed. I also dried a quantity of it for provisions upon my travel. After thus preparing ourselves, finding that our horses were irretrievably gone, we struck towards the mountains, with the mules alone attached to the wagon; and, travelling among them for five or six days, we came to the neighborhood of the mission of San Miguel, on the Salinas River. It was moonlight when we came in sight of the village, which we saw lying about a mile below us, with the shining stream not far off; all presenting a peaceful moonlight picture of great beauty.

It was certainly imprudent in us to attempt to

descend so steep a hill, as that upon which we approached the place, in the night time; but we wished to reach the river bank, and determined to try it. As we might have expected, notwithstanding all our precautions, and Drury's hanging to a hind wheel, we had not got more than half way down, when over went wagon, mules, bears, Drury, and all, tumbling everything helter-skelter; but, fortunately, injuring nothing seriously. It had been my luck to be upset more than once before; and I may say that I was used to it. Without delay, therefore, I went industriously to work, and gathered up the scattered articles and the frightened animals; and towards morning, having again got in travelling plight, pushed on to the river. The stream seemed shallow, and I thought I might as well cross and camp on the farther side; but, as it happened, we got into sand in the river, and, as I foolishly stopped to allow the mules to drink, the wagon wheels sank. When I urged the mules on again, I found that we were not only fast, but that the wheels had sunk over their hubs. There was no use geeing and hawing; and, in fine, all that could be done was to unhitch, drive the mules out, and carry the animals and goods to shore the best way we could. Luck seemed to be against us; but we worked on in spite of it, and succeeded, by dawn, in getting everything ashore but the wagon. Leaving that to take care of itself in the river, being very tired, we rolled ourselves in our blankets, and, weary and wayworn, soon fell asleep.

As the day advanced, the people of the mission beheld the curious spectacle we presented; and we were roused, after a few hours' sleep, by a troop of Spaniards and others, who came up laughing and making merry over our misfortune. We were well chastened by this time, and bore their sport with patience; indeed, we joined in the laugh, which was a good-natured one. When it was over, the people offered to help us; and, with their aid and that of several horses, we pulled our wagon out of the sands, and soon had it packed again. The people viewed my curiosities, and particularly the bears, with the liveliest interest, and seemed so much pleased that they invited me to dine with them. I would fain have eaten a civilized dinner, just for a change, but my expedition had left my garments in a rather unpresentable condition. I had therefore, on account of the shabbiness of my dress, to decline their generous offer, — and drove on.

On my way through the settled portions of the country, the people all expressed great curiosity to see my animals, and gave me milk to feed the small ones. For some reason or other, however, this diet did not suit them, and several died. As for the Lady and Ben and Rambler, they thrived well all the way. I allowed them to follow me at liberty a portion of the road, until we came in neighborhoods where dogs were kept, when I found it prudent to tie them up. This I did, not for their own protection, as they could vanquish any number of dogs, but to prevent difficulties with dog-fanciers, that irritable class of individuals, who are often more ready to fight for an affront to their puppies than for an insult to themselves.

We travelled on thus for several days, and at last came to a sideling hill which skirted the river. While passing this place, one of the mules balked, and suddenly wheeling down hill, we toppled on the brink. I saw in an instant that we must go over; and, dropping the reins, I jumped out in time to save myself; but the wagon tumbled on the mules, and then down into the river, making an almost perfect wreck, breaking the bed and tongue in several places, killing a young deer and elk, fracturing the leg of a small bear, and severely injuring one of the mules, which it dragged down with it. Here again was I the victim of misfortune; it seemed truly as if only bad luck was in store for me; and had it not been absolutely necessary for the preservation of my animals to exert myself with vigor, I should have been discouraged; but, as had happened twice before, we soon began getting the animals together, gathering up our scattered luggage, and repairing damages to the best of our ability.

After making a new tongue, mending the bed, and repacking the wagon, we drove on upon the main road towards San José. The injured mule, however, was so lame, that our progress was very slow, and we felt compelled to stop at the first ranch we came to, where I determined to lay over for a few days to recuperate. At this place, as it happened, the ranchero complained that he was greatly troubled by a grizzly bear that killed his calves; and he desired to know of me whether I could help him. I replied that I would gladly undertake to rid him of the troublesome visitor; and we forthwith proceeded to the corral, or cattle-pen, where he showed me the body of a calf which had been killed by the grizzly the previous night. Upon inspecting the tracks about the place, I found unmistakable evidences that the bear was a large one, not unworthy the honor of a meeting; and forthwith I made arrangements for an encounter with him.

The corral was a pen about five feet high, made of perpendicular wooden stakes, which were driven firmly into the ground, and lashed together with raw-hide strips; and it was in this enclosure that the calf lay. I directed the other calves and cattle to be driven out, so as to leave the body of the calf there alone, and, when evening came on, all the dogs about the place to be tied up, and the Spaniards to retire to their beds. As it grew dusk, I concealed myself, with Ben and Rambler, in a pile of logs near the corral, and commenced my watch.

It was a beautiful moonlight night, and I could perceive with considerable distinctness for some distance. I think it must have been about ten o'clock when the bear made his appearance. His step was bold and apparently fearless; but as he approached the corral, he raised his head and snuffed the air a number of times. For a few moments I supposed that he perceived us, but it soon appeared that he did not; for, approaching the side of the corral, he leaped over it without suspicion. As he went over, which he did with great ease, I could plainly see that he was a very large animal, and that it was going to be a triumph to kill him. I might have shot him as he went over; but it struck me as more prudent to let him fill himself first. It was with difficulty that I could restrain Ben and the hound; for, not having had a fight for some time, they were almost crazy to engage; but I kept them back; and the bear, being busy with his meal, did not observe our neighborhood.

As soon as I supposed he had eaten enough, I crept forward to the side of the corral; and, placing my rifle over the edge and taking fair aim at his shoulder, I fired. He fell, and upon my calling to Ben and Rambler, in an instant, they leaped the enclosure and were upon him. They all rolled and scrabbled together; and as soon as I could get a second load down my rifle, I sprang forward, and watching my opportunity, gave the old brute another ball, which, however, did not yet kill. Meanwhile the noise, which was terrific, aroused the Spaniard and all his household; and they all came running out with their dogs; but I peremptorily ordered them all back, and again turned to the scene before me. The wounded brute now had the hound in his mouth and was shaking him dreadfully, while Ben was doing his best to attract the enemy to himself. I at once jumped over into the corral, and rushing up, buried my knife in the brute's neck; when, dropping the dog, he turned upon me and tore my buckskins; but that was all the damage, for Ben, noble Ben, now redoubled his energies and drew the beast's attention from me. As he turned to Ben, I made several blows with my knife behind his shoulder, and in a few moments rolled him over as dead as his worst foe could have desired.

As soon as he expired, I called the Spaniards to see the individual that had been killing their calves; and, as they looked at him and then at me, they exclaimed, *Mucho bueno Americano,* — being highly delighted with the death of what they styled the infernal calf-killer. As the story of the exploit got noised about, I felt myself elevated into a personage of considerable importance among the rancheros of the neighborhood, and might have sported it in the region as a hero of the Hercules type; but playing the hero of this kind is out of fashion now-a-days, and, to use a homely but expressive phrase, "will not pay."

In a few days after the above incident, which was the last of what I call my adventures, we hitched up again and proceeded to San José, at which place I began to give exhibitions. Thence I went to Santa Clara, thence to the Red Woods, and from there came to San Francisco, where, in the course of the next year, I established the Pacific Museum. I have by degrees gathered all my animals together, and have them now, a goodly company, about me. As I look around upon them I am reminded of the freshness and freedom of the forests, and live over again in imagination the golden days when I trod, in pleasure and in joy, upon the mountain side. Lady Washington, Ben Franklin, — noble Ben, and his foster-brother Rambler; they are all here. The monster who rattles his chain in the cage yonder, and fairly shakes the building, is Samson; and the white-coated rogue by the side of the Indian dog is Funny Joe. The black and cinnamon bears, the panthers, wolves, foxes, wild cats, elks, deer, and other animals ranged around, all these I have sufficiently spoken of before; each recalls its own special adventure; and what there is of pleasure in reviewing an active career, in which I can recollect nothing to be ashamed of, that I enjoy.

As I come to the end of my book, I cannot but reflect that my life likewise approaches its close. I have looked on death in many forms, and trust that I can meet it whenever it comes with a stout heart and steady nerves. If I could choose, I would wish, since it was my destiny to become a mountaineer and grizzly bear hunter of California, to finish my career in the Sierra Nevada. There would I fain lay down with the Lady, Ben, and Rambler at my side; there, surely, I could find rest through the long future, among the eternal rocks and evergreen pines.

POSTSCRIPT.

To complete the foregoing narrative, a few words remain to be added. After exhibiting his animals in San Francisco for several years, Adams, as stated in the Introduction, removed to New York. He took passage with them on the clipper ship *Golden Fleece*, which sailed on January 7, 1860. The voyage required three months and a half. Upon arrival at New York he made a contract with Phineas T. Barnum and thenceforth exhibited in connection with Barnum's shows.

The reader will remember that in the spring of 1855 Adams had a severe encounter with a grizzly dam near his old camp in the Sierra Nevada Mountains. He was on that occasion stricken down by the brute, and, though he finally succeeded in killing her, it was not before she had inflicted serious wounds upon his head and neck. At the same time his bear Ben Franklin, who had materially assisted him in the fight, was also injured. Ben always afterward carried the scars of the conflict upon his face, though they did not in any respect disfigure him. As for Adams himself, when his scalp-wound healed, it left a depression about the size of a silver dollar near the top of his forehead, which looked as if the skull underneath had been removed.

When Adams went to New York, it was without Ben Franklin. That noble fellow, who had formed a

371

conspicuous feature of the Pacific Museum and was a great favorite with all visitors, had died from some unknown cause on January 17, 1858. The event not only affected Adams deeply, but was a subject of regret to the San Francisco public in general. It was noticed at considerable length by the *Evening Bulletin* of January 19, 1858, in an article entitled "Death of a Distinguished Native Californian."

After making his arrangement with Barnum, Adams gave exhibitions in New York for six weeks. Before the end of that time, however, he had become a very sick man. It was said that in the course of a severe struggle with one of his animals on shipboard, while doubling Cape Horn, the wound in his head had been torn open afresh. However this may have been, it is certain that, after his reaching New York, the wound became exceedingly inflamed; fever supervened, and Adams's condition of health became alarming. Upon consulting a physician, he was informed that he had not long to live, and was advised to cease labor. But he insisted upon continuing at work and made a new contract with Barnum to travel in connection with a circus and give exhibitions through Connecticut and Massachusetts during the summer of 1860. And, by sheer force of will-power, he managed, though with difficulty, to comply with his agreement.

On the completion of his contract Adams retired to Neponset, a small town near Boston, where his relatives resided. Upon reaching that place the sick man at once took to his bed; and he never rose from it again. The excitement of the exhibition ring had

passed away, and his vital energies sank. On the
fifth day, his physician told him he could not live until
morning. He received the announcement with apparent indifference; but at the request of his relatives
he sent for a clergyman.

According to Barnum—to whom we owe these last
particulars—Adams said to the clergyman that, though
he had told some pretty big stories in the exhibition
ring about his bears, "he had always endeavored to do
the straight thing between man and man." In answer
to questions about his faith, he replied: "I have attended preaching every day, Sundays and all, for the
last six years. Sometimes an old grizzly gave me the
sermon, sometimes it was a panther; often it was the
thunder and lightning, the tempest or the hurricane,
on the peaks of the Sierra Nevada or in the gorges of
the Rocky Mountains. But whatever preached to me,
it always taught me the majesty of the Creator and
revealed to me the undying and unchanging love of
our kind Father in Heaven. Although I am a pretty
rough customer, I fancy my heart is in about the right
place, and look with confidence for that rest which I
so much need, and which I have never enjoyed upon
earth." He then desired the clergyman to pray, after
which he took him by the hand, thanked him for his
kindness, and bade him farewell. In another hour his
spirit had taken its flight. It was said by those present
that his face lighted with a smile as the last breath escaped him—and that smile he carried with him into
his grave.